REVOLUTIONARY UNDERGROUND

Leon Ó Broin

REVOLUTIONARY UNDERGROUND

The Story of the
Irish Republican Brotherhood
1858—1924

Gill and Macmillan

First published 1976

Gill and Macmillan Ltd
15/17 Eden Quay
Dublin 1
and internationally
through association with the
Macmillan Publishers Group

7171 0778 7

Printed in Great Britain by Bristol Typesetting Co Ltd,
Barton Manor, St Philips, Bristol

To a stimulating friend,
Dr T. J. O'Reilly

Contents

PREFACE   ix

1 *Republicans and Home Rulers*   1

2 *The Irish National Invincibles*   24

3 *The Young Ireland Society*   36

4 *The Parnell Split*   46

5 *INB* versus *IRB*   60

6 *Commemorating 1798*   84

7 *Fred Allan and the* Irish Independent   97

8 *Arthur Griffith, an IRB Man?*   108

9 *The Castle in a Liberal Mood*   121

10 *The Rising of 1916*   140

11 *Michael Collins*   175

12 *The End of the Road*   206

REFERENCES   225

BIBLIOGRAPHY   234

INDEX   239

Preface

THIS book is about a secret society that for over sixty years considered itself to be fulfilling the function of watchdog on behalf of the Irish separatist tradition. A revolutionary society committed to winning Irish freedom by the employment of physical force, its membership fluctuated greatly. At times it ran into many thousands; at others the numbers were so low that it was said that they could all be fitted into a modest concert hall. This was the Irish Republican Brotherhood (the IRB), euphemistically called 'the Organisation', which, while preparing to strike a decisive blow to gain its ends, acted as a superior gingering element in Irish nationalist circles. 'It watched everything: it was in everything: and whenever there was an opportunity, however small, of doing anything to forward the separatist cause, it was there to do it. . . . Strange and transient committees and societies were constantly cropping up, doing this and that specific work. The IRB formed them, the IRB provided the money for them, and the IRB dissolved them when their work was done.'[1] This IRB began its life with an abortive rising in the 1860s; it ended its life in the aftermath of another rising in which, conspiratorially and practically, it played an important role. It was one of the parents of the IRA, ancient and modern. Its part was most significant in securing the acceptance of the Treaty negotiated with the British government in 1921.

The book, as I present it, is based to a considerable extent on what British government sources tell us about the IRB itself, its sister Fenian society in America, its personalities, its attitudes to movements like those for Home Rule and land reform, its internal rivalries, divisions and fluctuating fortunes. But this view of 'the Organisation' is balanced—not unsatisfactorily, I hope—by other material, published and unpublished, on which I have

A*

been able to draw, and from the results of my conversations with individuals.

The bibliography reveals my indebtedness to the directors and staffs of many institutions, particularly the Irish State Paper Office, the National Library of Ireland, the Archives Department of University College, Dublin, and the British Public Record Office, as well as to Mrs Michael Clifton, Seán Allan, Nevin Griffith, Mrs Alice Mac Eóin, Brigid Sweetman, the McCullough family and Maurice ('Moss') Twomey for allowing me to draw upon papers under their control.

There are others—some of them dead since I began my researching—whose varied help I must also acknowledge. They include Denis McCullough, Bulmer Hobson, Seán Mac Eóin, Joseph Sweeney, Ernest Blythe, Seán MacEntee, Claire O'Hegarty, Liam Deasy, Maurice ('Moss') Twomey, Risteárd Mulcahy, M. J. Costello, Dan Bryan, Dom Mark Tierney, Father Gearóid O'Sullivan, Seán Ó Lúing, Emmet Dalton, Liam and Kathleen O'Doherty, T. Desmond Williams, R. Dudley Edwards, Kevin B. Nowlan, Séamas Woods, May Cosgrave, T. W. Moody, Hugo Brunner, Thomas P. O'Neill, Mícheál Ó Raghallaigh, Con Farrell, Stephen Kearney, Seán Cronin, Pádraig Ó Maidín, J. A. Irvine, Martin Walton, John O'Beirne-Ranelagh, Pádraig Ó Fialáin, Colm Croker, Doreen Callan, Owen Dudley Edwards, Bríd, Bean Uí Eigeartaigh, and my wife Cáit and daughter Noirín.

Leon Ó Broin
Dublin
January 1976

Republicans and Home Rulers

1

REVOLUTION in Ireland today means to most people the Irish Republican Army, the IRA, something that links up vaguely in their minds with 1916 and all that. The IRA man, however, who knows anything at all about the history of his country, sees himself in a physical-force tradition that goes back a few years beyond 1800, the year in which, by British action, the old Irish Ascendancy parliament disappeared and Ireland and Great Britain were joined unhappily together. From the British point of view it was essential to take that action in order to keep the back door shut against invasion from the European continent. The ideas of the French Revolution had won many Irish adherents, and during the war with England efforts were made by the French to invade Ireland in support of the military organisation of the United Irishmen. This was a largely Protestant body that was concerned to achieve religious equality in a country where the Catholics, the overwhelming majority of the population, were the underdogs, and to carry through a radical reform of parliament. Equality for all citizens, perhaps more than liberty or forms of liberty, was the ideal that animated the United Irishmen. Their hopes and plans, however, came to nothing. The rebellion they initiated in 1798 was savagely repressed, their French allies were repulsed, and their outstanding leader, Theobald Wolfe Tone, who had travelled to Ireland with the French, was arrested and took his own life in prison when confronted with the ignominy of death by hanging.

Over the next fifty years some of the things the United Irishmen had sought were achieved by constitutional action, both outside and inside the united parliament of Westminster, under the leadership of Daniel O'Connell, a man who abhorred the use of physical force. Catholic emancipation came in 1829, tithes were later reduced, municipal government was cleaned up, and the police force became more impartial. O'Connell made a major effort to secure the repeal of the Act of Union and failed—it is most unlikely that any leader could have achieved this at the time—but he did demonstrate the potentiality that lay in democracy organised in support of parliamentary action, and it was this discovery that facilitated the parliamentary successes of later years. He found his support in a fundamentally conservative people, especially those who lived on the land, and in a clergy who were mindful of the needs of both faith and fatherland, of soul and body.

Nevertheless, the revolutionary idea persisted, and organisations that derived inspiration from the United Irishmen also made preparations underground and timed their revolts for when the enemy was at a serious disadvantage. England's difficulty was Ireland's opportunity. But the conspirators could misread the signs. In 1848 a revolutionary element among the Young Irelanders—a largely literary coterie ill equipped for military action of any kind—were betrayed by the easy success of the French revolution of that year and of the apparent strength of Chartism in Britain into believing that they could obtain by force what political action had failed to secure. They rose, if that is the word, when Ireland was suffering from the effects of the Great Famine, and were suppressed with ridiculous ease. Yet their courage in taking up arms was remembered and their incompetence forgotten. And from among their scattered followers two men emerged within a decade to direct the next attempt. One of these was John O'Mahony, a gentleman farmer and scholar who went to America and founded in New York the Fenian Brotherhood which derived its name from the Fianna, a pre-historic Irish military force. The other was James Stephens who, having worked with and studied French underground societies, returned to Ireland and established there in 1858 the Irish Revolutionary Brotherhood (IRB) which subsequently became the Irish Republican Brotherhood but was still known as the IRB. This was the counterpart of the American Brotherhood, and the term Fenian came to be applied generally to both organisations. However, the government authorities in Dublin Castle were able to distinguish between the two, seeing the IRB as a secret revolutionary society that aimed at putting an army

in the field, and the Fenian Brotherhood as an auxiliary whose
mission was to provide 'the sinews of war', to supply the Irish
army with arms and military stores, with officers, and conceivably
with reinforcements of men.[1]

After a setback in 1858 and 1859, as the result of the discovery
by the government of what was known as the Phoenix Conspiracy, a feature of which was the alleged threat of an American
invasion, the two organisations progressed with some measure of
association and took advantage of the situation that presented
itself to them at the close of the American Civil War. Trained
men in large numbers were then available for service across the
Canadian frontier or on Irish soil. But the British and Canadians
in concert, well aware of their plans, frustrated every move. In
1865 they swooped on the headquarters of the IRB in Dublin,
arrested most of the leaders and had them convicted on charges
of treason felony and sent to penal servitude. Stephens, having
avoided immediate arrest, was picked up later, but made a
dramatic escape to America where he tried to reunite the rival
factions into which the Fenian Brotherhood had split. He promised that 1866 would be a year of decision, a year in which,
with American assistance, he would personally lead a rising in
Ireland. But in December 1866 he abandoned the leadership
when the hopelessness of his intentions dawned upon him. A
rising was nevertheless attempted without him in 1867, the
initiative and overall direction coming from American army
officers, the principal of whom was Colonel Thomas J. Kelly.
Once more, however, the government was fully in command of
the situation, having been warned of what was going to happen
by spies and informers. Hundreds of men were arrested and released after a short interval, but the leaders taken earlier were
kept in prison, and with them a few others, including some
British army men who had changed their allegiance. Towards
the end of 1867 two notable events occurred in England. In
September a police van carrying Fenian prisoners in Manchester
was attacked and a police sergeant killed. Three men were
executed for complicity in this affair, and became, in Irish myth-
ology, the 'Manchester Martyrs'. In December a bomb went off
outside Clerkenwell Prison, where an important Fenian officer
was incarcerated, killing twelve innocent people and maiming
another 120. For that crime another Irishman went to the scaf-

fold, in what the Tory Chief Secretary for Ireland of the time, Lord Naas, hoped was the final spasm of the 'Fenian Fever'.[2]

In a 'Message to the Irish People' issued in June 1868 a body calling itself the Supreme Council of the Irish Republic sought to explain the circumstances in which 'the disastrous outbreak' of the previous year had been frustrated, and to give an assurance that, despite everything, the revolutionary future could be viewed with optimism. The Message threw the blame for what had gone wrong on the American Fenian Brotherhood, to whom it said it had been represented that the Irish Republican Army was almost completely equipped, the result being that the Americans entertained other projects and sent wholly inadequate supplies to Ireland. The Message also claimed that, while what had happened at Manchester was justified by the Law of Nations, the Clerkenwell business was beneath contempt, and were its perpetrators within the Council's control, their punishment would be condign indeed. The Message, now mentioning the Irish Republican Brotherhood for the first time, implored the Irish Americans 'in the name of Ireland, a perishing people, and God' to end their unhappy party differences; furthermore, it announced the rupture of formal relations with the Fenian Brotherhood. This rupture was to last until 1876 when, with much difficulty, a joint Revolutionary Directory was formed.[3]

In the general election of 1868 a Liberal government was returned, and William Ewart Gladstone was given the opportunity of implementing his declared policy of pacifying Ireland. He approached his task by securing the passage of two extremely important measures, a bill for the disestablishment of the Anglican Church of Ireland—this involved the removal of an important prop of the Union settlement—and another bill which laid the basis of a land code which, in the course of the next half-century or so, was to transfer the ownership of land to its occupying tenants. He aimed also at a reform of university education but did not succeed in bringing this about before he relinquished office in 1874. He had inherited from the Tories what was described as the remnants of Fenianism, the remnants of a movement which in 1871 his officials in Dublin Castle considered was 'rapidly dying out' and losing whatever popular support it ever had. The situation in America was not dissimilar. There, Fenianism had greatly declined as a result of the continuing divisions among its adherents. Armed sorties across the Canadian frontier had proved futile, and revolutionary hopes now rested on a modest organisation, the Clan na Gael or United Brotherhood, founded by Jerome J. Collins in New York in June 1867, to which John Devoy, 'the greatest of the Fenians',[4] was to impart enormous vitality on joining it about 1874.

Though small in numbers, low in morale, and distracted by the emergence of a popular constitutional demand for Home Rule under Isaac Butt, a Protestant lawyer who had spoken up for the Fenian prisoners in and out of court, the IRB somehow survived. In the June 1868 Message to the Irish People, it had been announced that the earlier losses had been repaired and that 'a duly elected representative Government' or Supreme Council had been formed which was in active and intimate communication with all parts of Ireland, England and Scotland. This Government or Council, it blandly claimed, derived authority from 'the Irish Republican Army and the Irish people within Ireland, and resident in England and Scotland'. In August 1869 this Government 'in Council assembled' adopted the first of a number of Constitutions of the Irish Republic. This one was to remain in force for four years.[5]

In January 1870, in another Address issued by the Supreme Council, supposedly 'to the People of Ireland' but really to the rank and file of the IRB, there was a franker admission that after 1867 the situation had been 'most deplorable . . . the once compact and powerful organisation [being] broken up into contemptible fragments, [with] nothing but discord and disorganisation on every side'. But, like the earlier Message, this Address strove to be optimistic. Reorganisation had been effective, and harmony virtually restored. Money had been misapplied with resultant loss of confidence but, even without American help, much had been done to procure arms, and if only the members would pay their dues regularly, in six months the Irish Republic would occupy a position far exceeding their wildest dreams. Strict discipline and prompt obedience to orders were called for, while the pledge of secrecy would have to be enforced in order to combat the mischief being done by loose talk. The members were to abstain from public demonstrations and political agitations of every kind until otherwise directed, but they were to make persistent efforts to obtain control of local authorities as a means of increasing republican power and influence. Raids for arms, on the other hand, were strictly forbidden : such silly exploits were fit only to excite unthinking boys; they did great injury to the cause and yielded utterly contemptible results.[6]

J. F. X. O'Brien, a young Corkman who had acted with conspicuous bravery in the 1867 Rising, was a close observer of the affairs of the IRB at this period. On his release in 1869 from Portland Prison he found 'the Organisation' vigorous and healthy, but in 1871, by which time he had become a member of the Supreme Council and possibly its President, 'the Organisation' was in decline, and by 1874 he was so dissatisfied with the way things were going that he felt obliged to quit the IRB altogether.[7]

Around St Patrick's Day 1873 a 'Solemn Convention of the Irish Republic' summoned by the Supreme Council was held in Dublin and was attended by some fifty delegates from the seven provinces and districts of Ireland, England and Scotland into which 'the Organisation' was divided. The printed report subsequently issued by the Council to the officers and men of the IRA—a very early example of the use of the well-known initials —indicated that a fresh start was being made following a period in which 'the Organisation' had suffered from persecution, slander, apathy, timidity and treason. The Council had itself been under attack from within the movement, and at the outset of the Convention it had resigned the authority which, as in 1868, it claimed it had received from the people. However, when details were given to the Convention concerning the civil, military and financial transactions of 'the Organisation', the resignation was not accepted and fullest confidence in the Council was signified. The details, described as being of a gratifying nature, disclosed that a very substantial quantity of war material had been accumulated, that an army capable of enlargement was in being, and that in every district there was a large balance of money on hand. Allegations against certain named individuals were, on investigation, dismissed, but certain other individuals were indicted with having 'laid hands on the funds of the Organisation, or otherwise misconducted themselves', and the Convention decided to make known the reputation of these 'wretches' far and wide.[8] O'Brien in his unpublished autobiography writes of an incitement to cast him and other colleagues out of the Council, of his defence of the 'Protestant Home Rule Association' being described as 'tawdry nonsense', and of men who had given indisputable proof of their devotion to the cause making away with money that had been given to them for safekeeping. Some of the trouble arose through groups having nowhere to hold their meetings except in public houses.[9]

The 1873 Convention discussed amendments to the Constitution and left the promulgation of the revised instrument to the Supreme Council. That instrument—the Constitution of 1873 —when duly issued, remained virtually unaltered until after 1916. It provided that membership was to consist of Irishmen, irrespective of class and creed, who were willing to labour for the establishment of a free republican government. While preparing Ireland for the task of recovering her independence by force of arms 'the Organisation', in time of peace, was to confine itself to the cultivation of union and brotherly love among Irishmen, the propagation of republican principles and the spreading of knowledge of Irish national rights. The decision of the Irish nation, as expressed by a majority of the Irish people, as to the fit hour for inaugurating a war against England was awaited (a provision apparently intended to prevent a recurrence of impulsive outbreaks like that of 1867),[10] but while awaiting this decision the IRB was to lend its support to every movement calculated to advance the cause of Irish independence, consistently with the preservation of its own integrity. (Thus the rank and file in Britain were kept away from 'the uproarious republican meetings' convened by Dilke, Bradlaugh, Odger and company, though the spread of the republican idea was welcomed.) Members, on being initiated, were required to swear an oath solemnly undertaking to do their utmost to establish the national independence of Ireland, to bear true allegiance to the Supreme Council of the IRB and Government of the Irish Republic, implicitly to obey the Constitution of the IRB and their superior officers, and to preserve inviolable the secrets of the organisation.

Membership was to be confined to persons whose character for sobriety, truth, valour and obedience to authority could bear scrutiny, and who could be relied upon to keep their mouths shut about what they learned within the Brotherhood. Members resident in towns or parishes were to be 'directed and governed' by an officer, entitled a Centre, elected by themselves. These Centres, in turn, were to be directed and governed by a County Centre, while each district where the Irish congregated in England and Scotland was to be directed and governed by a chosen District Centre. The overall government of the organisation was declared to reside in 'the Supreme Council of the IRB and Government of the Irish Republic' which was composed of eleven members: seven of them elected to represent the four provinces of Ireland, the North and South of England and Scotland, and four honorary members elected by the seven, to whom alone their names were to be known.

Enactments of the Government so constituted were to be the laws of the Irish Republic until the territory of the Republic was recovered from the English enemy and a permanent government established. These laws could embrace the levying of taxes, the negotiating of loans and the making of war and peace; and every act by a member of the IRB to subvert the authority of the Supreme Council was punishable—even by death as treason in time of war. The crime of treason was defined as any wilful act or word calculated to betray the cause of Irish independence and subserve the interest of the British or any other foreign government in Ireland to the detriment of Irish independence. The amended Constitution ventured to make a law, by declaring that in the Irish Republic there should be no state religion : every citizen was to be free to worship God according to his conscience. It also provided that the Supreme Council, to be elected every two years, was to have an unpaid Executive comprising a President, Secretary and Treasurer. Every member of the organisation was requested to give civil and military obedience to the Executive. Subject to the Supreme Council's control, the President was to direct the working of the organisation in all its departments, and he was declared to be 'in fact as well as by right the President of the Irish Republic'.[11]

2

The IRB, unlike the Fenian organisation in the United States, was a wholly oath-bound secret society. But how secret really was it? It certainly failed over many years to keep its plans, major and minor, to itself; and government agents, some of whom emerged from the ranks of the society to volunteer their services, were sometimes so plentiful that other offers to 'inform' had to be rejected. This was not always the position, but the government were usually well aware of what was cooking and who the cooks were. The conspirators, of course, reacted by reminding members of their commitment to secrecy and by disciplining spies and informers whenever they could. Pierce Nagle, for example, who betrayed the leaders in 1865, was found dead in 1879, lying under a standard of the Metropolitan Railway in Camden Town, London. He had been run through the heart with a large cheese-knife, on the point of which, as it protruded several inches from his back, was a paper which disclosed his name and the information that he had been killed as the penalty for his treachery.[12]

To tighten up their internal means of communication, John Devoy and his close collaborator Dr William Carroll constructed a cipher disguising the names of prominent Fenians and others that cropped up in their correspondence. Some of the assigned pseudonyms had a quizzical touch. John O'Leary became *John Knox*; Charles Kickham *St Colmcille*; Parnell *Emerson*; James Stephens *the Old Gent* or *the Old Ruffian*; and Patrick Egan *the Broker*; while the IRB became *Elder*; the Clan na Gael *Logan*; and the Revolutionary Directory on which the IRB and the Clan were joined in 1876 was known as *Elder and Logan*.[13]

In its domestic correspondence the IRB employed other forms of disguise, though whether it succeeded in concealing much thereby may be doubted. 'The Organisation', the colloquial term for the IRB, was in the 1870s commonly described in letters as *the firm* or *the business*. The members of the Supreme Council were *the heads of the firm* or *directors*. The President was *the Boss*. There were *meetings of shareholders*, otherwise *picnics*, and of *foremen of divisions*. The area covered by a provincial representative on the Supreme Council was an *agency*. Visitors to outlying *branches* were *travellers*. The Constitution of 'the Organisation' was *the trade rules*, while *stock* and *cargoes* meant only one thing, the arms and ammunition which the IRB sought to obtain and distribute. Terms of an entirely different character were also employed. It was not hard to understand what was meant, for instance, when a man, on being summoned to a meeting to review a situation, promised to attend at the *marriage* and give every assistance in his power towards furthering the prosperity of the *bridegroom*, or when a postal order was sent *for the use of the old man*, or when somebody formed *an intention of sending something to Granny*. The two sets of appellations came together when local *managers of the firm after taking stock declared the following result—subscribers 667, goods 116, cash £170* and that *a sum of £10 was sent to the trustees of the old woman*.

Although letters to Charles Guilfoyle Doran, the Secretary of the Supreme Council in the 1870s, were usually posted in the ordinary way to his residence in Queenstown or to the site of the Queenstown Cathedral where he was the clerk of works, sometimes an inner envelope containing the message was addressed to *L. Brehon*, which was Doran's pseudonym. That these letters were on IRB business could further be seen by the fact that they began with *My dear Friend*, a *friend* being a member of the IRB. Doran's correspondence indicates that a very large number of letters on IRB business went through the post in the ordinary way and that thereby the organisation's principals ran the gravest risks of discovery. If even a fraction of these had been opened, it would have given the government, as it gives us now, a fair picture of the state of 'the Organisation' and what its plans were. That this was not done may reflect the government's opinion that they had the conspiracy adequately covered otherwise and therefore had no need to depart from the normal custom of regarding letters passing through the Post Office as inviolable, a matter about which they had from time to time given assurances to parliament.

It would appear that the IRB resorted less to these devices for concealing what they were up to than their American counterparts did. Nevertheless the IRB was almost exclusively and at all times 'the Organisation' to its members, and as late as 1916 an intimation that a rising was about to take place was conveyed on a postcard which simply said that *Auntie was no better and might have to undergo an operation very soon.*[14]

3

The Constitution of 1873, as we saw, authorised the IRB, while awaiting the fit hour for inaugurating a war against England, to lend its support to any movement, consistently with the pres ervation of its own integrity, to advance the cause of Irish independence. This provision may have been incorporated in the Constitution specifically to enable the IRB to be associated in November 1873 with the formation of the Home Rule League over which Isaac Butt presided and at the inaugural conference of which two members of the Supreme Council, Charles Guilfoyle Doran and John O'Connor Power, proposed and had carried a resolution calling for the return at the coming general election of men earnestly and truly devoted to the Home Rule cause. Butt, it was alleged, had secretly assured Doran that, if by the end of three years Home Rule, giving Ireland some form of control over domestic affairs, had not been achieved, he would come back to Dublin and submit himself to the Fenian party. Home Rule was not achieved within the period, and the IRB thereupon decided to resume its opposition to the involvement of its members in parliamentary action. They did so as reports reached the Supreme Council of the damage being done to 'the Organisation' through the spread of the Home Rule movement.

We can accurately place the date of this decision, thanks to the survival of Doran's papers, for among them is a copy of a resolution of the Supreme Council passed on 20 August 1876 which runs as follows:

> Resolved that the countenance which we have hitherto shown to the Home Rule movement be from this date, and is hereby, withdrawn, as three years' experience of the working of the movement has proved to us that the revolutionary principles which we profess can be better served by our organisation existing on its own basis pure and simple, and we hereby request that all members of our organisation who may have any connection with the Home Rule movement will definitely withdraw from it their active co-operation within six months from this date.

Doran moved a resolution to the same effect at a Home Rule convention in the following November 1876.[15]

The Supreme Council was, however, deeply divided on this issue, and early in March 1877 four of its members were either compelled to resign or expelled: John O'Connor Power, Joseph Gillis Biggar, Patrick Egan and John Barry.[16] Two of these—O'Connor Power and Biggar, who conducted their IRB correspondence on House of Commons notepaper—belonged to the group in the House which flagrantly obstructed business in order to concentrate attention on Ireland's problems. They had found a valuable ally in a newly elected young Protestant landlord, Charles Stewart Parnell; and their efforts, combined with his, rapidly gained a great accession of support from among Irish people at home and abroad for this unusual form of parliamentary representation. Butt died in 1879, and after a short interregnum Parnell became the leader of the party. He owed his election largely to the efforts of John Barry, who had represented the North of England on the Supreme Council of the IRB and had built up the Home Rule Confederation of Great Britain into a powerful political machine.

Parnell had entered politics with all the determination that characterised his subsequent career. He was practically unknown and barely able to put two words together when he was defeated in March 1874 in a parliamentary by-election in County Dublin. He was successful a little more than a year later in County Meath, but in the interval he had sought support in Tipperary when the election there of John Mitchel, the Young Irelander and Fenian, was quashed on the grounds that he had neither received a free pardon as a felon nor had purged it by serving his term of imprisonment. Mitchel stood a second time and was returned triumphantly, but had the seat taken from him and awarded to his Tory opponent. That Tipperary was a county of advanced nationalist opinion had been demonstrated by his election and that of two other Fenians, Jeremiah O'Donovan Rossa and Charles Kickham, between 1869 and 1875; and it was the disqualification of Mitchel that caused Parnell, young and inexperienced though he was, to look for guarantees of support in the constituency. A fervent backer of his, the parish priest of Rathdrum, Co. Wicklow, wrote to the parish priest of Mullinahone in Tipperary, where Kickham, the President or Head Centre of the IRB, lived, strongly recommending 'a young man of great industry, great pluck and great promise'. His letter is among Doran's papers, and to find it there is surely amusing. An English observer would doubtless consider it 'very Irish' that two Catholic priests should be the means of introducing Parnell to the leading revolutionaries of the day.[17] Doran, the Secretary of the Supreme Council of the IRB, had worked hard to have

Mitchel elected, collecting funds, organising itineraries and speaking at public meetings. Other correspondents had suggested that Doran should meet Parnell personally when he came to Tipperary, and explore the possibility of giving him IRB approval in the event of 'the Organisation' not starting a candidate of its own.[18] We do not know if they did meet. If they did, it was probably Parnell's first face-to-face contact with an organisation which, in one way or another, and particularly in time of crisis, was to play an important role in his life, and after his death was to strive to perpetuate ideas which they believed he had shared with them. In 1876, when Parnell first went to America as a Member of Parliament, he did so in the company of the IRB man John O'Connor Power, with the intention of presenting the President of the United States with an 'Address to the American People' on the centenary of American independence. The Address, ostensibly 'from the Irish People', had been moved at an unimportant meeting of 'advanced nationalists' held in a Dublin suburb and organised by the local IRB under John Leavy.[19]

A matter that much concerned the Supreme Council in 1874 and 1875 was the negotiation of an agreement with the Clan na Gael for a joint Revolutionary Directory and for an annual subvention. The IRB badly needed money for such projects as the purchase of the *Irishman* newspaper from its impecunious and shifty owner, Richard Pigott, to whom they had given at least one loan in the hope of keeping him on their side. Money was harder to collect in America for Fenian purposes than formerly, and such funds as became available were required for American-based 'speculations' such as the rescue of Fenian prisoners held in Australia. Anyhow, the Americans did not appear to think very much of the IRB, whose talk of the rottenness and rascality of their American brethren had reached their ears.

Another IRB concern, apart from the Tipperary election, was the O'Connell centenary, which fell in August 1875. This they were glad to participate in, and a meeting of the Supreme Council was arranged to facilitate members who might wish to be present at the monster public meeting in Dublin.[20] The Brotherhood was disturbed, however, when it became known that the ex-Lord Chancellor, Thomas O'Hagan, 'a Whig placeman', was to deliver the address on behalf of the Irish nation;

and, under cover of a procession to demand the release of the Fenian prisoners, a protest was planned by the Dublin men. Some of these actually interrupted the O'Connell meeting and were later taken to task for going too far.

The split in the Supreme Council on the Home Rule issue is only too evident from the Secretary's correspondence. Kickham, the President of the Council, was critical of the 'weak-kneed nationalists' who condemned 'advanced' men. On the other hand, John Barry considered a speech by John Daly, who shared Kickham's views, as 'most reprehensible and mischievous'. Denis Dowling Mulcahy, an ex-prisoner returned from America who was trying to rally the IRB against Home Rule, complained of a speech by O'Connor Power in which he said that any Irishman who did not join the Home Rule Association was a positive enemy of his country and the cause they were fighting for. In a criticism of a federal policy put forward by Butt, Mulcahy said that a local parliament in Dublin would restore no national rights to Ireland, nor would it in the eyes of other nations take her out of the category of a dependency of Great Britain. If Home Rule restored to Ireland what the Anglo-Norman invaders and their successors had robbed her of, if it placed her in the proud position of America, then he was a thorough Home Ruler. It not, not. In the dying words of John Mitchel, he had made no peace with England. It was no wonder that foreigners should exclaim, 'Is it possible Christ died for this people?' when they read how fickle and inconsistent the Irish were, and how easily they became reconciled to misrule and wrong by the words of a plausible demagogue.

Mulcahy's anger increased as he learned of the difficulty Doran's organisers were experiencing in obtaining halls for his meetings in Cork, and from 'the patriotic people' of New Ross and Wexford. Home Rulers interrupted a meeting of his in Manchester, and a 'lower lot of ruffians' than he had ever seen in his life menaced the platform but were booted off. 'They brought me out much stronger on Home Rule principles than I intended to have spoken,' he said, 'but now that they have provoked me I mean to defend or be defeated. It is now war to the knife and blood to the buttocks. Irishmen have been demoralised and Ireland disgraced by Home Rule and Home Rulers.' Leavy, the Supreme Council Treasurer, hearing of the 'unseemly treatment' given to Mulcahy, proposed to make it up to him at a meeting he was organising for him in Dublin, but this was not a success. The spirit was bad, said Leavy, for demoralisation had borne its fruit. It would require careful, judicious but resolute treatment to repair the injuries created in their business by the 'unholy alliance'. It was being said in IRB circles in Britain that the learning of drill, which was incumbent on every member, was almost useless, as the men at the head of affairs would not begin anything until they were sure of success. It was being urged that the people of Ireland were not unanimous with regard to separation from England. And, as morale within 'the Organisation' suffered, reports began to arrive of clashes with Home Rule supporters. From London came word of 'a sharp tussle' in which the Supreme Council representative there got 'two very sick cuts in the head'.

4

On the American side of the Atlantic the Fenian elements were more active than their Irish counterparts. John McCafferty, an ex-prisoner of the British, prepared to kidnap the Prince of Wales and hold him as a hostage on a sailing vessel until his colleagues still incarcerated were released. The plan was dismissed by the Clan na Gael as impracticable, however, and the Executive adopted the alternative idea of employing a whaling boat, the *Catalpa*, to rescue Fenian prisoners held in Western Australia. This operation, in which two IRB men, John Walsh of Middlesbrough and Denis Florence McCarthy of Cork, played a part, was carried out successfully in April 1876. O'Donovan Rossa, another ex-prisoner, shared McCafferty's robust ideas and initiated a public Skirmishing Fund to finance attacks on selected British targets. And, as insurrections occurred in the Balkans as a prelude to the Russo-Turkish War, the Clan na Gael, in the belief that England would be drawn into the conflict, sent a delegation to the Russian ambassador in Washington and presented proposals for an expedition to Ireland. An informer told the British acting consul at Philadelphia that the Russians were as keen on giving aid to the Irish as the Irish were to receive it; General F. F. Millen, a member of the delegation, was optimistic about support from St Petersburg and predicted success in the event of a concurrence of war with Russia and an outbreak in Ireland,[21] but neither the informant nor the acting consul nor many other people knew that Millen had been, and perhaps still was, a British agent.[22] A second agent inside the Clan na Gael—this was the Englishman Beach, *alias* Henri Le Caron—was in direct communication with Robert Anderson, the watchdog on American Fenianism in the British Home Office, and he reported on 6 May 1878 that another in the series of Fenian incursions into Canada was on the way: it was intended to cross the frontier at two places in Michigan and Vermont. Reporting this to his brother, Samuel Lee Anderson, who held a similar position in Dublin Castle, Robert Anderson wondered if the Fenians had received some Russian pay to incite them to make a raid for which little preparation had been made.[23]

In the early stages of the Russo-Turkish War Kickham, the President of the IRB, told the members in a printed address that an opportunity appeared to be developing for which they should be prepared. Should England be forced into the war, and should such a providential chance for Ireland be allowed to pass, the cause to which they were vowed would be hopelessly lost for that generation. Some members had been misled by mistaken or designing politicians—in other words, the Home Rulers— and the impression that the organisation was the mere catspaw of parliamentary agitators had been embarrassing and paralysing. However, that and other impediments had been got rid of, and for the first time during many years the organisation had the entire and hearty co-operation of their transatlantic brothers. Members were asked to go to work, not noisily and excitedly like men taken by surprise, but with the cool determination of men resolved never to desert the ship, who had nailed their colours to the mast and cleared the deck for action.[24] The government, receiving a copy of Kickham's address almost as soon as it was printed, were hardly impressed. They were aware of the run-down condition of the IRB.

The Russian ambassador in Washington had also come to the conclusion that the IRB had not much to offer. There was no public evidence, he told the delegation that waited on him, of any separatist movement in Ireland: the Irish only seemed to be seeking minor reforms. Anyhow, his government would only enter into direct negotiation with Irish revolutionaries in the improbable event of Russia going to war with England. These remarks impressed Devoy and were a factor in his decision to launch the 'New Departure' tactics, to which we shall come presently, of urging the IRB to take part in public affairs and obtain control of parliamentary representation and local bodies.[25]

Robert Anderson, noticing some indications of a revival of Fenian excitement, became somewhat uneasy at the unparalleled dearth of information reaching him, and the idea entered his mind of bringing over to London an established informant from America—Le Caron, no doubt—though he knew that this was a risky business which was to be avoided if at all possible. On reflection, however, it occurred to him that if the Fenians were really becoming active, one symptom would be that informers would be more plentiful: in his polite words, there would be offers of intelligence. And, sure enough, the first of these offers now reached him.[26]

In Ireland also a valuable informant came forward; Desmond Ryan, a great authority on Fenian matters, suggests that this was John Leavy, who had represented the province of Leinster on the Supreme Council of the IRB and who, since Patrick Egan's resignation from the treasurership, had filled that position. The suggestion is hard to sustain. Leavy, a native of Westmeath who had been a member of an agrarian Ribbon society before joining the Fenians in 1865, personally directed IRB affairs in Dublin at this period, but found time to concern himself also with the organisation's business in the northern half of Ireland. He was among the most active IRB officers, and his many letters to Doran, the Secretary of the Supreme Council, show him as a critic of inaction, an advocate of a strong line against Home Rule and Home Rulers and of co-operation with Ribbonmen, whose activities in midland areas in the early 1870s had drawn the government's fire. He complained of the shortage of funds, and when the exchequer was exhausted he was obliged, he said, to dip into his own pocket to help out. But in April 1877 Leavy and some cronies were accused by W. F. Roantree, a leading IRB man, of applying money subscribed for republican purposes to their own use or of wasting it on 'paltry outrages on policemen or public statues'—a reference to the shooting of a policeman and the attempted destruction of the Albert Memorial on Duke's Lawn in Dublin.[27] Whatever the truth about the organisation's money, Leavy was given three months in jail for embezzling the funds of the Dublin firm by which he was employed, and this forced his resignation from the IRB. Some ten years later, in 1889, he turned up as a hostile witness at the Special Commission Court which examined the charges brought by *The Times* against Parnell and his colleagues. His relations were uneasy with what the police called 'the lower stratum' of Fenians, with men like James Carey, Daniel Delaney, Daniel Curley and Edward McCaffrey, who were to form the core of the Invincibles of whom we shall hear more presently. His criticism of 'paltry outrages' was probably aimed at them. If Leavy is to be believed, the group once threatened to take his life for not revealing to them where a meeting of the Supreme Council was being held. Carey, the leader of the group, ran a Home Rule club in York Street, Dublin, for men who came together at night to drill and practise the use of arms, a form of cover repeated through the whole of the IRB story. Carey's group, we need hardly say, was anything but a Home Rule club in the ordinary sense.

In 1877 John O'Mahony, the co-founder with Stephens of the Fenian movement, died in poverty in a New York garret, and his remains were sent home to Ireland for burial. They reposed for a day in Queenstown's Pro-cathedral, but when they reached Dublin, Paul Cullen, the Cardinal Archbishop, refused to admit them to the Pro-cathedral of the Dublin diocese. He had done the same in 1861 when the body of Terence Bellew MacManus was brought home. He then said that public funerals were reserved for those who had rendered great service to religion or country, and he questioned MacManus's claim on that score. The funeral, in his opinion, was an American 'diversion' to stir up trouble in Ireland.[28] But the Church ban did not prevent O'Mahony from being given a great public funeral which was designed, as Fenian funerals always were, 'to stir up the dry bones' of Irish nationalism. Dead Fenians were often better than live ones. The practice did not commend itself to Kickham, who was a pious man and unhappy about an essentially religious occasion being used for propagandist purposes.

In the same year, after long-drawn-out and acrimonious negotiations, the formal agreement with the Clan na Gael was ratified, enabling a joint Revolutionary Directory to be established to look after relations between the two bodies. It consisted of three men from the United States, three from Ireland, and one from Australasia, where Fenian settlers had started the IRB on a small scale. Owing to the difficulty of communication the Australasian part of the Directory became a dead letter, but the American-Irish combination worked well in practice for some time. Also in 1877 one of the IRB chiefs proposed to the Clan na Gael that a joint contingent should, in association with the Spaniards, capture the fortress at Gibraltar, but the Spanish premier, when approached, told the IRB–Clan na Gael envoys Dr William Carroll and James J. O'Kelly, and their military aides, F. F. Millen and Michael Kerwin,[29] that he could not entertain the proposal. British naval power forbade it.[30] An earlier and more ambitious enterprise also came to nothing : this was a plan to sweep the Atlantic clear of British ships with submarines which were being developed, with Clan na Gael moneys, by a former Irish Christian Brother, John P. Holland. On the success of this plan hinged an idea conceived by Dr Carroll that an army of up to 10,000 Irish-Americans should be ready at a month's notice to set off for an invasion of the homeland.

5

The idea of working with Parnell was making converts within the IRB, and James J. O'Kelly, a Fenian colleague of John Devoy's on the New York *Herald*, took the lead in advocating co-operation. He had met Parnell in Paris, had been greatly impressed by him, and believed that his idea of creating a political link between conservative and radical nationalists should be supported. Those who would not consider such a link would be content with nothing less than the moon and would not get it. The effect of Parnell's leadership, O'Kelly said, had already been tremendous; with the right kind of support and a band of *real* nationalists in the House of Commons he would remould Irish public opinion and clear away many of the stumbling blocks in the way of progressive action.

Devoy was won over by O'Kelly's estimate of Parnell's capacity, as was Michael Davitt, the one-armed Fenian, when, on his release on ticket-of-leave from Portland Prison in December 1877, he met Parnell for the first time. Davitt renewed his old connections and invited Parnell to join him in a reorganised IRB which would support an open movement on constitutional lines.

His concern was to wage war against landlordism, which he believed was at the root of Ireland's chronic land problem and was producing a condition of distress unexampled since the Great Famine of the 1840s. In 1877 there had begun a disastrous series of bad harvests and, with price declines and the restriction of credit, starvation and destitution occurred in parts of the country and sent rocketing the figures for agrarian crime and evictions. Parnell had no intention of joining the IRB, much though he valued Fenian support; and a promise of this support seemed assured when Davitt, with Devoy, returned to Europe from America with proposals for what was termed the 'New Departure'. This was described by Davitt as 'an open participation in public movements by extreme men . . . with the view of bringing an advanced nationalist spirit and revolutionary purpose into Irish public life, in a friendly rivalry with moderate nationalists'.

These proposals, though blessed by the Clan na Gael, failed to secure the approval of the IRB when they were produced in January 1879 to the Supreme Council at a four-day conference held in Paris and attended by Devoy. Kickham, the doggedly anti-deviationist President of the IRB, was not going to allow it to repeat its Home Rule League experiences. Even as the conference assembled in the French capital the Irish police were discreetly taking down enormous IRB posters that assailed the 'Constitutional Agitators and their Transatlantic Allies' and set out the case for the policy of resort to arms in terms that James Lowther, the Chief Secretary for Ireland, described as foolish rodomontade which would harm Mr Parnell and his following more than it would Her Majesty's Government.[31] In fact it harmed neither.

The Paris conference made some concessions. It agreed that individual IRB members, though they could not enter parliament, were free to take part in parliamentary politics or agrarian agitation. But the rejection of the main purpose of the New Departure proposals so offended Davitt, who represented the North of England on the Supreme Council, that he ceased to attend its meetings and was expelled in May 1880. 'He had been summoned to appear at a meeting of the North of England Centres to explain his connection with the land movement and to answer the charges of having misled the men of "the firm".'

He had not attended the meeting, and a letter of explanation from him being deemed unsatisfactory, he was asked to resign. Matt Harris and P. J. Sheridan were also 'shunted'. This and other information about the state of 'the Organisation' was improperly given to a correspondent of the New York *Herald* by either C. G. Doran or P. N. Fitzgerald, Davitt believed. The IRB, he said, was not in good hands.[32] By this time he had joined with Parnell in establishing the Irish National Land League, which became one of the most formidable popular organisations of the nineteenth century. The New Departure, thus translated into fact, swept Parnell into power as leader of a militant nation and broke the back of Irish landlordism.[33] It also almost wiped out the IRB.[34]

6

After the Paris conference Devoy went to Ireland on a visit of inspection and organisation of the IRB. He had with him Millen, the Clan na Gael's military expert, who travelled under the assumed name of General Morgan. From Ireland they went through England and Scotland and were not interfered with, perhaps because the government could rely upon Le Caron, their well-placed American agent, to obtain a copy of Devoy's report for them, while they maintained Millen's cover.

Dr William Carroll of Philadelphia, who was among the ablest and most devoted of the Clan na Gael leaders, had been in Ireland on an inspection visit immediately before Devoy's. He had had a couple of interviews with Parnell from which he formed the impression that Parnell was 'almost pledged to accept a position on the Council of the IRB.[35] The government had heard as much privately. They had also heard that Fenianism was 'nearly dead', with small farmers and country shopkeepers particularly apathetic.[36] The movement was certainly in very poor shape. In 1877 in the province of Munster, excluding Waterford, there were only 1,742 members, their equipment consisting of 348 'long' or 'short' weapons and 500 rounds of ammunition. In cash they had £259.[37] Since its beginning, Fenianism had had a pronounced urban character. A summary of the occupations of the persons taken into custody under warrants in connection with the Rising of 1867 showed that, out of a total of 1,086, only 118, or ten per cent, were farmers, farmers' sons or farm labourers.

Carroll on his inspection discovered that the IRB was in even worse health than he and his American colleagues had been led to believe, and this was a rather extraordinary state of affairs, considering that the government had for a long time left the organisation untouched. The trouble was internal. It arose in the first instance, he thought, out of the efforts of James Stephens to re-establish himself at the head of affairs with the help of a remnant of American Fenians under the hard-drinking O'Donovan Rossa, and Richard Pigott, the unscrupulous editor of the *Irishman*, a Dublin weekly. The quarrel over the expulsions from the IRB of men connected with the Home Rule Party was a second disruptive factor. Some of those expelled submitted quietly, but others began a war to the knife on the Supreme Council and succeeded in reducing the membership in the North of England substantially. A third element was an inefficient Secretary to the Council who was also the representative of the province of Munster. That province, where the national spirit was perhaps stronger and more intelligent than in any other part of Ireland, had gradually been let fall into a state of partial disorganisation. Leinster similarly had suffered from the neglect of local officers and personal squabbles. Three of the best-organised counties, Dublin, Louth and Wexford, seceded from the Supreme Council, believing the oft-repeated story that the Americans had given their allegiance to Stephens. There still remained with the Council Ulster, Connacht, Munster and a portion of Leinster, as well as Scotland and the South of England; but work in these divisions was almost paralysed, and the attention of the members distracted, by repeated visits and communications of a conflicting nature from contending factions, all of whom claimed to be 'working for Ireland'.

Carroll first succeeded in gaining over the Leinster men to the Supreme Council by telling them 'the real truth' about the state of things in America. 'A competent and energetic man was elected representative for the province and the process of winning back Stephens's followers was satisfactorily begun.' Carroll also reconciled the North of England, thus completing the union of the whole seven provinces of the IRB—Ulster, Leinster, Munster, Connacht, South of England, North of England and

Scotland—though the organisation in two of them was considerably shattered by the ordeal through which they had passed. The Supreme Council itself was then reorganised and an efficient Secretary elected. The final position, then, was that the Council commanded the allegiance of about 24,000 men, compared with over 40,000 a few years before. The process of arming, however, had been neglected in the interim and would have to be pursued with greater vigour and with financial assistance from the United States.

When Devoy arrived on 1 April 1879 he found that the IRB was just beginning to breathe a little more freely and to feel that it was again a solid living body. By July when he left, new elections, he claimed, had taken place in every Circle in every province, and, from the highest to the lowest, every officer had been either replaced or re-elected. Arms were flowing in and training in their use had begun again. This was being done with circumspection lest a hitch would spoil everything. He hoped to live to see the military honour of Ireland, which had been tarnished by two bloodless failures, in 1848 and 1867, restored to its old and proud position.

Devoy travelled through all seven IRB provinces, attending county meetings at which County Centres were elected and making the personal acquaintance of the men who could speak for the Districts. As opportunity offered he met the rank and file at their Circle meetings, which were held in all sorts of out-of-the-way places and in all kinds of weather. He also attended provincial conventions, returning to meetings of the Executive of the Supreme Council—the President, the Secretary and the Treasurer—to report what he had seen and to make whatever recommendations he thought the situation demanded. He found in the rural districts 'a great tendency to looseness and a great want of system'. The people were by nature easy-going and careless but exacting on their leaders. They expected too much from the Supreme Council without stopping to inquire where the Council's resources were to come from. He concluded that it would take long training to make the IRB, as a whole, a self-reliant, self-supporting organisation, and to make the members in the rural districts understand that much more was necessary to sustain a great political movement than a mere willingness to risk life and liberty.[38]

B

The Irish National Invincibles

I

IT CAN be assumed that in their perambulations Carroll and Devoy preached acceptance of the New Departure. This affected the assistance given by Fenians to the campaign of the Land League which also drew support from isolated underground groups such as that which in April 1878 murdered Lord Leitrim, the most persistent of Irish landlords in the pursuit of his own ends, and his clerk and driver with him, on a lonely Donegal road. In Mayo, Davitt's native county in which the Land League began, there had been unmistakable signs of revolt against rack-rents and capricious evictions. Ribbonmen, for decades loosely organised in a secret society, sporadically made themselves felt in various parts of the country. To contain them in Westmeath and neighbouring areas, special legislation, hurriedly passed, superficially achieved its purpose, but, in the wake of Lord Leitrim's murder, the Resident Magistrate for County Westmeath informed Dublin Castle that the Ribbon organisation was just as powerful and as prepared for action, when necessary, as he had found it about fifteen years earlier.[1] Outside the cities and towns, therefore, it was land and the problems associated with it which commanded the attention of people rather than the abstractions of the IRB leaders, the Kickhams and the O'Learys. They felt they could be better occupied removing the stumbling blocks in the way of the redistribution of farms, low rents and fixity of tenure.[2]

The Land War, for it was nothing if it was not that, went on for a long time, but the Land League proper had quite a short life. It came into being, as we saw, in October 1879; it was suppressed by the government two years later in reaction to a manifesto directed to farmers to withhold their rents, and was never revived. Davitt's ticket-of-leave was rescinded, and Parnell and other leaders were arrested and lodged in Kilmainham Jail, an action which raised Parnell's reputation with the Fenians and further incensed the people. The non-payment of rent led, of course, to more evictions, and these, increasing from 1,732 in the first quarter of 1881 to 6,496 in the third and to a total of 17,341 for the whole year, produced a state of frenzy. 'The country stood at bay,' a contemporary nationalist writer noted, 'and driven from constitutional and open movement, with speech and writing and organisation suppressed, with every day adding a new wrong and a new insult, with wholesale eviction, exile and starvation once more confronting the nation as in the dread past, the population resorted to the secret organisation and the revolting crimes which have been the inevitable and hideous brood of despotic regimes.'[3] In the nine months between January and October 1881, when Parnell went to jail, there were forty-six violent attacks, consisting of nine murders, five cases of manslaughter, and thirty-two of 'firing at the person'. In the following six months there were no fewer than seventy-nine violent attacks, comprising fourteen murders and sixty-five cases of 'firing at the person'.

One would not be disposed to describe any of Gladstone's regimes as deliberately despotic; yet it is true that his second administration, formed after the general election of 1880 in which sixty-eight Home Rulers were returned, proceeded to deal with the chronic problems highlighted by the Land League with measures of drastic coercion as well as of reform. Things came to such a pass by April 1882 that Parnell, using a member of his party, Captain Willie O'Shea, as intermediary, was glad to come to terms with Gladstone in the so-called Kilmainham Treaty. This enabled the government to release Parnell, to relax coercion, to improve a land measure before the House of Commons, and to give protection to tenants in arrears with their rents; in return, Parnell promised to use his influence to calm the country and to secure the general acceptance for the amended land bill.

A number of personal factors were involved in the settlement. Parnell was anxious to secure release from prison not only in order to regain control over the disorderly elements among his following but also because of his entanglement with Captain O'Shea's wife, Katharine, who had just given birth to their first child. Gladstone knew little of Parnell's personal life, but he had got to know O'Shea rather well and found him useful in the course of the proceedings leading to the Kilmainham settlement. The terms of that settlement were not, however, to the liking of W. E. Forster, Gladstone's Chief Secretary, and Earl Cowper, the Lord Lieutenant, and they both resigned in protest. They failed to carry any other member of the government with them, however, for what they sought was quite unobtainable, a penitential public declaration from Parnell discountenancing the intimidation in which the Land League was implicated. Gladstone knew that if the Irish leader appeared as an open critic of a section of his own people, his power to co-operate would quickly disappear.

Cowper and Forster were replaced as Lord Lieutenant and Chief Secretary by Earl Spencer and Lord Frederick Cavendish, and Gladstone was not sorry to make these changes. Cowper had not seemed equal to the responsibilities of his office, and Forster, he thought, was a very impractical man in a position of great responsibility, and with no adequate conception of public liberty. That was the popular Irish view of the man, too. It was particularly the view of a band of assassins, calling themselves the Irish National Invincibles and operating mainly in and from Dublin, who had repeatedly failed to 'get' Forster before he left the country.

2

The burden of watching all secret society activities in the Dublin Metropolitan Police (DMP) area rested on Superintendent John Mallon of the G Division. By any reckoning he was a remarkable man. A native of Meigh, Co. Armagh, Mallon was educated in Newry Model School, served an apprenticeship with a drapery firm in Newry, was rejected for admission to the Royal Engineers, and then joined the DMP in 1858 at the age of nineteen. First under Superintendent Daniel Ryan and subsequently by himself he directed the detective force and played a major role in countering the Fenians. His unique qualities were recognised by Earl Spencer: 'We depend in Dublin on one man, Mallon; were he to die or be killed, we have no one worth a row of pins.'[4] He had a finger in every pie, and exploitable contacts by the hundred. In November 1881 he had a visit from a man he suspected of being a member of the executive of the suppressed Land League who feared that a warrant had been issued for his arrest. 'This,' in Mallon's words, 'was a gentleman above the middle class, a sensible well-to-do business man.' The information he proceeded to give, Mallon stressed, he gave not as an informer but as one who had seen the error of his ways. He told Mallon that the Land League executive had been pushed into issuing a no-rent manifesto against their better judgment and that Fenians and Ribbonmen were involved in the Land League outrages. It required great efforts to restrain them; and Patrick Egan and Thomas J. Brennan, the League's treasurer and secretary, were largely beyond control. This was particularly true of Egan, who was a former member of the Supreme Council of the IRB. Egan kept the pent-up passions of the active Land Leaguers in reserve and when it suited him he gave them the word, saying in effect: 'Look, there's the target; do as you please.' The men in America who subscribed money controlled by Egan did so for revolutionary purposes and were looking for results. The accounts were in a dreadful state and nothing like a decent attempt had been made to audit them since Egan went to Paris to avoid being arrested.

Egan and Brennan, the visitor continued, were probably the only two leaders that ever fraternised with the Fenian element in Dublin, who were too contemptible for any respectable and intelligent man to have anything to do with. The antagonism between Land Leaguism and Fenianism was not correctly understood. It arose from jealousies among the officers of both organisations in the first place, and from the different bases upon which the two organisations worked. At no period was a thorough fusion of principle so likely to take place as now. Moderate men were every day being taunted with the absurdity of constitutional agitation. The intention to assassinate persons in high places existed, but this was not at the suggestion of the Land League executive, who had always opposed any such idea. They could not control, however, the fanatics who accepted as inevitable and for the good of the cause that the Prime Minister (Gladstone), the Home Secretary (Harcourt) and the Chief Secretary (Forster) should be 'removed'.

George Talbot, the Chief Commissioner of the DMP, affirmed the general truth of this information. Things were in the hands of unscrupulous miscreants whose movements it was necessary to watch, and to do so he was sparing no effort. All the precautions at his disposal would be taken.[5] But these were anything but sufficient. Indeed, on 6 May 1882 the man to whom he gave this assurance, the Under-Secretary, Thomas Henry Burke, was brutally murdered in Phoenix Park in Dublin, and with him Lord Frederick Cavendish, who had taken up office as Chief Secretary that very day in substitution for Forster. A small close-knit group of men, mostly of the artisan class, had assembled in the park with the intention of killing Burke, but when he came into view he was not alone, but walking arm-in-arm with Cavendish. Nevertheless, the attack was pressed home with surgical knives and Burke fell to the ground. Cavendish tried to counter the attack with his umbrella but he too was cut down. In a matter of minutes the grisly business was over; the assailants made their way back to the city and left black-edged cards at the newspaper offices. These said that the deed had been done by the Irish Invincibles, the first time that particular body had been heard of.

Suspicion naturally fell on the Dublin IRB men, among whom Superintendent Mallon recognised there were men wicked enough to have killed Cavendish and Burke; but he looked beyond them for a person or persons capable of both planning the crime and providing the money to sustain the perpetrators of it, and their dependants, should they run into trouble. In this fashion he focused attention on Egan, the Land League treasurer, who, he believed, had directed the Land League's conspiracy from his Paris headquarters, probably with Thomas Brennan, the League's principal secretary, who had been directly concerned with the attempt to blow up the Albert Memorial in the city. They were both known to be critical of what was termed the Parnell surrender, the Kilmainham Treaty; but, that apart, they were determined to dispose of Ireland's principal enemies, as they saw them, by strong-arm methods. By degrees Mallon added other names to the category of the superior officers of the Invincibles, including Frank Byrne, the secretary of the Land League of Great Britain, who had an office in Westminster, P. J. P. Tynan, who in later years wrote a book about the Invincibles, John McCafferty, John Walsh and P. J. Sheridan. All these men had Land League and Fenian connections.

The Phoenix Park murders were trenchantly condemned by the Irish Parliamentary Party—indeed, Parnell was so horrified that he offered to resign his seat if Gladstone considered it necessary for the maintenance of the government's position that he should do so—and by outstanding IRB men like Kickham, the President of the Supreme Council, and John O'Leary, another of the original Fenian chiefs, who since his release from prison had been living in Paris. Kickham denounced the Invincibles as 'Fenians seduced by the Land League', and O'Leary saw what had happened in the Phoenix Park as a Land League crime, conceived by men who had all once been Fenians, who had not acted as Fenians but in the teeth of what any responsible Fenian would in the least countenance. They were 'murderous ruffians'. John Devoy in America also condemned the act but thought it possible that the Invincibles were moved by a misguided patriotism. The Celtic nature revolted at the bare idea of assassination, he said, while it welcomed, as the Fenians did, the thought of conflict in the open field.

None of the 'superior officers of the Invincibles' were ever brought to book, but the actual group that did the killing was. They were discovered largely through the ingenuity of Superintendent Mallon, aided materially by informing from within their own ranks, especially by James Carey, and they were either hanged or sent to long terms of penal servitude. There is evidence to show that their activities were not confined to the Phoenix Park or, for that matter, to the city of Dublin.[6] In killing T. H. Burke they had got rid of one of the most dangerous men in Ireland, from their point of view. They had listed Mallon and Samuel Lee Anderson also for execution, but both survived. Anderson, however, died in 1886 when only forty-nine years of age. The strain of his office had undermined his health, forcing him to retire prematurely with a knighthood conferred on him by Lord Spencer in recognition of his work in the suppression of crime and criminal conspiracies.[7]

The search for the Invincibles was going on when Charles Kickham died in August 1882. He had been President of the Supreme Council of the IRB since the reorganisation of 1873, if not from an earlier date.[8] He was given another of the great Fenian funerals, with a graveside oration by John Daly of Limerick, a strict-observance Fenian like Kickham himself; and among those in the cortège were the entire Supreme Council and practically every County Centre in Ireland. The presence was especially noticed of John Ryan, the head of the IRB in Southern England; John Torley representing Scotland; Dr Mark Ryan, then living in Brighton, representing Connacht, and Robert Johnston of Belfast representing Ulster. In Devoy's judgment, Kickham was the finest intellect the movement had produced on either side of the Atlantic. He was recognisably a superior person, sensitive, cultured and deeply religious; and he had an unusual capacity for expressing in prose and poetry his love of country people and their traditions. He did this though hampered by poor sight and stone-deafness as a result of an explosion, which made it necessary for those who wished to communicate with him to resort to sign language. But, like other superior persons at the higher levels of Fenianism, one wonders how capable he was of directing revolutionary activities, or how much he really knew of what went on 'down below'.

We do not know who immediately succeeded him at the head of the IRB. It may have been John O'Connor, who had been the Secretary of the Supreme Council since the resignation of Charles Guilfoyle Doran from that post in 1877. The presidency passed later (probably in 1885) to John O'Leary. O'Leary was, like Kickham, a cultivated man. He was interested in literature and dispensed considerable influence in letter-writing and conversation. He represented Romantic Ireland to the poet Yeats, and to Dublin Castle their idea of what a Fenian should be—a man who believed in honourable warfare, who was prepared to wait until the IRB could march an army into battle with flags flying and pipers piping, which might be never. He certainly was an odd figure to have at the head of a republican organisation, because he was fundamentally not a republican at all, his own predilection being for monarchy. He had spent a long time in prison and in exile which had attenuated his membership of the Supreme Council; but he was very much of the movement, and the importance of his opinion was recognised when he was brought into the vital Council talks in Paris in 1879. He and Kickham were in close agreement on the undesirability of having anything to do with parliamentary agitation, and his election as President ensured that that was to remain the policy of 'the Organisation' through what was left of the 1880s.

3

The suppression of the Land League and the Prevention of Crimes Act, passed in 1882 to deal with situations like those created by the Invincibles, facilitated Parnell's strategy of deflecting public attention from the land question to that of Home Rule. This issue, backed by a new popular organisation, the Irish National League, held the centre of the stage from 1883 till 1887, and in the first two of those years Parnell showed himself rather infrequently in public, being much concerned with his personal problems. It was during this time that Mrs O'Shea gave birth to the second and third of his three children, and that he began to make use of her as a go-between with Gladstone on political business. Through these years there is little evidence of IRB activity other than through its front literary societies. The country was still disturbed, especially in the period immediately following the Phoenix Park murders when, in the words of a leading IRB man of a later generation, 'coercion, eviction and retaliation were let loose over the land like so many wolves'.[9] The retaliation was directed mainly from the United States where the Clan na Gael and an American version of the Irish National League had passed from the control of John Devoy and Dr William Carroll into the hands of an utterly unscrupulous character, Alexander Sullivan.

Contrary to what Devoy wished, Sullivan provided cover for the 'skirmishing' campaign for the use of dynamite against English cities, O'Donovan Rossa declaring that for that purpose he was in favour of 'dynamite, Greek fire, or hell-fire if it could be had'. In 1883 and 1884 there were explosions at the Local Government Board Offices in Whitehall, at the *Times* office in St James's Square, at Scotland Yard, and on the underground railway system at a number of stations; and on a day at the end of January 1885 tremendous explosions occurred almost simultaneously in the Tower of London, Westminster Hall and the House of Commons. The wreckage wrought in the Commons was very great. These operations, to counter which a Special Irish Branch of the London Metropolitan Police was created, were not performed without cost. On a dark December night in 1884 when three men, who had crept up in a boat, were

B*

placing a large packet in position under one of the arches of London Bridge, its contents exploded, injuring the massive masonry hardly at all but blowing the boat and the three men to pieces. One of the men was William Mackey Lomasney, the central figure in many Fenian exploits in the city and neighbourhood of Cork in the 1860s.[10] He was, in Devoy's phrase, 'a fanatic of the deepest dye'.[11]

Before the Prevention of Crimes Act was due to expire in 1885, Spencer, the Lord Lieutenant, asked the cabinet what their wishes were regarding it. His personal view was that it was not safe yet to drop the act, though conditions in the country had greatly improved. Fenianism was still completely organised, however, and, although not active, it awaited an opportunity when England went to war to create serious difficulties for her. The strongest organisation in the country was probably the National League, he said. In its avowed objects it was constitutional and legal, but many of its members were not only Fenians, but men of desperate character who were either ready to commit crimes themselves or who belonged to secret societies organised for murder and outrage and used the League to cover their proceedings. Life and property were still threatened; at the end of December 1884 a thousand police had been employed in 275 posts to protect individuals. The Crimes Act should therefore be renewed but, in doing so, the government should promise further measures of a remedial character; and he mentioned specifically local government, the purchase by occupiers of their holdings of land, and the reform of central government, by which he meant replacing the post he himself occupied by a Minister for Ireland and the acquisition of a royal residence to which the Queen and members of her family could resort from time to time.[12]

In June 1885, however, the government, unable to compose internal differences on these and other matters, allowed themselves to be defeated; and when they returned in February 1886, after a caretaking spell by the Conservatives under Lord Salisbury, they were prepared—at least Gladstone and some of his colleagues were—to consider giving Ireland a form of Home Rule. In the new parliament Parnell's party held the balance of power, and Unionism, a counter-movement to the nationalism which Parnell represented, began to manifest itself.

4

Whether Liberals or Tories were in office, the Royal Irish Constabulary (RIC) and the Dublin Metropolitan Police (DMP) continued to supply the basic information about the state of Ireland on which the government relied, and this in turn depended in large measure on what their informants told them. The RIC kept a register for the years between 1884 and 1891 which showed payments, most of them small, to a number of IRB men, and to Fenians who supported Stephens, and to each of these was given an identifying cognomen. (I have seen no corresponding register for the DMP area or of payments to informers living outside Ireland.) Many of these informants were dropped when found to be drinking too heavily; that was a primary sign of undependability. The highest paid was 'Nero', a resident 'in a good position' in the South-Western Constabulary Division : on him Colonel Alfred E. Turner, who was engaged as a Special Commissioner of Police in uprooting agrarian crime, reported that he was worth any amount for the information he supplied about coming events, the movements of prominent nationalists and their intentions. He accordingly received £205 in 1889, including one payment of £100 by special authority. In the same Division, and in the same year, £60 was paid to 'Mary Sullivan', who was a member of the IRB, the Gaelic Athletic Association which had been founded in 1884 and infiltrated by the IRB, and the Irish National League. It was chiefly through his help that the Plan of Campaign, by means of which the Irish Nationalist Members of Parliament John Dillon, William O'Brien and Timothy Harrington organised combinations of tenants to achieve reduced rents from reluctant landlords, was combated on the Kenmare estate. 'Mary Sullivan' also enabled the police to break up a conspiracy to boycott—the practice of moral coventry which was first applied in 1880—to check a 'Cattle Manifesto' and to arrest three conspirators. 'Quentin' in the South-Eastern Division received a regular yearly stipend of £100. He was described as 'a sworn IRB man of good standing' whose services were most valuable in connection with the IRB and every movement in his county. It was true that he was inclined to generalise too much, but he was undoubtedly a useful man and his intimacy with leading Fenians meant that he would be of great use should the IRB become active. Changing their tune, the police decided in 1890 to 'drop him quietly', paying him meanwhile by results, but the final entry against his name indicated that he was 'giving rather better information latterly'. Among other informants—'informers' the people preferred to call them—were 'Lake' an IRB Centre in West Cork —'a man of considerable position and influence'; 'Jennings' in Cork city—'one of our oldest and most reliable men' (he was a leading Stephensite Fenian who had been imprisoned on political charges); 'Hood', also of Cork city, 'one of our most reliable men'; 'Essex' in Armagh—'an old IRB man and friend of O'Donovan Rossa'; and 'Joe Duro' in East Galway, who was simply described as 'Inner Circle, IRB'.[13]

This RIC register was seen in Dublin Castle as a guide to the sources from which information might be fairly expected from time to time. Some of the best informants, it was noted, did not give their information for money, and for that reason were not under control; but men of the class of 'Quentin' and 'Nero' were looked upon as special agents who could be directed to follow up matters and clear up points on which further knowledge was required. When in December 1890 the Under-Secretary, Sir Joseph West Ridgeway, lamented the great dearth of news at that time—though this, he confessed, might be due to inaction on the part of the secret societies—the special agents were asked to report fortnightly, and the police officers who 'controlled' them were directed to keep a form of diary showing where the 'special men' had been on each day during the fortnight, and the nature of the business on which they were engaged.[14]

Some informers, particularly really important men like Pierce Nagle, John Joseph Corydon, Godfrey Massey, John Devany, George Reilly and James Meara—these in the 1860s had driven many nails into the Fenian coffin—had to be maintained, with their families, as they hid themselves away outside Ireland under assumed names. They were a dissolute lot for the most part and whined a great deal about the inadequacies of their annuities. When their demands for more money were not met and they threatened to employ legal aid, or when there was the likelihood of their being brought to court for not paying their debts, they were told very bluntly that they not only ran the risk of having their position made public and their personal safety thereby endangered, but also of having their pensions entirely stopped by the government.[15] The government knew how to handle them. These pensions, Robert Anderson at the Home Office high-and-mightily thought, were based on the theory and object of withdrawing from public notice men whom necessity had compelled the government to use in loathsome work; they were not meant as rewards for villainy.[16]

The Young Ireland Society

I

THE MEMBERS of the IRB, at various stages of the organisation's existence and regardless of its condition, armed themselves as best they could, drilled with an eye always on the possibility of revolt, and involved themselves in agitation towards that end. They did this commonly from within national organisations with which they felt some kinship, and which they also used as recruiting grounds. They also operated at times through open or front societies of their own creation. The National Brotherhood of Saint Patrick in the 1860s was one of these and the Young Ireland Society of the 1880s was another. This Young Ireland Society had its headquarters at 41 York Street, Dublin, and had branches in parts of the country and in Britain. W. B. Yeats, who joined it in October 1885 and was profoundly influenced by it, has much to say about the society in his *Reveries over Childhood and Youth*.

The minute books for 1884–85, which fortunately have survived, cover the meetings of the committee (or Circle) which ran the society as a whole, as well as the open meetings held in York Street. Whatever the society said to the world at large about its objects, the authorities in Dublin Castle were never in doubt about them. They described the society as having been founded with the object of retaining a foothold in politics for the IRB, then threatened with extinction by being absorbed by the National League. No indication of that appeared in the society's syllabus, however. What did appear were selected extracts from Davis, Tone and Parnell; these, and the lectures and discussions generally, revealed the society's nationalist character. It showed itself particularly in the way the society worked up attendances at the annual Manchester Martyrs commemoration; its care of, and promotion of visits to, the graves of the patriot dead; and its criticism of the Lord Mayor of Dublin for his 'slavish' attitude to a visit from the Prince of Wales. The society had an exaggerated sense of its importance. The meetings were open to the press, but on a couple of occasions individual journalists were asked to withdraw either because their papers had failed to report an earlier meeting or had not done so to the committee's satisfaction.

More indicative still of the society's character as a front for the IRB were the collection taken up for the defence of its vice-president, Frederick J. Allan, when a prisoner in Kilmainham on a treason felony charge, and the arrangements made for giving John O'Leary a worthy welcome on his return to Ireland in 1885 after many years of imprisonment and exile. Allan escaped conviction in connection with what was known as the 'Paris letters', documents describing IRB movements and finances and which were said to contain references to people who had been involved in the Phoenix Park murders and in another one at Barbavilla Demesne near Collinstown, Co. Westmeath.[1] The letters had been sent by registered post to a Paris address and returned through the dead letter office. On his release Allan was active again in the society, lecturing on Emmet, the leader of the abortive rising in 1803, and expressing a nationalist reaction to a lecture on internationalism.

The society's minute books give the names of the committee members, all of whom it may be assumed were IRB men; they include, notably, John MacBride, who was a particularly lively and outspoken member. It also gives the names of newcomers to the branch meetings. Among these, joining in November 1884, was a Trinity graduate, T. W. Rolleston, who subsequently read papers to the society and took part in the discussions—he favoured the restoration of Grattan's Parliament as a stepping-stone to complete independence—and a medical student, Denis J. Coffey, who in later times was to be the first President of University College, Dublin. From another source we know that the man who was to become the first President of an independent Ireland also attended some of the meetings and spoke to the papers. This was Douglas Hyde, then a student of Trinity College, Dublin, who had already begun to acquire a reputation as a scholar in the field of Irish language and literature.[2] The society had no qualms about circulating all the Nationalist Members of Parliament for subscriptions to the Allan Defence Fund, but their regard for them individually depended on how extreme they appeared to them to be. Of John Dillon, who was actually the society's president in the 1884–85 session, William O'Brien, the Redmond brothers, John and Willie, and Dr J. E. Kenny, Parnell's doctor, they had no doubt; but there were others, among them Tim Harrington and Frank Hugh O'Donnell, whom they obviously disliked.

The arrangements for John O'Leary's return comprised a series of public meetings in major centres where there were active branches of the society, beginning with one in the Rotunda in Dublin. In all these places O'Leary spoke on the theme of 'Young Ireland—the Old and New', and it was noticeable on each occasion that his remarks received few cheers in comparison with those given for the parliamentarians who shared the platform with him. To that extent one senses that the organisers' intentions had misfired. The meetings in Manchester and Glasgow especially give a clear picture of conflicting policies and personalities. In the former place O'Leary told his listeners that he wanted to talk about two things—oath-breaking and dynamite or, to put it more plainly, perjury and murder. His views on dynamiting were already known to his listeners. From his exiled home in Paris he had written to the *Pall Mall Gazette* in March 1884 a letter in which he said that 'all these Invincible and dynamite doings' were utterly abhorrent to his whole nature. 'I have often told my countrymen', he wrote, 'how fervently I feel with Davis that

> Freedom comes from God's right hand
> And needs a Godly train
> And righteous men must make our land
> A Nation once again.'

But he denounced John O'Connor Power and the other ex-IRB men who, as he saw it, had forsworn their allegiance to Ireland by going into parliament with Parnell and bending the knee to the English Queen, and he reiterated his sense of shame as he regarded the hideous folly and awful criminality of dynamite and dynamiters. O'Donovan Rossa was the main offender on this score. He had begun as an honest enthusiast : he had ended as a somewhat unscrupulous madman. Rossa, Patrick Ford and their skirmishers had ceased to believe in the Fenian idea of fighting England fairly. It was useless talking to them about a moral issue. They were consumed by a hatred of England, and morality did not seem to be important any more. 'Taking their policy as it stood, I told them', O'Leary said, 'that they could not materially injure and were very little likely to frighten England : that they would certainly bring large loss of employment, and in the long run probably large loss of life on their countrymen in England.' But they would not listen to him, and there the matter rested, but he did know that, like all moral diseases, this one would have to be cured by moral remedies. No sin could cast out sin. Dynamite, assassination, revenge or union with frauds or robbers, even to obtain good, were all equally reprehensible. No sin could possibly restore Ireland to true freedom, but only to a more deadly slavery.

At Glasgow he spoke to what the newspapers called a mixed audience, of whom some cheered and others hissed when the name of Parnell was mentioned. The chairman, referring to the earlier meeting in Dublin, said that one of the Members of Parliament on the platform there had patted O'Leary on the back, telling him that he had fallen behind the times, that he was a Rip Van Winkle who did not understand what was wanted in the modern Ireland. 'The procession is moving on,' he was told, 'and if you want to keep up with it you must trot out.' To repeated cheers and hisses the chairman made it perfectly clear that the people for whom he and O'Leary spoke had no intention of keeping up with the procession; they were opposed to any policy other than that of Wolfe Tone, Robert Emmet and the Fenians of the 1860s, which meant that they had no faith in either parliamentary agitation or dynamite. There was uproar when somebody on the platform made an offensive reference to Parnell, and further interruptions and cheers when O'Leary rose again to speak to a vote of thanks. A number of men present, he said, had cheered Mr Parnell, and he could have no earthly objection to their doing so. He (O'Leary) had not been a Land Leaguer, nor a National Leaguer, but if Parnell was what he thought him to be the other day when he spoke in Cork, he could not see why they should receive his name otherwise than kindly. Mr Parnell had said that the Irish people wanted Grattan's Parliament, and that no man had the right to fix the boundary to the march of a nation. If Mr Parnell went on in that way, more luck to him.

But this did not imply that O'Leary or the IRB had changed their opinion of parliamentary agitation. At the Dublin meeting Charles McCarthy Teeling, who had become vice-president of the Young Ireland Society in place of Fred Allan who was in Kilmainham Jail, had put their point of view in the crudest terms. Their aim, he said, was to put the British government out of Ireland, and the way to accomplish this was not by cringing and begging in an alien parliament. They would never get anything that way. If they wanted to win national independence, they would have to fight for it. If they had not the pluck to fight for it, they would have to do without it. McCarthy Teeling, a flamboyant young man who had fought for the Pope and who always rode a white horse in the nationalist processions, was given to forceful utterances of this kind.

O'Leary's attitude to the Irish-American dynamiters caused dissension within the Young Ireland Society. Following the Rotunda meeting some of the members opposed the printing for circulation of O'Leary's speech, and later on John MacBride, in the presence of O'Leary, moved, though without success, that the printing be not proceeded with because of what O'Leary had said about O'Donovan Rossa; the society, he insisted, should not be made a platform from which to denounce an Irish patriot. It may have been these remarks which provoked a violent incident described by Yeats in his *Reveries*. O'Leary had become the president of the society in succession to John Dillon, whose health was poor, and in a letter to the newspapers he repeated his condemnation of the Irish-American dynamiters. This provided McCarthy Teeling with an opportunity to retaliate against O'Leary for telling him that attempting to oppress others was a poor preparation for liberating his own country. He moved a vote of censure, in the course of which he said that while he himself did not approve of bombs, he did not think that any Irishman should be discouraged from using them, and was ruled out of order by O'Leary. And when members nearby threatened to throw him out, he lifted the chair on which he had been sitting, swung it round his head and defied all and sundry to do so. He was ejected nevertheless, and when a special meeting was called to expel him from the society, he gathered his supporters outside the committee rooms with the intention of preventing any such decision. They made a lot of noise but failed to effect an entry.

2

A succession of dramatic happenings kept the public mind focused on the activities of the Irish Members at Westminster. There was the national monetary tribute to Parnell and the Vatican rescript condemning it because the collection and presentation seemed to condone illegal and sinful methods of achieving desirable objectives. There was the debate in 1885 on the extension of the franchise. There was the subsequent general election which the Irish Parliamentary Party used to protest strenuously against the whole system of government as it affected Ireland and to demand its reconstitution on new foundations. And there was the failure of Gladstone's first attempt at Home Rule for Ireland in 1886 and the consequent return to power of the Conservatives.

At that time, in the official view, the IRB was numerically strong and well organised : in Dublin alone, it was said, there were about 10,000 members, but this is probably an exaggerated figure, even if it includes members of the Young Ireland Society. The policy for the moment was not to stand in the way of Parnell and the National League. In a circular letter issued in June 1886 the Supreme Council declared that Parnell had no commission to accept in their names the concession of a parliament such as that outlined in the Home Rule Bill, but that the proposals, inadequate though they were, were by no means to be rejected. They represented progress. It was the duty of IRB men not merely *not* to seek to hamper the efforts of the Gladstone–Parnell combination but to assist them as far as they could.[3]

O'Leary from time to time explained his position. As an IRB man he *aimed* at securing a republic, but he was not a doctrinaire republican. He saw Parnell as the only leader who could make a success of constitutional action. In any event, Parnell was 'the man on the horse' and should be allowed to take the fence. When a Home Rule parliament was a possibility in 1886, O'Leary was uncertain as to his ultimate position, but the defeat of Gladstone's proposals disposed of that problem and left him with the problem of the republican extremists. He opted to shun them as far as possible. They included some of O'Donovan Rossa's men who, without much success, went about in Ireland looking for recruits and also 'guerrilla' Invincibles whose hero was Joe Brady, the most notorious of the Phoenix Park killers. This second crop of Invincibles was broken up in gangs who distrusted one another. They were armed, most of them, with good revolvers; and, under a capable leader, they could be really dangerous, the police thought.

From America the news was of divisions in the Clan na Gael. Supporters of Alexander Sullivan and John Devoy were opposing each other with great bitterness, with the result that the whole organisation was weak and short of money. Dynamite was out of favour; but there might be assassinations.[4]

3

During most of the Conservatives' term of office, which lasted from 1886 till 1892, the Chief Secretary for Ireland was Arthur James Balfour, who declared it his intention to be as ruthless as Cromwell in dealing with disorder and as thorough a social reformer as Parnell or anyone else could desire. His reforms, though real, were obscured by the coercive measures with which the name of 'Bloody Balfour' is popularly linked. There was fresh and permanent crimes legislation, the administration and the police were reorganised and strengthened, meetings were proclaimed, prosecutions of priests and press conducted, the Irish National League was suppressed, and the activities of the Plan of Campaign were opposed with great determination. The results were considered satisfactory. Balfour told the cabinet in January 1889, in a report on the general political condition, that agrarian crime was lower than in any year since 1879; this he ascribed to their own coercive legislation, the Pope's rescript and the improved attitude of landlords to their tenants. Yet, he noted particularly, the IRB was steadily gaining ground at the expense of a declining National League, and were finding in the Gaelic Athletic Association (GAA) the nucleus of the army with which they hoped to put an end to English dominion.[5]

To meet this situation a serious reorganisation of the counter-secret society work was undertaken, and both the Royal Irish Constabulary and the Dublin Metropolitan Police were issued with lists of suspects arranged in three categories, A, B and C. On the A list were entered those suspects who were to be 'shadowed' continuously by policemen specially detailed for that purpose. The suspects on the B list were to be 'ciphered', which meant that their movements were to be telegraphed in cipher from place to place so that they could in that way be kept under general police surveillance. On the C list were local suspects whose activities the police were required to 'note'. The A list was headed by William O'Brien, MP, John Dillon, MP, Dr Joseph E. Kenny, and John Kelly, a leading National League organiser. On it were two leading IRB organisers in Belfast, Robert Johnston, a timber merchant, and Daniel McCullough, a publican, and a third IRB man who was 'probably the most dangerous Secret Society man with whom we have to deal'. This was Michael O'Hanlon of Downpatrick. On the B list were Michael Davitt, John O'Connor and James O'Kelly, as well as eighteen others, fourteen of them 'leading IRB organisers'. These were Michael J. Seery, a traveller; James Boland, a pavier; John Clancy, a sub-sheriff; James O'Connor, J. J. O'Shea and F. J. Allan, journalists; James Rourke, a baker; John Sullivan, an auctioneer; Joseph G. Bolger and C. McCarthy Teeling, clerks; David Breen and J. C. Foley, travellers; Eugene Davis, a journalist; and Thomas F. Geoghegan, a photographer.[6]

4

Parnell's prestige never seemed higher, nor Irish hopes of achieving Home Rule brighter, when in March 1887 *The Times*, in a series of articles on the subject of 'Parnellism and Crime', began the publication of some letters which, on their face, showed that the Irish leader had condoned the Phoenix Park murders at the time they occurred. A Special Commission, with roving terms of reference, established, however, that the letters were forgeries. They had been concocted by Richard Pigott, the former editor of advanced Irish weekly newspapers, who, when his perfidy was discovered, hurried off to Madrid and blew out his brains in an hotel bedroom. Parnell's triumph and exculpation was widely acclaimed, not least by the Liberal Party, with whom the Irish MPs were closely allied.

But at that point, almost as if the move was held in reserve against the possibility of the *Times* series failing to destroy Parnell, Captain O'Shea brought an action for divorce against his wife and cited the Irish leader, the 'uncrowned king of Ireland', as the co-respondent. No defence being entered, judgment was given to O'Shea. This produced a situation to which Gladstone, for the Liberals, reacted by saying that while he had no wish to appear as a censor of morals, he was absolutely convinced that it would be useless to continue to advocate Home Rule if Parnell remained at the head of the Irish Parliamentary Party. That party then quarrelled and divided most bitterly over the retention of Parnell, and the Irish people followed suit. Repudiated by a majority of his parliamentary colleagues (of the three former members of the Supreme Council of the IRB who had entered parliament, one, J. G. Biggar, was dead, another, John O'Connor Power, stood as a Liberal in the general election of 1885 and was defeated, the third, John Barry, voted to depose Parnell), Parnell took the fight to Ireland where, in early by-elections in North Kilkenny, North Sligo and Carlow, quarter was neither asked for nor given. Parnell lost these contests but continued to defend his position with the help of the IRB against a combination of the majority of the Irish Parliamentary Party, the Irish National League, and the Catholic clergy who found his consorting with Fenians as reprehensible as his misalliance with Katharine O'Shea. A Parnell Leadership Committee was formed in Dublin with an executive which included Joseph K. Bracken, John Wyse Power, Fred Allan and Henry Dixon. John O'Leary and P. N. Fitzgerald were co-opted later. These were all senior IRB men. It was the same elsewhere wherever local Leadership Committees were set up. In Belfast, for instance, Robert Johnston was the chairman. In London Dr Mark Ryan was a vice-president.[7]

In the Kilkenny election campaign Parnell issued an inflammatory 'appeal to the men of the hillside', by which he meant all men like the IRB in the physical-force tradition. He called on them to rally round him as their fathers had rallied round the insurgents of 1798, and to withhold support from a faction which would make the Irish people the servants of a foreign power. He was no mere parliamentarian, he declared later. When and if he found it useless and unavailing to continue parliamentary agitation in order to obtain Home Rule, he would return at the head of his party and take counsel with the Irish people as to the next step. John Redmond took up this cry and proclaimed that

Parnell's fight was the same fight that had been carried on for centuries against the English enemy. These utterances came as a profound shock to moderate people and increased Parnell's alienation from former colleagues and churchmen, but they brought many Fenians to his side. John O'Leary wrote to the papers strongly in his support. James Stephens declared for him; so did Dr Mark Ryan and John Devoy.

The result inevitably was that Parnellites, Fenians, IRB men and 'hillsiders' almost became synonymous terms. Men who formerly refused to have anything to do with parliamentary politics, or touched them with reluctance, became engulfed in parliamentary action. They were sustained by even more uncompromising speeches from Parnell. In Navan he told an audience that though they were 'men of royal Meath', someone in the distant future might have the privilege of addressing them as 'men of republican Meath'. And to close friends he foreshadowed the Sinn Féin policy of later days of withdrawing the Irish MPs from Westminster and resorting to civil disobedience.

But Parnell did not live to develop these lately adumbrated ideas which were so strikingly at variance with his talk, when negotiating a flimsy Home Rule measure with Gladstone, of a 'final settlement'. He was dead, of hypertension, within a year. Not so the political split, which was kept alive and greatly aggravated by his sudden and unexpected demise. For a decade there were Parnellites, deriving much of their energy from the IRB and led by John Redmond, and various factions of anti-Parnellites who acknowledged the leadership of Justin McCarthy, John Dillon, William O'Brien or Tim Healy.

4

The Parnell Split

IN THE early period of the struggle the *Freeman's Journal*, which had been Ireland's principal Catholic daily, fought for the Parnellite cause with abandon. It took to lecturing the bishops for daring to condemn Parnell and oppose his leadership; and so anticlerical did the paper become that Dr William J. Walsh, the Catholic Archbishop of Dublin, warned his flock that it was endangering the purity of morals of the people of his diocese. The Parnellites also expected to be able to rely on *United Ireland*, which William O'Brien, on going to America before the split, had left in the care of Matthew Bodkin, the editor, and James O'Connor, the sub-editor, who was an old IRB man; but these men, though they put their views temperately to their readers, took the anti-Parnellite side. This was not good enough for Parnell, who believed that a paper in which he had any interest whatever should speak out unequivocally on his behalf. So on the morning of 10 December 1890 he arrived in Dublin by the mail boat and after a scanty breakfast set out with a few stalwarts to effect an eviction. At the office of *United Ireland* he called for Bodkin and ordered him to hand over the premises. Bodkin refused, whereupon a young man who stood head and shoulders over the crowd which had gathered and appeared to be their leader—this was the IRB man Long John Clancy, the sub-sheriff—stepped forward and called out: 'Matty, will you walk out or would you like to be thrown out?' Matty Bodkin, wisely, walked out.

That night, while the city was alive with frantic oratory, and newspapers were being seized at Kingsbridge railway station by armed men and flung into the Liffey, Tim Healy and the evicted sub-editor James O'Connor got together a band of their supporters, marched them to Lower Abbey Street, recaptured the

United Ireland building in the name of William O'Brien, and reinstated O'Connor. Not to be outdone, Parnell returned later, followed by a crowd of men armed with sticks and crowbars—many if not most of them from the IRB—and, knocking violently on the door, demanded entry, which O'Connor, opening on the chain, staunchly refused. Scarcely was the word out of his mouth, however, when Parnell plunged at the door with his shoulder, and the men at his back made an instant dash at it. O'Connor resisted as best he could, dodging blows from sticks and iron bars that were shot through the partly opened door. One of these smashed his glasses. For fifteen minutes the attack was held off while Parnell, baffled and like a raging lunatic, tried to leap over the railings. His friends held him back, but taking their cue from him, they jumped down into the area, smashed the kitchen window, and rushed upstairs. One of them went to open the hall door and Parnell, literally blind with rage, struck him a violent blow in the face with a stick. O'Connor and his helpers were turned out, and Edmund Leamy, a journalist MP who had stood by Parnell, was installed in the editorial chair. From America O'Brien, when he heard what had happened, cabled to Bodkin that it was mournful to think that a paper which for ten years had borne all the assaults of Dublin Castle should receive its worst stab from the leader he had all but worshipped.

These developments forced the anti-Parnellites to start a daily paper of their own to counteract the influence of the *Freeman* and *United Ireland*. Money was collected at home and abroad, spacious offices were taken in Dublin, machinery of the most improved pattern was installed, and on the 7 March 1891 the first number of the *National Press* was offered to the public. By the time Parnell married Mrs O'Shea four months later the shareholders of the *Freeman* saw that their paper had taken an unpopular line. The *National Press* was sapping its foundations, taking away its subscribers, capturing its advertisements, and threatening to bring the whole concern down in ruin. An explosion in the premises in October 1891, for which nobody was brought to book, only gave the paper publicity. A change of direction for the *Freeman* was urgently necessary. A general meeting of shareholders was therefore held, and a motion in favour of a change of policy was carried by a considerable majority. A new board of directors was appointed, and with a hop, step and jump the *Freeman* abandoned Parnell and joined the seceders.

The situation called for a newspaper on Parnell's side, and though his health was deteriorating rapidly, Parnell moved to establish one. This was the *Irish Daily Independent*, intended to be the organ of a national party independent of Gladstone, the Liberals and everybody else. The appearance of the first issue on the 18 December 1891 was facilitated by the employment of a staff of Parnellites including Fred Allan from the *Freeman*, but by that time Parnell was already more than two months dead. His funeral to Glasnevin, in the organisation of which the IRB were especially active, was long remembered. In fog and rain his body was carried, first to the old Parliament House in College Green and then to the City Hall where it was laid for a while beneath the statue of O'Connell, the Liberator. Thirty thousand people filed past the coffin there, and then led by two thousand men from the IRB-infiltrated Gaelic Athletic Association carrying draped hurling sticks, a mighty procession which took four hours to pass trudged its way to the graveside. W. B. Yeats was in Dublin, but shrank from going to the funeral because of the vast crowd. He knew, however, of the savage mood of many of the mourners and told his sister in a letter that people were breathing fire and slaughter. The wreaths bore such inscriptions as 'murdered by the priests', and a number of Wexford men were heard promising to 'remove' a bishop and seven priests. The morrow would bring cooler heads.

John Devoy was greatly impressed by the drive and capacity shown by the IRB in organising Parnell's funeral and announced to his Clan na Gael followers that a 'complete and satisfactory union' had been effected with the IRB. He urged the necessity to co-operate with such men who held out 'the possibility of good results'. By this he meant that they should profit by the divisions in the 'open' movement and recognise the likelihood that the Parnellites would become absorbed by the IRB. The Royal Irish Constabulary saw things differently. They told the government that the IRB had itself suffered serious damage in consequence of the Parnell split. It was true that the majority of the members had become Parnellites and were to the fore in the bitterly fought by-elections in Kilkenny and Carlow, but in every one of the constabulary's divisional areas instances were known of leading

IRB men taking the anti-Parnellite side. The Young Ireland Society had also declined in parallel with its controlling body, and from the same cause. Some branches had collapsed, others existed only in name. Most of them had gone Parnellite, but it was noted that a shift in the opposite direction had occurred in Belfast and that the branch there had lost many of its members.[1]

The number of IRB Circles was unchanged in 1893 as compared with 1892 but the number of members 'in good standing', that is to say who attended meetings and paid their subscriptions, dropped from 11,000 to 8,000. These were police estimates,[2] and even the lower figure for the whole country may well have been exaggerated. Mallon, speaking for the Dublin Metropolitan Police area—he was now the Assistant Commissioner—made the extraordinary statement in October 1892 that he knew only fifty active IRB men and could put his hands on every one of them. These were all members of the National Club, the Nally Club, the Independent Labourers' Club, or the Amnesty Association, or were on the staff of the *Irish Daily Independent* and *Evening Herald*. A couple of years later he put the figure up to 200 or 300. These were chiefly fitters, printers, compositors, smiths and warehousemen, and they were 'a dangerous lot'.[3] He commented on the fact that the leading members of the IRB were unable to show with accuracy the numerical strength of the organisation. That was not the case before 1879 when each County Centre furnished returns to the Supreme Council of the strength in men and material in his area. Some of these had fallen into the hands of the police.

Mallon reported that towards the end of 1891, in the weeks following Parnell's funeral, the Supreme Council and the Dublin Directory had been re-established but, through dissensions and lack of money, they were seen to be 'inoperative within a twelvemonth'. One member at least of the Directory had been discarded. Mallon set out the officers of the Supreme Council as he knew them to be in 1891. They were: John O'Leary, President; C. J. O'Farrell, a grocer, of Enniscorthy; Robert Johnston, a Belfast timber merchant; Walsh, a miller from Castlebar; W. McGuinness, a publican from Preston, Lancashire; Dr Mark Ryan of Chelsea, London; and the Secretary, John Wyse Power, a pressman. On the Dublin Directory he named James Boland, a foreman pavier as Chairman, with James Mullett, a publican;

Michael Glina, John Nolan and John Menton. On Mallon's list, when it was referred to him, Major Nicholas Gosselin, who was in charge of Irish secret service work at the Home Office, had little comment to offer. The Dublin Directory he did not know, but as regards the Supreme Council he could say that it might exist on paper but only in that way. He never knew of Walsh of Castlebar or Wyse Power being on it, and he understood that J. O'Hanlon of Downpatrick had replaced Johnston of Belfast as the Ulster representative. P. N. Fitzgerald had represented Munster for years and, according to his information, did so still, and it was said by way of surmise that he had made independent contact with one wing of the divided Clan na Gael. Sir Joseph West Ridgeway, the Under-Secretary in Dublin Castle, when he saw Gosselin's minute, inquired (23 Nov. 1892) whether it was to be inferred that the IRB no longer had a real governing body and was told that his inference was correct.

In the wake of the general election of 1892 which brought the Liberals back to power but ended disastrously for the Parnellites and affected IRB membership, two aspects of the revolutionary movement were observed by the police. Some of the senior men of the Young Ireland Society were now closely identified with the production of the newspapers Parnell had brought into being in support of his policy of independent opposition; and there was also in Dublin a rowdy element which appeared to be in a condition of perpetual aggressiveness since the death of 'the Chief'. As time went on it became clearer that both of the groups were connected within the IRB, educated men like John O'Leary and Fred Allan and some less literate on the one hand—the sort of persons who frequented the public meetings of the Young Ireland Society—and a working-class element on the other, for whom Mallon, despite his own modest background, never concealed his contempt. His attitude was affected no doubt by his experience of what he called 'the ragged and unwashed' inhabitants of Dublin's back streets who rallied to the rescue of every drunk the police struggled to arrest.[4]

2

At the end of December 1892 the government were given particulars of 'a dynamite outrage of a most serious character' that occurred late on Christmas Eve in Exchange Court, a *cul de sac* which formed the boundary between the Detective Office on the periphery of the Castle and the City Hall. A time-fuse attached to a bomb had been set to go off at about the hour when policemen not on special duty attended roll-call in the office, and the explosion when it occurred was heard to a distance of five miles. It stunned for a minute one or two persons on the streets nearby as well as the police inside the Detective Office. A number of civilians and police officers had arrived almost together on the scene, to find a shapeless mass lying in Exchange Court, and this, on examination, proved to be the body, or what was left of it, of Constable Sinnott of G Division.

The case fell to be investigated by Mallon. He obviously believed that the explosion was politically motivated, which was why he first put himself in touch with his regular secret agents in the city, 'the persons who ought to be well informed on such matters', but they knew 'nothing specific'. They could only point to the extremist characters who frequented the National Club, the Nally Club, and Mullett's public house in Lower Bridge Street. There was a distinct family likeness between the Exchange Court explosion and two others that had taken place about a year earlier, one at the *National Press* office, the other at the GPO. The explosions in each instance were produced by materials of a crude character, and there was no evidence that any complex mechanism had been used such as would require skill to prepare or manipulate.

Mallon believed that the persons engaged in all these cases were 'of the very low stratum' of the underground IRB who had been unusually active since the Parnell split. Looking for a motive for the Exchange Court affair, he thought it might have been an act of revenge for the death of P. W. Nally a month earlier in Mountjoy Prison. Nally, a Mayo man, had been found guilty in 1883 in connection with what was popularly known as the Crossmolina Conspiracy and sentenced to ten years' penal servitude. At the inquest the jury, in returning a verdict, declared that the treatment to which he had been subjected in Millbank Prison and subsequently in Downpatrick Jail for refusing to give evidence on behalf of *The Times* at the Special Commission had shattered his naturally strong constitution and left him susceptible to the typhoid fever to which he succumbed.[5] However, it was not possible to identify anybody positively from a description the police had of the man who set the fuse in Exchange Court. It appeared to apply to a number of men Mallon named belonging to the Labourers' Club, including Thomas Dunne and Jackie Nolan. Dunne, a compositor who had produced a short-lived sheet called the *Labour Advocate*, was the founder and secretary of the club and was suspected of two attempts in June 1892 to burn down the offices of the *Dublin Figaro* which had published an article reflecting on John Clancy. It was more likely that Jackie Nolan was involved and, though he could pin nothing on him, Mallon thought that, with one Pat Reid, Nolan had perpetrated the explosion in Exchange Court, had been the principal in the earlier attempts, and that, with Reid and James Boland, he had been concerned in the planting of a bomb in Dublin Castle.

In March 1893 Nolan left for America in the company of John Merna, another member of the Nally Club, and during their absence some person or persons unknown to the police made an abortive effort to damage the exterior of the Four Courts. Nolan and Merna returned to Dublin in November having, it was said, undergone a course in the use of dynamite, and were almost immediately involved with the police over an attempt to blow up Aldborough Barracks and the murder of their colleague Pat Reid. At about eleven o'clock on the morning of Sunday 26 November a soldier noticed in the barrack yard, close to a ten-foot wall adjoining a street, an old tin uniform cap box wrapped in a handkerchief and connected to a fuse with a detonator cap. The fuse was scorched as if it had been lighted; the box contained fuller's earth saturated with glycerine. At about 1 a.m. next morning a report like a pistol shot was heard by policemen nearby, and in the centre of the carriage row in the same street opposite the Phoenix Club, a suspicious rendezvous, they found a small piece of burning fuse. Two men were seen going into the club just before the noise was heard, and shortly after 1 a.m. Pat Reid and Walter Sheridan, both of them well-known IRB men, left the premises. Sheridan was drunk, thus providing the police with an excuse for arresting him. On being searched, a box of detonators was found on him of the same pattern as that in the box in the barracks. The piece of burning fuse found in the street also corresponded with that attached to the box.

Unlike Sheridan, Reid had nothing on his person to incriminate him and was allowed to go free, a circumstance which may have convinced his companions that he had betrayed Sheridan. (We shall see later what Major Gosselin of the Home Office thought of this.) Reid was tried, the police believed, by an IRB vigilance committee, and shortly after 7 p.m. on 27 November he was shot dead in Cardiff Lane near Sir John Rogerson's Quay. Three men in angry conversation were seen to enter the lane and to stop for a few minutes close to a street lamp. Two revolver shots were heard, and Reid was found bleeding from a wound in the neck. Death must have been almost instantaneous. His clothes were searched at the hospital and £7 in cash was found, but no documents of any consequence. He had shaved since the morning, evidently for the purpose of disguise, and as he had several shirts with him it was surmised that he had been making his way to the South Wall with the intention of leaving the country on one of the outgoing steamers. The police established to their own satisfaction that Nolan, Merna and Denis P. Seery had been in Reid's company on the day he died, and they brought all three in for examination. Mrs Reid said that her husband, when leaving the house, told her he was going to meet a man named Nolan who, with another friend, was to see him off to escape the police who were looking for him. She had given him the £7.

Mallon told his chief, the Commissioner of the DMP, that Nolan and Merna had suspected Reid of treachery because he had visited them while they were in America and again in Dublin on 25 November. He had spent the greater part of 26 November in Nolan's company, while Nolan and Merna kept together the whole of the 27th until after the murder. A description of Reid's companions, received immediately afterwards, fitted Nolan and Merna with fair accuracy. Merna, formerly a grocer's assistant, was known to be a very active IRB man and a member since 1881 of the Dublin vigilance committee of the organisation. In December 1891 he had convened a meeting in a pub in a back street at which it was decided to 'remove' a man named John Luccan who was suspected of giving information to the government. The police averted his murder and, under examination by Mallon, Merna, whose confederates at that time were James Boland, Pat Reid, and Jackie Nolan, practically admitted the facts. He had been implicated with Nolan and Reid in the earlier explosions.[6]

3

Nolan and Merna were charged in January 1894 with the murder of Reid, but the prosecution failed to establish their guilt. The defence was organised by Fred Allan and paid for out of a 'Fair Trial Defence Fund' of which he was chairman. Allan gave evidence on behalf of the accused and swore that he was with them at the National Club at the time the murder was committed. Long afterwards the police were told that Nolan and Merna were in fact in the club that night, and that the revolver with which Reid had been shot was taken from them there.[7] And in IRB circles it was said that the revolver was afterwards lodged in Allan's safe, and that, when quizzed on this point by Mallon, he pulled the keys from his pocket and said: 'If what you say is true, here are the keys of the safe—go and find the revolver.' The bluff was successful. Mallon did not take the keys, and Allan returned them to his pocket.[8] As for Nolan and Merna, they, on being discharged without prejudice, went immediately to America and were received by William Lyman, the leader of a wing of the Clan na Gael and the man behind the *Irish Republic*; this paper advocated the use of dynamite, in the manufacture of which Nolan and Merna were given further instruction.[9]

In October 1894 Merna returned to Dublin and was given a small job in the *Irish Daily Independent* office. Nolan came back the following February and he, a fitter by occupation, was also taken on by the *Independent*, as a chief machinist, it was said, at thirty-five shillings a week, though subsequent events showed the inaccuracy of this report. He was described to the police as 'an awfully bold, forward and half-mad sort of fellow' who was capable of any nastiness for which he was paid.[10] He had once been a boxer of some competence but was now a physical wreck. Nevertheless, he was 'active' and very determined. Merna, by contrast, had appeared in court as somewhat of a weakling. He had not done well when he first went to the United States on a solo visit, and was so 'very naked' on his return that his wife had had to buy an outfit for him.[11] But things were now looking up for him, and for Nolan. They had plenty of money, supplied, the police believed, by the American Lyman whose tools they had become; and Nolan, who lived with his mother in a small huxter's shop in James's Street and had otherwise no visible means of support nor the likelihood of respectable employment because of his reputation as a murderer, was observed to be spending freely, as much as five shillings a day, on cigars and drink, and was well dressed.

The police were at all times intrigued by Fred Allan's connection with Nolan and Merna, particularly the extent to which he was a party to the Reid murder, which looked very like the traditional Fenian 'removal' of a spy or informer. They found it hard to reconcile anything of this sort, or what he had done for Nolan and Merna afterwards, with the religious person Allan was supposed to be. Nolan and Merna were obviously useful fellows to have on one's side in the turbulent situations that frequently arose between rival factions, and especially when an effort was being made by Lyman from the other side of the Atlantic to swallow up the Parnellite–IRB agglomeration. Mallon thought it not unlikely that supporters of the conflicting forces might start shooting each other.[12]

4

Allan, the son of a Board of Works official, had been a clerk on the Great Northern Railway before taking to journalism on one of the *Freeman* group of newspapers, the *Evening Telegraph*. He was known by the police to attend lectures and reunions where advanced political views were canvassed, and after the arrest and conviction of the Phoenix Park murderers in 1883 he was said to have formed with P. N. Fitzgerald and other IRB men a society called the Avengers. This is doubtful. However, he was arrested, as we have seen, in 1884 on a treason felony charge, the case collapsing in the police courts when a principal witness for the prosecution disappeared. The authorities likewise failed to secure a conviction against Fitzgerald on a somewhat similar count. An interesting feature of Allan's defence was the briefing of Tim Healy, later to be such a thorn in Parnell's side, who came straight from the Lord Chancellor's court, the day he was called to the Bar, to plead his first case.

After his discharge, Allan's employer, Edmund Dwyer Gray of

the *Freeman*, may have asked him not to put himself forward in the future in political matters. At any rate, although he was known to have been a delegate in 1886 at the GAA convention in Thurles when the association was captured by the IRB, he was not in the news again until the *Freeman* threw Parnell overboard in 1891 and dispensed with virtually all the departmental heads. Parnell then took these men over and Allan became the manager of the *Irish Daily Independent*. He was accepted as a leading spirit—perhaps *the* leading spirit—among extreme nationalists; and it was noted, in the series of biographies of secret society personalities the police liked to keep up to date, that, apart from being a Methodist, he was interested in theosophy and contributed occasionally to socialist and anarchist journals in London and New York.[13] In October 1895 he was described as a person of gentle manner who felt keenly any dishonourable act done by an IRB man. He was the effective head of that organisation and would sacrifice his life for his country, but he would not hesitate to commit murder for the same good cause. He had had a private office constructed for himself in the *Independent* building where any one calling on him had to be announced before being admitted. All the leading IRB men of Dublin came to see him there, and it was often said by his brethren that he possessed the brains of Robert Emmet, the young United Irishman who had staged a rising in 1803.

The *Independent* offices in Middle Abbey Street were undeniably the centre of IRB activity. Much of the information received by the government pointed that way. In one report[14] it was even said that John E. Redmond, who led the Parnellite party in and out of parliament, and who had succeeded the dead 'Chief' as chairman of the *Independent* newspapers, was a Fenian, as was his brother Willie. So also were M. J. Manning, the editor of the *Weekly Independent*, and J. W. O'Beirne and John O'Mahony of the *Evening Herald*, all three members of a group which, with Allan, 'constituted the inner Circle of the IRB'. This report also drew attention to the very large proportion of Fenians among those employed in the various branches of the *Independent* newspapers; some of them had joined since they went into employment there. Allan was receiving £4 a week as manager, which was not sufficient wages for a man in such an elevated position, 'but he took the post at that [figure] by consultation with the Redmonds so that he could always be present in the office and thereby keep all letters relative to Fenianism in his own hands'. John O'Leary, an increasingly shadowy figure, was writing the history of the Fenians and had placed the first chapter in Allan's hands for publication in the *Weekly Independent*.

Whether John Redmond himself was or was not an IRB man, he certainly knew how Allan stood in that regard. That is evident from the few letters that survive of their correspondence. Allan, in one of these, complained of the boycotting of the P. W. Nally anniversary by the *Independent* newspapers, an action he claimed that would be likely to have serious repercussions. 'The men are full of indignation over it. They would, I know, neither grumble openly nor pass resolutions but if the papers ever want the fighting men of Dublin, or of the West again, we may rest assured that the boycott of poor Nally will not be forgotten to us. It was simply idiotic.' In another letter, written during the preparations for the 1798 centenary, he told Redmond of 'a quiet talk' he had had with John O'Leary and others when it was decided that it would be most judicious to stick to an original arrangement of not inviting Members of Parliament, like Redmond, to join the committee. He explained :

> There was an attempt to rush the committee from the other side; and the only way to prevent it was the adoption of the arrangement I refer to. We have nearly a three-fourths majority of the provisional committee now and so long as the other side don't suspect us, we can get the control of the executive. . . . O'Leary is writing to you formally . . . but as he'd hardly care to go into explanations I thought it better to write to you privately to let you know how things really are.[15]

5

Among the revolutionaries of 'the lower stratum' that required special police attention was James Mullett, who had served a long sentence for his involvement in the Phoenix Park murders. He had a pub in Bridge Street, and a police agent heard there of a proposal, ascribed to Mark Ryan, the IRB notability who practised medicine in London, for a revival of secret warfare. Though Mullett was discredited in some quarters and had been put out of the Amnesty Association and the Parnellite and anti-Parnellite movements alike, he was said to be quite capable of any wickedness, and his house was the focus of all that was mischievous in Dublin city. Nolan and Merna were intimate with him. A committee on Invincible lines, the police were told, had in fact already been formed in a public house at 114 Abbey Street by other well-known characters, including James Boland and T. F. Corcoran; and the Home Secretary (H. H. Asquith) and the Chief Secretary (John Morley) were mentioned for 'removal'. But when a meeting was called to discuss the 'when' and 'how', Boland was absent through illness, and Corcoran, though present, was drunk. Nothing in consequence was done; but at another gathering when Mullett was present the police agent heard of a plan to stage an explosion at the Chief Secretary's house in Kingstown or at a club in Pall Mall in London. Mallon expected that Merna would be one of the operators in this business, along with a Patrick O'Loughlin, who, for the time being, was believed to be the most reckless ruffian the police had to contend with. Nothing came of this plan either; and Mallon observed that, while the new Invincibles might grow as their predecessors had done, there was a feeling of relief abroad that leading men like Fred Allan and P. N. Fitzgerald were now strenuously opposed to any form of outrage whether against persons or property. He had no doubt that since the Parnell split several hellish schemes, of which the authorities had no inkling, had been concocted and dropped. Conspirators were at sixes and sevens.[16]

Mallon did not remember—and his experience went back to the 1860s—a time when constitutional politicians and secret society men alike were as divided as they now were. The divisions among the politicians were only too obvious. Whereas at Parnell's death there had been Parnellites and anti-Parnellites, the latter body had divided further. It was almost publicly known what the secret society men were up to, although they professed to be operating under cover. They were suspicious of, and watching, one another. They might try an outrage on some government official—Mallon had even heard his own name mentioned as a possible candidate for extermination—or on some individual in the constitutional movement; but they were more likely to injure themselves. It would not surprise him at all if James Boland, who led a group in the Invincible camp, was assassinated.

His brother, J. P. Boland, was suspected of being a spy. Davitt had said that he was. So had Tim Healy. The people who managed the Phoenix Club had said the same, and Fred Allan of the *Independent* was fighting shy of him. 'If we have a murder during the winter my impression is that James Boland or some member of his following is likely to be the victim.'[17] With this reasoning Major Nicholas Gosselin, from his vantage point in the Home Office, agreed generally. The secret society men were more absorbed in competing with each other than in organising a conspiracy as a whole.

At the head of the factions was a 'new movement' to which the government's American informants now frequently adverted. This was the Irish National Alliance (INA) or Irish National Brotherhood (INB), which was directed by a large element of the Clan na Gael under William Lyman, and led in Britain and Ireland by Dr Mark Ryan. Another faction were the Stephens-ites, a party of old Fenians that looked back to the 1860s when James Stephens's was a name to conjure with. They met in a house in Upper Abbey Street, and tried to get young men to join them in the pretence that they were a benevolent association; but their designs were not very serious. A third faction was the resurrected Invincibles, who also met in a house in Abbey Street. James Boland was in this gang along with four ex-Invincible convicts, James Mullett, Dan Delaney, Edward McCaffrey and William Moroney. They had access to the meetings of the INB, which was curious, Mallon thought, but he supposed that it was probably because the same extreme policy suited them both.[18]

These were by no means the only groups on which the police kept an eye. Indeed, they watched with unvarying assiduity every organisation, constitutional, quasi-constitutional and extremist, nationalist or agrarian, including the trades and labour societies. They regularly recorded the estimated strength of the IRB, as we have seen, and of the Ancient Order of Hibernians, the Irish National League, the Irish National Federation, the Young Ireland Society, the GAA, the Irish National Foresters, the Independent National Club, the National Society, the Army of Independence and the Knights of the Plough. A 'Gaelic League' had just been founded with the object of de-anglicising Ireland and saving the Irish language. It seemed in its inception a polite society, but it too, in time, was looked at critically by the police.

I.N.B. *versus* I.R.B.

I

THE 'new movement' which began to be talked about in 1894 derived directly from the split some ten years earlier in the American Clan na Gael. Alexander Sullivan had become the head of the Clan and, with two relative nonentities, Michael Boland and Denis Feeley, constituted a 'Triangle' which speedily incurred the strenuous opposition of John Devoy, Dr Philip Henry Cronin and Dr William Carroll. Under the direction of the Triangle the Clan became very much of an American political machine, securing jobs for supporters and amassing power and prestige for Sullivan in the Republican Party. He was an expert manipulator, was able to 'fix' juries in cases brought against his 'boys', and could always count on the aid of the police. This was evident when an investigation was called for into the assassination of Dr Cronin in 1889. The captain of the Chicago police precinct in which the murder occurred put the investigation in the hands of Dan Coughlin, one of his officers who had actually supervised the operation, and he, naturally, failed to find the murderers. Coughlin was later sentenced for his part in the crime.

The Triangle had put into circulation an allegation that Cronin was a British spy and was, therefore, deserving of death at the hands of patriotic Irishmen. In fact he was murdered in order to gain possession of a report he had compiled of an inquiry into charges levelled by Luke Dillon and John Devoy against the Triangle for their treatment of men sent to England on dynamiting missions in the early 1880s, their breaking of the connection with the IRB, and their lavish expenditure, amounting to embezzlement, of Clan na Gael funds. Cronin, in the committee of inquiry, voted to find the Triangle guilty of these charges and kept a record of the evidence after the secretary had destroyed the official one. The Triangle believed that he carried this document around with him and that no copy existed. The belief was erroneous. To provide against the probability of an attack such as was made on Cronin, three copies of his record had been made and Devoy held one of them. Sullivan, who had not scrupled to get rid of people who were a danger to him sought to have Devoy assassinated, but the man on whom he relied to do the job quailed when it came to the crunch, though he entertained a deeply felt grudge against Devoy for alleging that he had been a 'peeler' in Ireland, a dreadful thing to say of an emigrant Fenian. Devoy knew very well that his life was at risk and never went to Chicago, Sullivan's stronghold, without a gun.

The manner of Dr Cronin's death could hardly have been uglier. He was summoned from his home in Chicago one evening in May 1889; several weeks later his naked body, bearing marks of violence, was found in the catch-basin of a sewer. He had been murdered by three Mayo men, two of them former members of the IRB who had joined the Clan na Gael on coming to the United States. Martin Burke, who struck the first killing blow with an ice-hatchet, had lived for several years in America; the others were comparatively recent arrivals. All three had had it drummed into them that proof existed of Cronin's betrayal of the Irish cause, and on the evening of the murder one of the assailants, as he wrapped up his brickmason's chisel, said in his children's hearing that it would remove another Le Caron. (Le Caron had recently appeared at the Special Commission in London to testify to having spied for years, at the highest level, on American Fenianism.)

Devoy, never one to mince his words, called Alexander Sullivan the bastard son of an English army officer named Fortescue. Putting it more colourfully still on another occasion,[1] he said that the chief of the Triangle was the cross-born offspring of an English cad, born in a British camp, nursed in a British barrack with the Union Jack flying over it, fed on British rations and educated in British schools. There was nothing Irish about him except his name, which did not properly belong to him. Of the other members of the Triangle he said that Michael Boland fought at Ridgeway in the Fenian raid on Canada in 1866, but later deserted his men in the face of the enemy. He was a crooked lawyer who fleeced his clients in Louisville and had to get out of the city because nobody there would trust him with business. Denis Feeley was a member of the Coburg Battery which served against the Fenians during the Canadian raids. He was a shyster lawyer who made his living by five- and ten-dollar cases, and was only the tool of a tool. What a combination, said Devoy, to have charge of the interests of Ireland in America and to presume to speak in the name of the Irish people! But bad though Boland and Feeley were, they were utterly insignificant, in Devoy's eyes, beside Sullivan. He was the arch-enemy of the Irish cause. He had severed the Clan's connection with the IRB, and had conducted a dynamite campaign, borrowed from O'Donovan Rossa, of which the Supreme Council of the IRB disapproved, within the territory over which the Council exercised jurisdiction. He had substituted a policy of terrorism in England for the old one of preparing for insurrection at a fitting opportunity, the terrorism being aimed at forcing concessions from the British government rather than winning national independence, which could only be secured by driving the English out of Ireland. He had split the Clan na Gael, retarded its progress for many years, and made impossible the work on a larger scale that could only be done by a unified movement. And he had planned the murder of Dr Cronin, the event which divided the Clan into Cronin and anti-Cronin factions.

In the course of time the headship of the anti-Croninites effectively passed to William Lyman, a protégé of Sullivan. He was a domineering, stubborn man with none of Sullivan's ability. He had originally had a small plumber's shop in Boston and belonged to Rossa's organisation. In New York he joined the Speranza Club, a Clan na Gael centre, and was its president at the time the dissension arose over Cronin's death. By a practically unanimous vote the club took the Croninite side, and Lyman in disgust started a rival body. By the time the 'new movement' began he was recognised as an extensive building contractor, performing, Devoy alleged, a tight-rope dance from one building to another. He had no capital but was able to raise money by mortgages and to get supplies on credit through the influence of Republican Party politicians who believed he could deliver the Irish vote to them at election times. Rightly or wrongly, Lyman certainly gave the impression of being unusually well-to-do. He owned and directed from New York the *Irish Republic*, which

became the official mouthpiece of the 'new movement' under
the editorship of Charles O'Connor McLaughlin, a young
Galway graduate, whom Devoy unfeelingly described as a bum.

2

The divisions among their American brethren were bound to
create difficulties for the IRB. Should they support the 'new
movement' or not, or confine themselves to doing whatever they
could to effect a reconciliation between the opposing wings of the
Clan? The various moves are not clear, including the line of
policy pursued by P. N. Fitzgerald, who attended a Clan convention in Philadelphia on behalf of the IRB; but it is most
likely that the Croninites, led by Devoy, managed to explain to
Allan why the IRB should have nothing to do with the INB.[2]
This was the line the Supreme Council followed, but some leading IRB men adhered to the 'new movement'.

The principal one among them was Mark Ryan, and he was
joined by his brother Patrick, by Anthony MacBride, the brother
of John MacBride whom we met earlier in the context of the
Young Ireland Society, and by a Dr O'Brien, all of them medicos
practising in London. Mark Ryan became the 'European' leader
of the INB in October 1894. He was financed directly by
Lyman, which enabled him to put the Fenian James F. Egan
on the road as a paid organiser shortly after his release from
prison. A notable adherent was the young W. B. Yeats. He was
introduced to Dr Ryan by T. W. Rolleston and, though dreading
a revival of Fenianism, he inconsistently joined a body which he
described in terms that would have better suited the IRB at that
time: 'a secret organisation to continue both the Fenian propaganda and the parliamentary movement'. Dr Mark Ryan was
not an able man, in Yeats's patronising opinion, but he exercised
great influence through having befriended many Irishmen. He
tolerated fools gladly because of a naturally indulgent nature,
and had a naive and touching faith in men better educated
than himself. 'His associates in this new secret society', said
Yeats, 'were almost all doctors, peasant or half-peasant in origin,
and none had any genuine culture.'[3] From this company
Rolleston quickly extricated himself when the young poetess
Alice Milligan, herself caught up in the INB, told him she had

c*

dreamed he was in danger of arrest, but Yeats carried on and featured in time in the police reports as 'a literary enthusiast, more or less of a revolutionary',[4] which was not an unfair description of him at that time. He could find in the 'new movement', however, only one man sufficiently educated to interest him or understand what he was talking about. 'His name was, I think, Sellers, and he was a member of the Primrose League, an extreme Unionist body, but satisfied some love of disguise by combining it with Fenianism.'[5] But there was also a woman member, the beautiful Maud Gonne, who excited Yeats's interest and led him into unusual situations.

It was some time, strangely enough, before Yeats discovered that the organisation he had joined represented one of the violently opposed sections into which Irish-American revolutionists had split over the murder of Dr Cronin, and that his newfound friends represented the supposed murderers. The discovery did not worry him. After all, he said, the murder had taken place years before; the court had acquitted Alexander Sullivan, the accused man; how could they in Europe, with all that water between them, re-try the case?[6] He satisfied himself, anyhow, that he was on the right side, and when he met Sullivan's wife he wrote an article for her, 'something about Dr Cronin'. He told a friend that Mrs Sullivan was not sure that Cronin was dead at all. In any event, he seemed to have been a great rascal, and it was a very becoming thing to remove him—that is, if he was really dead and if the body found in Chicago was not somebody else's. A spy had no rights.[7] Callous talk of that kind was nothing new in revolutionary circles. Lyman's *Irish Republic* (13 Sep. 1896), for example, discussing the alleged perfidy of the parliamentarians John Dillon and William O'Brien, hinted strongly that they should be 'removed'. A dead traitor was a national blessing.

By May 1895 sufficient progress had been made with recruiting in Ireland to enable the INB to be formally established there. This was done at a meeting in Blessington Street, Dublin, which Mark Ryan and Pat O'Brien, MP, attended. Approval was given to a constitution and set of rules drawn up by John O'Mahony of the *Evening Herald* and J. A. O'Sullivan of the London Amnesty Association, and a copy came into the hands of the police. They were seen to be similar to the constitution and rules of the IRB, though it was noted that the INB exacted a pledge from members instead of an oath. Otherwise—and surprisingly—the INB appeared to the police to be the more secret body.[8] The police also noted that none of the extremists attended the meeting, though an outrage or two would have strengthened Lyman's hands for a convention he was planning to hold in America. They were present in force, however, at a meeting held in the *Independent* office.[9] There was something here which Major Gosselin and Assistant Commissioner Mallon tried to explain. The IRB position was clear enough : they were involved as Parnellites in parliamentary agitation and simultaneously were committed to outrage. The INB position was confused. From the American end came denunciation of parliamentarians and the plotting of outrages which it was Major Gosselin's business to frustrate, but on the Irish side of the Atlantic the INB's dynamite policy was kept in cold storage. Gosselin read this into a circular issued by Dr Anthony Mac-Bride which stressed that the blowing up of houses and defenceless women that had occurred before—presumably at Clerkenwell—was not what they had in mind.[10] Mallon concurred : 'The men in Dublin who are the recognised promoters of the INB do not appear to favour outrage, or to be of the class who would commit outrage themselves. The men of the IRB, who are to all appearances in direct opposition to the INB, do favour outrage, and they embrace all the men who are reputed to have taken part in every outrage that has been committed in Dublin for the past thirty years.'[11]

3

So as not to confuse the reader we have thought it well to describe the 'new movement', wherever possible, simply as the INB (Irish National Brotherhood) even where the INA (Irish National Alliance) is the form used in the source from which we are drawing, and which may be intended to distinguish between the 'open' and 'secret' forms of the movement. In September 1895 the 'new movement' held a convention in Chicago, which was attended by delegates from various parts of the United States as well as by Henry Dobbyn of Belfast and John MacBride of

Dublin, though Dublin Castle understood that MacBride represented nobody but himself. The convention adopted 'Irish National Alliance' (INA) as the name of the open movement that was to replace the American Land League, and made Lyman the chairman of its ways and means committee. It also made him president of what was called an auxiliary military order of brotherhood (INB). This body had, of course, already been at least a year in existence, and since it had failed to win over the IRB, it had begun to assail that body in the person of Fred Allan, employing the *Irish Republic* particularly for that purpose. Allan had his own papers in which to reply. In one of these[12] he rejected out of hand the allegation that he had considerably modified his views on Irish affairs. 'From the time I took up the creed of John Mitchel, as a lad of sixteen,' he said, 'my views have never altered and I must confess to even less faith in constitutional movements now than I had then, having seen their features for myself. . . .' And, obviously answering a criticism for adhering to the Parnellite element in the Irish Parliamentary Party, he added that he was a Parnellite on the two broad questions of clerical and English dictation.

The circular of invitation to the Chicago convention attacked the IRB for keeping the organisation in being for some day in the distant future when a general rising might become a practical possibility, and for its association with the parliamentary Parnellites under John Redmond :

> Away with men who would fain postpone the battle; they are cowards. Ignore them; they are like snakes in the grass. The time is now to hit, not tomorrow. Each day but adds a galling link to the chain that already binds our land. . . . Away with the creatures who perplex themselves and others with evil forebodings and impending failures. . . . There is an unanimous feeling among men who have been associated with the Irish cause that, as a means to the advancement of Irish Independence, parliamentarianism has been tried and found wanting. Ireland cannot fight England in England.

At the convention itself the principal speakers, including O'Donovan Rossa, the dynamiter, emphasised that the aim of the new movement was nothing else but revolution. England was encircled by enemies. To secure terms from France and Russia who were about to fall on her, Ireland should have trained soldiers to put at their disposal.[13]

When some of the statements at the convention were copied into the Irish newspapers, Fred Allan wrote immediately warning the Irish people to beware of the trickery of hitherto obscure men who had been thrust to the front by the notorious Triangle. If these men were in earnest, they had a peculiar way of showing it.

> If they want a constitutional agitation they will find it hard to better the principles of the Parnell movement, based as they are upon independence of all English parties. If they fancy revolutionary methods—well, revolutions are not made by distributing circulars or holding public conventions. I think I may say too that if the people of Ireland ever turn again to revolutionary methods, it will not be under the guidance of the creatures of the notorious Triangle.

And Allan, no doubt well schooled by Devoy, directed attention to the fact that the 'new movement' had been condemned as a fraud and a sham by the Irish Confederated Societies at a meeting in Chicago earlier in the year. The 'new movement' had been considering holding a Robert Emmet commemoration in Dublin. As a Dubliner, Allan professed to be appalled at the idea. 'I may safely say', he wrote, 'that no tools of that body which has brought lasting discredit upon the Irish cause in America will ever be allowed to hold a demonstration in the Irish metropolis in the name of Emmet. Fancy the murderers of Cronin organising an Emmet demonstration in the Dublin streets.'[14]

It was Devoy, of course, who brought the so-called Irish Confederated Societies together in Chicago in March 1895 to condemn the 'new movement' and to bolster his own untiring efforts to expose Alexander Sullivan. Resolutions were adopted protesting against 'the attempt by a non-descript aggregation of professional politicians . . . to present the chief of the infamous Triangle . . . as the leader of the Irish movement, as a man worthy of trust and confidence'. Devoy went further. When Sullivan was about to address a meeting of his own in Chicago, a messenger boy stepped onto the platform and handed him a letter whose contents visibly affected him. The letter enclosed an article from the *Irish Cause* entitled 'Answer, Mr Sullivan' in which emphasis was laid on the need for purity in public life, and which recalled Davis the Young Irelander's appeal for a godly train of righteous men. Eight pointed questions took some of the pep out of the speech Sullivan had intended to deliver.

4

The IRB from November 1894 were observed by the police to be making very strenuous efforts to resist the 'new movement' and to rebuild their own organisation. The necessary directions emanated from the offices of the *Irish Daily Independent*. Allan, manager of the *Independent* newspaper group and Secretary of the Supreme Council, was very much to the fore. He had settled differences he had had with P. N. Fitzgerald. He was among the leading figures in the movement for amnesty for political prisoners. He spoke at public meetings for that cause and was the author of a long series of newspaper articles in which he described individual cases of prisoners and the circumstances, often disreputable, in which they were convicted. He had visited Portland Prison in 1893, and one of his articles incorporated a letter from a prisoner there. This was Thomas J. Clarke, *alias* Henry H. Wilson, who acknowledged Allan's sympathetic interest in him. Allan presided over the Dublin meeting that welcomed O'Donovan Rossa home after many years of exile. Their hearts, Allan said, went out to the old, stern, indomitable and unconquerable Fenian leader. The occasion was an obvious IRB one: apart from Allan and Rossa, the speakers were men whose names kept recurring in the police reports.[15]

The INB's attacks on Allan continued. The instructions given to McLaughlin, the editor of the *Irish Republic*, Devoy said, were to blackguard everyone that Lyman disliked, to brand as a traitor to Ireland any person who refused to bend the knee to the paper's bumptious, swaggering and ignorant owner.[16] And the articles to a large degree were based on 'copy' received from Patrick Tobin and D. P. Seery of Dublin, two men who had conceived a dreadful hatred of a former close colleague. Responding to his criticism of what transpired at the Chicago convention, the *Irish Republic*[17] described Fred Allan as the bleary-eyed, psalm-singing cad who had the temerity to write to the *Irish Daily Independent*, in the office of which he eked out a living, denouncing men who had met in Chicago to start anew the battle of Irish liberty. Nothing was half so funny as this miserable shadow of a man attacking, with all the venom usually associated with abortion, the veterans who had travelled thousands of miles to unfurl again the flag of Irish nationality. Who, the paper asked, was this Allan anyhow? And the answer was given in a series of assertions. He was a poor devil given a job for pity's sake when on his uppers in the streets of Dublin, a man with whom true and tried men like John O'Leary would not sit in the same room, a man pledged to the British government, a man strongly suspected of being familiar with the backstairs of the Castle, a man who, when he knew he would be arrested, carried documents in his pocket that might be of value to the government, a man who augmented his pittance from the *Independent* by dipping into the balances of funds raised for the erection of monuments to national heroes. He had attacked the convention's plans for a Robert Emmet celebration; yet not a word had been spoken at the convention, the paper said, on that subject. The Dublin men who were present hoped to celebrate the occasion with arms in their hands. Fred Viper Allan could be solemnly assured that those Dublin men would not sully their lips with his name. It was traitors like him that invariably brought ruin to the Irish cause.

That article, patently ridiculous though it was, caused what Mallon described as a stir: 'Printers and compositors in two or three of the principal newspaper offices and some members of the National Club had regular scrimmages over the affair.' Detectives shadowing Allan and Nolan 'and that lot' laid reports on their movements on the Commissioner's table first thing each morning.[18] The IRB were known to be doing their utmost to counter the activities of James F. Egan, the INB organiser. Allan, in his capacity as Secretary of the Supreme Council, had formed a vigilance committee, headed by Jackie Nolan, to watch Egan closely. From three different sources, one of them 'Alpha', a regular informant on IRB–INB matters, the police were told that the assassination of Egan was contemplated, and Gosselin in London said he had excellent reasons for believing the accuracy of this report. It was also likely that Mark Ryan, the leading INB man in 'Europe', would share the same fate. But how was Nolan, their potential assassin, to be restrained? Gosselin suggested that he should be arrested as a suspicious person having no visible means of existence, but Jones, the Dublin Police Commissioner, thought that this would be injudicious. Mallon, who wanted Nolan 'checkmated', described the IRB man's circumstances :

> His mother has a shop [in James's Street], sells papers etc. and he lives with her and is provided with food and lodgings. We don't know what his income is and we don't know what assistance he renders her. He leaves home every morning between 10 and 11 o'clock and returns there several times during the day. He visits the office of the *Independent*, drives on the van with papers, some of which are delivered at his mother's house, and he is rarely out later than 11.30 p.m. He is very often under the influence of drink, but he is a cute drunken man and he makes no disturbance, so that we could not sustain any charge against him, but [under] the present system of supervision by which he is met at every point at different hours and under different circumstances he will find it difficult to commit crime. Between excessive drinking and worry and the manifest desire of respectable people to shun him he is not likely to bother us much longer and it would not surprise me if within a short time he found a resting place in the Martyrs' Plot in Glasnevin.[19]

Gosselin, on a second sight of the file, said it spoke well for the dignity of the law when a murderer and a would-be murderer would not even be asked how he got his living; but the Attorney-General, John Atkinson, ended the discussion by advising that, as there was no evidence that Nolan had committed any offence or was a vagrant within the meaning of the statutes, nothing could be done. It appeared to him that Major Gosselin was merely complaining about the inadequacy of the law of the land. So Jackie Nolan continued to walk the streets of Dublin, to drive on the *Independent* van, and to worry the police.

Mallon thought that Allan at this time was losing ground, and a speech of his in November 1895 in the Kilkenny Workmen's Club was taken to mean that he was not satisfied that the IRB were doing enough to defend themselves against the INB. A meeting of the Supreme Council held on 23 December was said to have been considering a union between the two organisations, but Major Gosselin was unaware of any wish on the part of the leaders of the American factions to come to terms; and 'without American money and American gas the home organisations would soon come to an end'. Talk of a general tendency towards an amalgamation was again reported in May 1896, but Allan was said to be the obstacle.[20] The only thing that united them was the amnesty issue. Pat O'Brien, MP, the secretary of the London Amnesty Association, was observed to be on friendly terms with Allan, and they were understood to have revived the idea of carrying off a young member of the royal family and holding him as a hostage until the men imprisoned since the 1880s for dynamite outrages were released.[21]

5

Fenianism, in its Irish and American manifestations, had been condemned explicitly by Pope Pius IX in 1869 and before that by the Irish bishops in 1863. Paul Cardinal Cullen, the Archbishop of Dublin and Primate of Ireland, affirmed in 1865 in a famous pastoral the desire of the Irish people to be 'great, happy and free' but insisted that they should never seek to realise those aspirations by means bad in themselves. The Church in Ireland had precedents, therefore, when in the late 1890s it found it necessary to intervene to thwart the recruiting efforts of the rival brotherhoods (IRB and INB) and of agrarian societies which perpetrated outrages under cover of darkness. In Athlone priests at Mass warned young men of the dangers they would incur by joining clubs which were covers for secret societies.[22] They had in mind the Oliver Bond Club started in the town by prominent IRB men.[23] Similar warnings were given in Dundalk[24] and in churches in Counties Cavan and Donegal. In Miltown Malbay[25] at the end of a mission one of the clergy preached a sermon on secret societies and moonlighting and cursed those who took part in them. He prayed that the hand of the person who fired into his neighbour's house or injured his property might be withered before he left the spot. He then called on all the young men present to hold up their hands and promise faithfully that they would not join secret societies or take part in crime. In the excessively crowded chapel the police noticed a large number of moonlighters, all of whom raised their hands.[26] A Young Ireland Society recently formed in the town and 'run on very extreme lines' collapsed. This result was brought about partly by the opposition of the clergy and partly through dissensions among the members, some of whom declared themselves followers of F. J. Allan, while others were against him.[27]

The IRB in County Monaghan were 'considerably stirred up' in November 1895. Performances by a travelling company of a play about the United Irishman, Lord Edward Fitzgerald, were turned into Fenian demonstrations. A local fife and drum band, which consisted chiefly of IRB men, attended the show and played rebel tunes.[28] In Oldcastle, in a neighbouring county, a young man was stabbed in six places by a member of the IRB. He had refused to join the IRB and was accused of being an informer. A doctor, who was himself an IRB man, swore at the trial that the wounds were not serious and generally made light of the matter.[29] There was considerable activity in the early months of 1896 in IRB circles in County Wexford. Eighty-seven members were enrolled in the Gorey district, the work directed by Charles J. O'Farrell of Enniscorthy, a member of the Supreme Council. He had attended the meeting of the Council in Dublin a few days before Christmas and there received orders to leave nothing undone to strengthen the organisation.[30] Nearly four thousand persons turned up at the Wolfe Tone anniversary demonstration at Bodenstown churchyard organised by the Young Ireland Society.[31] The speakers struck a common note: parliamentary politics had had their trial and failed; the young men of Ireland should revert to the old Fenian policy and emulate Wolfe Tone.[32]

In October 1895 a conference of clergy of the diocese of Clogher condemned the 'new movement' recently inaugurated at Chicago and decided that any emissaries from the United States who might visit Ireland in furtherance of it should be exposed. The Ancient Order of Hibernians (AOH) was also condemned as a secret society of sinful tendencies; between it and the much weaker IRB there had been great animosity in County Cavan. The AOH regarded the IRB as enemies of their country and lost no opportunity of assaulting them. When the IRB began to recruit actively a fight developed at Swanlinbar fair which the police had to stop. The parish priest warned against both parties the following Sunday. A similar situation arose at Kilgolagh fair in the following month. The Bishop of Clogher felt called upon to denounce secret societies and to warn his people, young men especially, to have nothing to do with them.[33]

The demand for the release of political prisoners was the order of the day; and the police noted that the Limerick branch of the Amnesty Association was being conducted in the interest of the INB. That body's advocacy of amnesty, besides being a cloak to conceal its real nature and objects which were known to comparatively few, was a means of inducing many persons who sympathised with the cause of amnesty to support the INB and to squeeze all the IRB people out of the branch. An American tour by the INB organiser J. F. Egan, backed by Lyman, had been successful, and a large portion of the moneys collected by him for amnesty purposes had gone to Dr Mark Ryan of London to be used in promoting the INB.[34]

The Lenten letters of the Bishops of Dromore and Derry for 1897 continued the denunciations of secret societies generally, and Cardinal Logue, the Archbishop of Armagh and Primate of All Ireland, declared in his pastoral that he had learned with extreme pain that the promoters of secret societies, taking advantage of the unhappy political confusion in the country, had renewed their efforts to regain a hold on some foolish and unwary members of his community.[35]

6

Allan's name continued to crop up in the police reports. In July 1896, in his capacity as president of the Nally Club, he marched at the head of about three hundred of the worst suspects in Dublin. He did so again in August, when the club paraded with a brass band to honour the release from prison of John Daly, the Limerick Fenian. The *Irish Republic* continued to attack him : he was now, it said, attempting to destroy J. F. Egan's amnesty mission. Tireless, Allan was reported to be pushing the IRB organisation in Ulster.

The INB was also trying to expand, according to a police informant who passed under the cognomen of 'Shandon'. Their numbers were increasing all over the country, and especially in

the West. And they would do better still were it not for the
tyranny of the priests, Dr Patrick Ryan told his brothers Mark
and Michael after a visit. A sign pointing in the same direction
was that Joseph K. Bracken of Templemore, Co. Tipperary, a
leading IRB man, had gone over to the INB. He would not
have done so had he not been assured that that was the winning
side. He was now quarrelling with P. N. Fitzgerald, but this was
mainly because he had not been paid for a headstone he had
erected over the grave of an IRB man, M. J. Seery. (Joseph
Bracken was the father of Brendan (later Viscount) Bracken, the
intimate friend of Winston Churchill and member of his wartime
government.)

As 1897 opened there were reports of local conflicts between
IRB and INB groups, but Jackie Nolan, to whom the police
reports continually returned, was not particularly busy during
most of the year. At the end of it, however, he was looking for
'stuff', and both Mallon and Gosselin, from their different positions, learned that he and his comrades in the Nally Club had
something on hand and had established a vigilance committee—
an ominous sign. In March a growing impression that the IRB
in Dublin were putting the INB in the background was confirmed when they opened the North City Gymnastic Club in a
room of the old European Hotel where sections of the Brotherhood met. Subsequently Allan held a somewhat private meeting
in his own house of 'the bad lot', but this did not imply that
Allan would admit any of them into his inner circle.[36] The Nally
Club had an evil reputation and was the one the Catholic clergy
had probably in mind when from the altar they denounced a
dangerous society that had its headquarters in Dublin.

Both parties had begun to gear themselves to celebrate worthily
the centenary of 1798. The *Irish Republic* started a fund for the
erection of a statue of Wolfe Tone in Dublin, and W. B. Yeats
became the president and Dr Mark Ryan the treasurer of the
Centenary Association of Great Britain and France. But when a
representative *national* committee was formed in Dublin with
John O'Leary as a chairman acceptable to both sides, it was
noted in Dublin Castle that overall control rested in the hands of
the IRB and Fred Allan. A few INB men had been adopted in
order to preserve the appearance of neutrality, and to attract the
comparatively few members of that body that remained. And, as

might have been expected, there was a good deal of dissension.

Meanwhile the *Irish Republic* continued to snipe away. When John Redmond gave a public lecture on the theme of '98 the paper criticised what he said. Allan, reporting to Devoy, wrote:

> The articles in the *Irish Republic* . . . are disgraceful lies. There was not a single word in Redmond's whole lecture that could offend the most extreme man. As a matter of fact, the lecture was delivered to clear off the debt on a monument which was to be erected over one of our fellows here, Michael Seery, and our boys feel greatly riled over the *Irish Republic* articles, as they looked upon it as a generous act on Redmond's part to lecture for us.

Allan added that the '98 business was getting on very well, though he supposed the whole thing would end with speech-making, demonstrating and flag-waving. 'Still,' he said, 'it may put a little national spirit into the young men here, and God knows they want it.'[37]

7

When he was appointed to his special post in the Home Office in 1890, Major Gosselin discovered that the whole system by which the surveillance of Irish-American secret societies was conducted was 'rotten'. Hoare, a British vice-consul, had been the agent in charge in New York, but only one of his informants or sub-agents was a member of the societies they were supposed to be watching. A complete reorganisation was called for. At Gosselin's suggestion, the Secretary of State removed Hoare; this enabled the other ineffectives also to be got rid of. Gosselin then appointed a man named Gloster Armstrong to be his American agent, and, under cover of the Mexican Land Company of which he had been secretary in London, Armstrong opened an office in New York and took over the direction of five men Gosselin sent him. All of these had been connected with 'the extreme party' at home, and four of them managed to worm their way into the 'very heart of the American conspiracy'.

By 1896 Armstrong had seven men employed, 'every one of whom were members and some very deep in the confidence of the leaders'. They kept their eyes particularly on the anti-Cronin party led by Lyman, whom Gosselin described as a fanatical hater of England, a man who ruled with a rod of iron and who was reputedly losing some five thousand dollars a year of his own money on his paper. Gosselin had said earlier that Lyman —and it is interesting to compare his story with Mallon's which we have seen already—had spent a great deal of money 'trying to do something in Dublin (murdering certain officials) by means of two men Nolan and Merna, but I was able to foil all their plans, the result being that these men shot a fellow conspirator, a man named Reid, believing he was the informant. I may say the real man is quite unknown and unsuspected.'[38]

Lyman had prepared an elaborate scheme for bombing attacks on the Canadian frontier, the object of which was to cause friction between the governments of the United States and their neighbours. Gosselin claimed that he warned the Colonial Office about this in advance and later heard that the scheme had failed through the plotters losing their nerve. Lyman had also planned to send a large group of dynamiters to England, under Tynan the Invincible, which included Edward Ivory, J. F. Kearney, T. Haines and a man called Cooney nicknamed 'the Fox'. Cooney had played a part in the murder of Dr Cronin in Chicago, and while the dynamiting campaign was being arranged, Lyman chose him to kill Joseph Chamberlain, the Colonial Secretary. Fortunately for Chamberlain, Gosselin got word of what was on foot and immediate counteraction was taken. But Cooney sneaked back to New York and one of Gosselin's informants had to fly for his life.

Gosselin also claimed to have scotched the dynamiting campaign and had the leader Ivory arrested. He was charged at Bow Street Police Court with conspiring with Tynan, Kearney and Haines in July 1896 to cause an explosion of a nature likely to endanger life and cause serious damage to property,[39] and a British agent in America, Merrick Shaw Copeland Jones, was produced to give evidence against them. Like Le Caron before him, Jones disclosed that, while working as a secret agent in the United States, he had met Ivory, Tynan and others with Lyman, on whose instructions they were acting, at the *Irish Republic* office and in various revolutionary circles. The case was suddenly dropped on the disclosure of a possible *agent provocateur* element in it, and Ivory was released. On his way back to America he visited Dublin and was seen in his hotel there by three INB men, Patrick Tobin, Stephen Holland and Louis Ely O'Carroll. Otherwise little notice was taken of him. Tynan, who had been arrested at Boulogne at the instance of the British government, avoided extradition and got back to the safety of the United States.[40]

Before appearing before the world in his true colours the British agent Jones had himself visited Ireland. His first call was to the *Freeman's Journal* office in Dublin where he met two INB men, the brothers Stephen and Dan Holland. He spent a morning with Dan, whom he had known in America, and that afternoon they called to the *Independent* office to see Nolan and Merna in the hope of winning them over to the INB. Both of these men had belonged to Jones's 'Camp', or Circle, when in New York city, but had returned to the IRB fold, apparently out of a sense of their indebtedness to Fred Allan, who had done so much for them over the years.

From Stephen Holland Jones got a picture of the INB position in Dublin. There had been fifteen Circles in the city, five of them under his own direction, but through lack of money and organisers, attendances had dropped considerably and only two now survived. Circles usually met in the houses of individual members, and the place of meeting was constantly changed. Occasionally they forgathered in the National Club, unknown to the staff there. Holland's position as a sports writer on the *Freeman* enabled him to do some organising, which he usually did when travelling to report Gaelic Athletic Association matches. There were plenty of good young recruits to be had, but they required to be visited frequently and directed. Many of the groups he started had petered out. The president of the GAA, F. B. Dineen, who was a commercial traveller, was similarly able to move about freely without attracting the attention of the police, while employed at a salary by the INB, but he did not appear to have been any more successful than Holland in 'building up the country'. At the Railway Clearing House Jones learned from Patrick Tobin, to whom he was introduced by Dan Holland, that the affairs of the Brotherhood were in a bad way, the reason being that the London people, Dr Mark Ryan and company, were trying to run the business from there but were not putting up enough money for the support of the organisation, such as it was, in Ireland. Tobin had been called to a meeting in London within a few days, but he would not go as his expenses had not been sent.

Jones went to Belfast which had been a moderately strong IRB area, and renewed acquaintance with Henry Dobbyn, whom he had met at the Chicago convention as the delegate from the North of Ireland. Dobbyn had returned to Ireland fully convinced of the superiority of the 'new movement'. He, together with John MacBride, who was now in the Transvaal, and Robert Johnston were regarded by the police as its principal backers. Dobbyn, a severe critic of Fred Allan,[41] had recently been sentenced to two months' imprisonment, reduced to a fine of £20, for assaulting an IRB man. He brought the visitor to his house for a chat, and Jones once more heard the complaint that the organisation was losing ground from lack of funds. If Lyman would only send £50 for a start, Dobbyn would be able within six months to show good results in the way of arming and organising in Donegal, Antrim, Derry and South Armagh. A man named Crummy had tried to organise Donegal but had had to give up when the money ran out. Dobbyn himself had distributed the bulk of a consignment of rifles in Donegal and Derry, using a carrier who had his yard next door to his house and who was a member of the organisation; there were forty rifles left in the house as he spoke. There were many Presbyterians near Belfast, he said, who held 'advanced and extreme views'.

On the following day, a Sunday, Dobbyn brought Jones to a secret meeting held at the top of what he understood was the Crown Building; on the street door, as he went in, he noticed a brass plate with the names Steele and Milligan. He was also able to remember the names of eleven of those at the meeting. One of them was Crummy the organiser, another was Harbinson, a retired soldier whose father had been hanged as a rebel, and another still bore the name of Gonne. Dobbyn seems to have done a great deal of the talking, and a point that Jones must have particularly noted, having regard to his own double role, was that somebody called Morgan was alleged to be sending weekly reports to Dublin Castle. Dobbyn introduced Jones as 'a Brother from America who occupied an important position' and invited him to speak. 'In doing so,' Jones told Gosselin, 'I said that I was in no way a delegate from the USA, but was in Ireland on private business, but when I returned to America I would be happy to bring anything they might wish under notice of our leaders.'

That afternoon Dobbyn introduced Jones to Miss Johnston, whose brother had visited 'our camp' in New York some two years before, and from her he gathered the name and address of 'an important man in the Secret Organisation' in Liverpool which he gave to Gosselin. The following day he was introduced to 'Miss Milliken' (i.e. Alice Milligan), but all he recorded of their conversation was that she had met Mrs Lyman when, with her husband, she visited Belfast in 1892. And he concluded his report to Gosselin by saying that the information from Dobbyn and his associates had been secured without any exertion on his part.[42]

Jones, when in Ireland, got the republican reactions to the affair with which Ivory was charged. In the eyes of the INB man Patrick Tobin it was a foolish business. Men should have been employed who could have made a success of the explosion; money spent on failures destroyed the confidence of the men at home in the men at the head of affairs in the United States. There were plenty of good men in Ireland who could do the job if the Americans would only put up the money. On the very day that Ivory was arrested he was to have attended a meeting in Glasgow at which a plan for the government of the INB in the United Kingdom was to have been arranged. Dobbyn had gone over for the meeting, but finding himself being followed by a detective, he surmised that something was wrong and made for the Belfast boat, leaving his bag behind him in the hotel: he was worrying about the forty rifles he had left at home.[43] He complained that the Ivory business had done a great deal of harm, especially in Glasgow; and a police report added that in Manchester also the arrests had disorganised secret society circles. Gosselin commented that 'these heroes are easily frightened'. In the North of Ireland the effect of Jones's appearance in the witness box was cataclysmic; and the constabulary reported at the end of 1896 that, since the débâcle, very little had been heard of the INB.

The IRB reaction, on the other hand, was one of pleasure. Allan was said to be exultant, and in a circular letter signed by

Devoy and others the following pointed reference was made to the Ivory incident:

> You will hardly need to be informed that no member of our organisation had anything to do with the recent disgraceful exhibition of blundering, incompetency and treachery which the newspapers dignified with the name of 'dynamite scare' by which four men were simultaneously arrested, on information supplied from America, in three different countries and a store of explosives seized in a fourth.[44]

8

The British agent Jones had met two, if not three, unusual women in Belfast. The first was Anna Isabel Johnston, the daughter of Robert Johnston, a timber merchant in a big way in the city who had represented the North of Ireland for many years on the Supreme Council of the IRB. She was better known as the poetess Ethna Carbery, and with Alice Milligan, the second of the trio, Jones's 'Miss Milliken', she had begun in January 1896 to produce the periodical *Shan Van Vocht* in which through prose and verse they sought to serve the cause of Irish freedom. The title was taken from a popular song of 1798 and was a reminder of the significance of the approaching centenary. For an allegedly revolutionary journal the *Shan Van Vocht* was a mild and inoffensive affair and made little or no effort to identify itself with the 'new movement'. It ran for less than three years, and in its first issue commended the advice of a correspondent in the Transvaal, addressed to nobody in particular, to learn to shoot straight. It colourlessly reported meetings of miscellaneous associations and literary societies which INB personalities attended. But it was only in the ninth issue that the INB's front association, the Irish National Alliance was mentioned by name. This was in a report of a manifesto setting forth the Alliance's policy which, reduced to simple terms, was to reject the parliamentary humbug of the past seventeen years and to look to revolution for redemption. The magazine made no comment of its own on this, but did reproduce part of a commentary from the *Irish Republic* of New York which declared plainly that a Home Ruler should be regarded as inimical and dangerous to the cause of nationality as were the royalists during the American War of Independence. James Connolly, the socialist, wrote some articles for the magazine, including one in which he asked if Irish republicans could be politicians. John MacBride and Arthur Griffith were obviously staunch supporters, and when Griffith went to South Africa at the end of 1897, the farewell occasion in the Celtic Literary Society was noticed. Griffith and William Rooney were the prime movers in this society which, like the IRB-inspired Young Ireland groups, took the writings of Thomas Davis as its testament.

It is reasonable to assume that the person Jones simply called Gonne in his list of those he saw at the INB meeting in Belfast was also a woman—in fact, Maud Gonne, a 'daughter of the gods, divinely tall and most divinely fair', later immortalised by Yeats. It is surprising that he did not remark on the presence of a woman at a Fenian meeting—in the 1880s, certainly, the Castle view was that the IRB were never 'foolish enough to admit petticoats into their order'.[45] But the INB may have had other ideas or provided exceptionally for Maud Gonne, who was said to have been initiated into the INB by Dr Mark Ryan. In a passage of her autobiography Maud Gonne brings all three women and Yeats together :

It had been one of our late nights in my rooms over Morrow's Library [in Nassau Street, Dublin], for Anna Johnson [*sic*] and Alice Milligan from Belfast were staying in Dublin and Anna had read us some of her poems and we were full of almost envious admiration of some numbers of the *Shan Van Vocht*, the daring little paper Anna and Alice were editing. They were so different but worked so well together—Anna, tall and romantic, with her long face and tender dreamy eyes —Alice small, aggressive and full of observant curiosity. I thought Dublin would have to look to its laurels if it were not to be outdone in literary journalism by Belfast. Willie Yeats had read his play, *The Countess Kathleen* [sic]; he wanted to have it produced in Dublin and he wanted me to play in it. He said he had written the part of the Countess Kathleen for me and I *must* act it. I was severely tempted, for the play fascinated me and I loved acting, but just because I loved the stage so much I had made the stern resolve never to act. I was afraid it would absorb me too much to the detriment of my [political] work. I knew my own weakness, and how, when I got interested in anything, I was capable of forgetting everything else. House-building, evicted tenants, political prisoners, even the fight against the British Empire, might all disappear in the glamour of the stage. It was the only form of self-discipline I consciously practised. 'I am a horse that has to wear blinkers to prevent being side-tracked—I must not look to the right or the left.'[46]

From the day she entered the Irish movement this daughter of an English colonel who had figured for a time in Castle society in Dublin kept the Irish and English police forces busy reporting on her multiple activities. She was a most unusual person, though Gosselin dismissed her by saying that 'Every man of standing amongst secret society men knew she was a woman with a past.' This was a milder description, however, than one by a priest which the police recorded. But neither she nor her cranky revolutionist friend Cipriani, who made anticlerical speeches to the Irish in France, were to be taken seriously, Gosselin suggested.[47] There were some things the police may have missed, however—for instance, the part she played in preventing Tynan's extradition from France. She did this, working through the father of two of her children, Lucien Millevoye, a Boulangist deputy and editor of *La Patrie*. His great ambition was to win back Alsace-Lorraine from the Germans, for whom he nourished a loathing which he shared with the English, the vanquishers of his kinsman and hero, Napoleon. He said to Maud one day: 'Why don't you free Ireland as Joan of Arc freed France? You don't understand your own power. To hear a woman like you talking of going on the stage is infamous. . . . Have a more worthy ambition: free your own country, free Ireland.'[48]

Maud Gonne started a monthly paper *L'Irlande Libre* in Paris in 1897. Its objects were to strengthen the bonds of sympathy between France and Ireland and to make the Irish cause better known. Though small in size—funds being low—she secured promises of contributions from celebrated French authors and hoped that representative Irish writers would also write for her. She wrote to Tim Harrington, erstwhile Secretary of the Irish National League and a principal author in 1886 of the Plan of Campaign for the protection of tenants through collective bargaining with their landlords, and asked him for something on the subject of the evicted tenants.

By the way, [she added] do tell me when you write of a Mr [McCarthy] Teeling from Dublin who turned up in Paris the other day and announced that he was sent by the *Irish National Party* to attend the St Patrick's banquet in their name to denounce Miss Gonne as a spy in the pay of the English and German governments. He called on the Secretary of the St Patrick's Association, the Comte de Cremont, to announce his intention. His ardour was somewhat damped by being told if he did anything of the kind he would be turned out by the waiters. He attended the banquet but contented himself with drinking to England's confusion without mentioning me.[49]

Commemorating 1798

I

FOR ABOUT ten years the idea of celebrating the centenary of the 1798 Rebellion had been in the air and was talked of by all shades of nationalists as a time to demonstrate their strength. According to Major Gosselin, the extreme men had hopes that the occasion would unite them all in a single solid revolutionary body similar to the United Irishmen they were commemorating, but each section secretly hoped that in the march of events they would assume the leading place. Gosselin watched the position outside Ireland with particular care; and he noted that the '98 Centenary Association of Great Britain, which was largely an INB affair, drew its inspiration and considerable cash from Lyman in America.[1] Money from the same source was also reaching Ireland through Dr Mark Ryan, and this accounted for the great activity of Tobin, Seery, Hoctor, Butler, James Mullett, Edward McCaffrey and a host of others who were always in evidence, Superintendent Mallon said, when money was stirring. Feelings were running high between the INB and the IRB, and some of the latter were threatening the INB men for taking members away from them.[2] By the end of 1897 there were local centenary committees everywhere,[3] and many clubs, which were really only fronts for the two subversive organisations, had been formed, particularly in Dublin, to work up popular enthusiasm.[4] Visits were paid by these clubs to the graves of the patriots, and to that of Richard Robert Madden, the historian of the United Irishmen,[5] and an informant said that disloyalty had never been so rampant.

The Queen's Diamond Jubilee fell in 1897, and various extreme groups set about upsetting the arrangements for its celebration in Dublin. Maud Gonne, dragging Yeats after her, conspired with James Connolly to prevent the illuminations of shop fronts by cutting off the electricity supply. She led marchers to where United Irishmen were interred and set crowds wild with her oratory. She had a magic lantern installed outside the National Club and from it statistics were projected on to a white screen showing the evictions and deaths from starvation that had occurred during Victoria's reign. In a mock funeral devised by her a coffin with 'THE BRITISH EMPIRE' painted on it was paraded through the streets, and black flags carried by the 'mourners' bore the names of Irishmen hanged for treason. The police intervened as the 'funeral', led by a band which played a dead march on cracked instruments, passed by the City Hall where the Executive Council of the '98 Centenary Committee was in session. Heads were broken in baton charges, and, with the processionists running for cover, Connolly ordered the coffin to be thrown into the river nearby. Yeats managed to take the reluctant Maud across the town with him to the National Club, and as they were drinking tea behind closed doors the police charged again, this time to break up the crowd that had gathered to look at the magic lantern pictures. A woman was killed and, as news of this spread through the city, some thousands of pounds' worth of plate glass were smashed in shops that carried jubilee decorations.

Another example of disloyalty was observed at a reception given for the opening of the Empire Theatre on the site of Dan Lowrey's Music Hall. Fred Allan, T. O'Donovan and E. T. Stewart of the *Independent* were there and deliberately remained seated when the toast of the Queen was proposed. Some time later James Connolly, the two O'Briens (William and Daniel) and the two Lyngs (Thomas J. and Murtagh) with six or seven other socialists appeared on the gallery to make a demonstration but, seeing the police around, they contented themselves with hissing slightly. Mr Findlater, the chairman of the Empire Company, was not abashed. He had initiated the playing of 'God Save the Queen' at the end of each performance, and the practice would be continued, not through cussedness or obstinacy, but simply to raise the tone of the theatre. His aim was to obliterate the name of Dan Lowrey which was a synonym for rowdyism and playing to the gallery. But the police were not happy. Jackie Nolan was preparing an explosion, and what was more natural than that it should be in the Empire Theatre? Indeed, he might have thought of doing this earlier in order to make it impossible for the Lord Mayor's carriages and military escort to pass in and out of the Castle yard nearby.[6]

On the last night of 1897 there were torchlight processions in Dublin, Cork, Belfast and Limerick to inaugurate the centenary. In Dublin about 5,000 people marched with bands, among them representatives of the local clubs carrying lighted torches. The procession, which started at eleven o'clock at night wound up at one in the morning. Occasional cheers were given, and on passing the Empire Theatre some hooting and groaning took place, but the proceedings, on the whole, were orderly. In March a monster meeting was held in the Phoenix Park, attended by between ten and twelve thousand people and marshalled by the Irish National Foresters in regalia but, with the exception of W. B. Yeats of London and Anthony Mackey of Castleconnell, none of the speakers aroused any enthusiasm. The authorities, as always, were interested in finding out what accession of strength the rival organisations were gaining as a result of these demonstrations, and Robert Anderson in the Home Office gave Major Gosselin[7] the gist of a return Dr Mark Ryan had furnished to Lyman. This had come through an informant and showed that at that time the INB in Great Britain and Ireland had 10,000 members, distributed as to 300 in Britain, of whom fifty were in London, and the rest in Ireland. The Irish membership comprised 6,000 in Dublin, 1,800 in Cork, 1,800 in Belfast, 800 in other parts of Ulster, and a balance of 1,100 was distributed throughout the country. The numbers would be greater, Dr Ryan said, were it not for the priests, and progress in Limerick had been particularly affected by the opposition of the bishop there.

Mallon and Gosselin laughed at these figures. There were not five hundred INB men in Dublin, and the William Orr '98 Club, their principal stronghold, had recently been unable to muster sufficient strength to expel IRB men from a meeting and had had to put up with their interruptions. Mallon had heard a hint that Dr Ryan was himself preparing to withdraw from the INB.[8] Another sign that the 'new movement' was in serious trouble was the collapse in July of the organisation in Belfast as the consequence, it was said, of the bad management and personal unpopularity of Henry Dobbyn. This strengthened the ranks of the IRB who were availing of the '98 movement to draw secret society men of every hue together,[9] no doubt with the intention of collaring them.

2

A lot of attention was paid by the police to the current activities of men recently released from English prisons. The first of these was James F. Egan, 'an ill-tempered little man' who, having organised for the INB and Amnesty, mainly in England, had been appointed Sword-Bearer to the Dublin Corporation. He had joined the IRB at the age of twenty-one, had got a clerical job in Birmingham, married a woman of doubtful character, and went to jail with John Daly of Limerick in 1883 on a dynamiting charge. On coming to Dublin to take up his sword-bearing job, he was met by about two hundred people who formed a procession headed by a band and a dozen torch-bearers; but the police noted that enthusiasm was lacking and that there was a marked absence of the IRB element: the fact that Egan had worked for the INB was not to be forgotten. Egan travelled subsequently to London to make contact with another of the released men, H. H. Wilson, whose real name was Thomas J. Clarke, and returned to Dublin with him and Daly. Gosselin told the Inspector-General of the RIC that Clarke was evidently an important man, as a number of London suspects assembled at Euston to see him off. Egan's concern was to ensure that Clarke and Daly adhered to the INB, but in this he was unsuccessful. In Mallon's phrase, Clarke and Daly were irreconcilables. Daly was an 'extraordinary bad type of man', but so long as dissension existed Mallon did not fear a conspiracy. As for Clarke, he was speedily seen 'all over the place', emphasising the need for work instead of speeches about Irish independence, and was overheard criticising Daly for not having the right men about him. Daly was said to have assumed the lead in all nationalist matters, and was aspiring to control the Limerick City Council, but in this he would be strongly opposed, and his success was therefore doubtful. He nevertheless possessed influence which he demonstrated by boycotting a lecture given by John Redmond, MP, the Parnellite leader.

The minds of Irishmen were occupied at this time (1898) by the system of local government on the British model which the

D

Tory Chief Secretary Gerald Balfour had introduced; and Daly was believed by the police to be seeking to secure power and influence in the new councils, no doubt for ulterior purposes. The possibility of war between France and England was another factor to which the police adverted. It might provide the long-looked-for opportunity which an unscrupulous leader could turn to account. This raised a question as to where the monumental old Fenian, John O'Leary, stood at this time. Gosselin believed that O'Leary was looked upon by the IRB as a fossil, occasionally useful but no leader. He was just an old crank full of whims and honesty. Mallon agreed : this was exactly the description the Dublin police had applied to him for years. At the same time O'Leary was the boss figurehead of the Executive Council of the '98 Centenary Committee, and his views had been strictly endorsed on recent occasions. In connection with a visit of John Redmond to Dublin, for example, the Executive Council had adopted a letter of his to the press in which he directed all '98 associations to ignore a request to attend a reception for Redmond. Any individual member of the '98 club had, of course, a perfect right to receive anybody he liked, O'Leary said, but a '98 association, as such, had no business whatever to mix or meddle with party politics.[10]

Earl Cadogan, the Lord Lieutenant, was the recipient of anxious anonymous letters about the continuing '98 celebrations. One writer, an old lady in County Wexford whose relatives suffered at the hands of the insurgents in the rebellion a hundred years before, feared a similar outbreak and suggested that reliable troops and police should be stationed in the county. A demonstration had been announced for Wexford town and it had been made clear that all windows not illuminated would be broken. The police had no doubt that the lady's fears were genuinely entertained, but they did not think there was any reason to apprehend disturbances. The absence of American visitors and the great lack of funds had knocked the bottom out of the celebrations.[11] The outbreak of war between the United States and Spain, an exceedingly unfortunate event in the eyes of the revolutionaries, had prevented the expected influx of Irish-Americans.

It was felt, nevertheless, by the organisers, even before half the year was out, that the anniversary had done much good. For some time there had been little life in secret societies, a Scotland Yard man 'listening with an apparently incredulous and in-different air' was told by a friend. The youth of Ireland had become indifferent. Little interest was being taken in 'extreme work'. The minds of the people were engrossed with parliamentary factions and the original objective—the independence of the country—was being lost sight of. The '98 movement had changed all that. From one end of the country to the other '98 literature had been distributed, vivid descriptions given of the various incidents of the rebellion in which the patriotic angle was always emphasised and the leaders eulogised. To any person having a knowledge of the Irish people at home, more especially the youth of the country, the result was patent. He knew for a fact, the friend said, that Sligo and Leitrim were being diligently worked over by secret society agents with considerable success. A force working unwittingly in the same direction was the clergy. In their anxiety to stamp out Fenianism they were discouraging meetings of the GAA and driving the members into the arms of the secret society men.[12]

3

In August Mallon sent the Commissioner of Police a copy of the first eight-page issue of the *Worker's Republic*, a new paper edited by James Connolly of the Irish Socialist Republican Party and financed by Maud Gonne. It might live for six months, Mallon said, and was likely to have a limited circulation.[13] In fact, it lasted only until October,[14] although it was revived in the following year. The paper, which was offered to the public as 'a literary champion of Irish Democracy', advocated an Irish republic, the abolition of landlordism and wage-slavery, and the co-operative organisation of industry under representative governing bodies. Connolly's contributions, largely based on the speeches he regularly delivered in his clipped accent in Foster Place, dealt with the capitalist origin of war and with contemporary aspects of religious sectarianism. Irish-American Catholics, he stressed, were distinguishing themselves in the war against Catholic Spaniards, while Protestant workers in Belfast were striking against Protestant employers.

The first number of the paper was sold to the crowds coming

into Dublin for the laying of the foundation stone of a '98 memorial, an event linked particularly with the name of Wolfe Tone. Connolly saw Tone as a man whose social ideas, realisable only in a socialist republic, were such that he would have been a rebel even had he been an Englishman.[15] He stood breast-high for the men of '98, but he was highly critical of those who had united the centenary movement with what he called the bogus organisation associated with the name of Mr Tim Harrington, a reference to the association of the Parnellite MP with the foundation of the United Irish League. That organisation, Connolly declared, had distorted the meaning of 'United Irishmen' into a 'union of class and creed'. How feasible was it to unite in one movement underpaid labourers and overpaid masters?[16]

The police reported on Connolly's appearances as a matter of course. They noted, for example, an occasion when, to a crowd that was neither large nor appreciative, he made some mischievous observations. It was the usual twaddle, they said, that could be heard any Sunday in Hyde Park or on the Green in Glasgow, but there was a difference in the effect. Listeners in London and Glasgow would take no serious notice of what was said; but in Dublin, unfortunately, disaffected people associated what was said with treason and disloyalty.

4

The Wolfe Tone demonstration on the 15 August 1898, the high point of the centenary celebrations, was the biggest thing of its kind seen in Dublin for years. Some thirty thousand people lined the streets to watch a procession organised by Fred Allan that took over two hours to pass from the General Post Office to the site of the projected memorial at the top of Grafton Street. Mallon was impressed: this was indeed a monster IRB turn-out. The result of it would be an absorption of all revolutionary associations by the IRB followed by an attempt to shape the course of the constitutionalists. The INB were not permitted to take an active part.[17] On the eve of the demonstration the IRB held two important meetings at 15 D'Olier Street at which decisions were taken, Mallon said, to continue the organisation with a purely revolutionary programme. They also 'talked a lot about the Local Government Bill, [and about] organising against the present Nationalist Members of Parliament and members of Municipal and Poor Law bodies. They all spoke strongly against clerical influence. No reference, directly or indirectly, was made to unlawful methods (outrage).'[18]

The INB also met in Dublin on the same day. Dr Mark Ryan was there with Henry Dobbyn, Patrick Tobin, Dan and Stephen Holland, Louis Ely O'Carroll and some others. They discussed the possibility of throwing in their lot with the IRB, who, as Mallon had earlier reported, showed no disposition to enter into a compromise.[19] Indeed, it was only at an all-party centenary dinner given by the Lord Mayor that the two sides showed up in each other's company, John O'Leary, Fred Allan, John Redmond, MP, and William Field, MP, sitting down at the same table as Dr Mark Ryan, W. B. Yeats and Maud Gonne.[20]

The newspapers gave elaborate accounts of the IRB demonstration and the speeches, one of which, by William Rooney, was unique, being given entirely in the Irish language. A few days later the police had a mild sensation to report. A bust of Wolfe Tone which had been placed on the site of the projected memorial had been knocked over, decapitated, and the head taken away. This had been done, apparently, by some students from Trinity College, but the Commissioner of Police felt inclined to blame the INB. They were jealous because Fred Allan had 'bossed' the Wolfe Tone procession, and they had taken the chance offered by the temporary absence of the watchman to mutilate the bust, thereby throwing ridicule on the whole affair.[21] (In passing, two things might be noted: first, that the Wolfe Tone Memorial Fund Committee was for a long time a public organisation through which the IRB worked, and second, that the foundation stone laid at the top of Grafton Street was in about 1929 removed by the Dublin City Commissioners, with the approval of the Minister for Local Government, an old IRB man. It now occupies the central position in the Wolfe Tone Memorial Park between Jervis Street and Wolfe Tone Street.)

Mallon grew more and more contemptuous of the revolutionaries as the year of commemoration drew to a close. The erection of the Wolfe Tone memorial was a laughing matter, he said. It was estimated to cost £14,000 but only £561 had been collected. The Americans would not part with their money, and if the parliamentarians and some others who had subscribed £5 each had their money back, they would not part with it so readily. Twenty thousand copies of an appeal had gone out, and Mallon passed one up to the Commissioner which had been received from a cynic who doubted if the signatures would draw the cash. Mallon knew all the signatories, the first of whom was John O'Leary; the others, with three exceptions, were also secret society men. No one, he said, would trust the secretaries with a £20 note, and the treasurers were 'not much'.[22] The first subscribers, surprisingly, included W. J. Walsh, the Catholic Archbishop of Dublin, and T. M. Healy, MP, who, from being the bitterest of Parnell's enemies, was to become the first Governor-General of the Irish Free State.[23] The Archbishop subscribed, not because of any particular affection for Tone but because the '98 celebrations had done something unusual at that time in bringing together so many representative Irishmen for the accomplishment of a common purpose.[24]

A return of the approximate strength of secret societies prepared for the government at the end of 1898 told a tale that Gosselin found hard to believe. It showed that there were then 513 IRB Circles in existence with a total membership of over 25,000, of whom 8,500 were in good standing. The INB had 10 Circles and 1,270 members, 470 of them in good standing. There were 9 branches of the Young Ireland Society still going with 1,400 members. The relative positions of the two wings of the Irish Parliamentary Party appeared in the same return. The Irish National League (the Parnellites under Redmond) had declined to 6 branches with 615 members of whom 160 were in good standing, while the Irish National Federation (the anti-Parnellites led by Dillon) had 221 branches, and a total membership of 27,400, a third of whom were effective. Understandably the '98 centenary associations outstripped them all with 31,000 members, a figure that was thought likely to decline rapidly.[25]

The '98 celebrations spilled over into 1899. In June of that year a memorial was unveiled at Ballina to the French general Humbert who led an expedition to Ireland in 1798, and a quarrel broke out among 'prominent suspects' who attended the ceremony. Gosselin commented that the spectacle of one leader throwing a jug of water at another would have been an edifying one for the French visitors.[26] He also thought it was a good sign when the National Club in Dublin closed because the members could not pay the rent. It had been maintained by extreme nationalists but suffered very much in consequence of the Parnell split. Its directors since then had been Dr J. E. Kenny, John L. Carew, John E. Redmond and T. C. Harrington—all Parnellite MPs. Other centres of Parnellism also threatened to close down.

5

The split in the American Clan na Gael came dramatically to an end in 1899 with the expulsion of William Lyman, at an INB convention held in Buffalo, for having treated the organisation in a 'suicidal manner'. There was a shortage of $22,000 in the funds; for a year and a half he had had no relations with their friends in Ireland; and, despite every effort, including the employment of men to watch his house, it had not been possible to locate him or to induce him to give up the books.

His expulsion opened the way to the reunion of the opposing forces for which Devoy had worked for years. With enormous determination he had traipsed over large areas of the United States speaking to individuals and groups, and had plied both his own supporters and the opposition with long circular letters setting out the facts as he saw them and acclaiming that the light was spreading and honest men returning to their old allegiance. In May 1899 at a conference in New York representatives of both sides of the Clan began to discuss reunion. There were further meetings in August at Atlantic City and in September at Philadelphia, where final agreement was reached. The only thing that could have kept them apart was the Cronin murder, and this difficulty was resolved by a joint declaration absolving the INB from responsibility for the death of 'an upright and honourable Irish patriot upon whose memory unwarranted attacks had been made'.[27]

A Clan na Gael convention held in Atlantic City in July 1900 at which the agreement to reunite was ratified, put an end, Devoy declared,

> to dissension and discord that had prevailed for fifteen years. . . . It gave the Clan a new birth. . . . It accomplished much more than the unity of two warring sections of an Irish Revolutionary Organisation. It restored the union between the

Irish in Ireland and their exiled kindred in America which had been broken by selfish, short-sighted and faithless men, and renewed that candid co-operation between the two which is absolutely essential to the final achievement of National Independence. It was by long odds the best and most representative Convention which the Clan na Gael (then 33 years in existence) had ever held. . . . Not one member of the Triangle was there. Chicago had a larger representation than any other big city, but Alexander Sullivan was not a delegate, and was no longer a member of the Organisation. . . . Mike Boland, Sullivan's right-hand man in the work of destruction, was not a delegate, had no place in the Organisation, and seemed to be forgotten. Power acquired by trickery and fraud is always short-lived. Poor D. C. Feeley, of Rochester NY, the weak member of the Triangle . . . had quietly dropped out, his little Club was dead. . . .[28]

An INB delegate from 'Europe' had explained to his American confreres in 1899 why their numbers were so small. They had, however, in the southern and eastern parts of Ireland an organisation of six or eight of the leading men in every parish, who could be depended on to carry their areas with them when necessary. In the western and northern areas, where they were regarded as parliamentarians, it was hard to recruit men. In Scotland they had a good working organisation, 'in fact the best of any with the exception of one other place [London], and in that said place our organisation is made up of the brightest lights of the present age, literary and professionally [*sic*]'. The reference to Yeats and the company of medical men is obvious in this grossly exaggerated report. The police view was that since the end of 1897 very little had been heard of the INB. The '98 commemoration movement, so largely an IRB affair, had absorbed everything; and from the beginning of 1899 the elections to county and district councils, pursuant to the recent Local Government Act, had had an effect.[29] The *Shan Van Vocht* had died in October 1898, the *Irish Republic* a few months earlier.

At the Atlantic City convention in 1900 two envoys were present from 'the home organisation' but, according to custom, they did not appear at the General Assembly nor were their

names disclosed : their reports were given to a Foreign Relations
Committee, which heard that the news of a settlement in
America had reached Ireland, and that both sides of the divided
Irish had come together and sent Patrick Hoctor and Dr Anthony
MacBride to represent the re-constituted IRB whose President,
as before, was the venerable John O'Leary, now in his seventieth
year.

Effectively the American agreement, 'practically on IRB
terms', had left the INB in Ireland without a *raison d'être*. Some
of its members had joined or rejoined the IRB, but men like
W. B. Yeats who were not considered to be serious revolutionaries were quietly by-passed. Arthur Griffith, the editor of the
United Irishman, on his return from South Africa, was approached to rejoin but asked for time to consider the matter. 'He
suspected persons had influence in the organisation about whom
he had grave apprehensions and who were mystery-mongers and
mischief-makers.' George A. Lyons who tells the story, and who
was in a position to know what he was talking about, says that
it was 'quite true that some old degenerate remnants of the once
great Fenian Movement had developed a form of spy mania,
and careless talk went round when these men met in a certain
kitchen in Cuffe Street and started swapping pints over their
reminiscences'.[30]

The spy mania could have tragic results. There was the case
in 1883 of John Kenny, an IRB man, who was seen going into
Dublin Castle. He had legitimate business there, but it was concluded that he had become an informer and, having been secretly
tried in his absence, was sentenced to death. Joe Poole, another
IRB man, hearing of the decision, set out to warn his friend that
a firing party lay in wait for him. He took the wrong road,
however, and missed Kenny, who walked into an ambush and
was killed. Poole was arrested, was found guilty of the murder
of the man whose life he had endeavoured to save, and was
hanged. The affair, involving the deaths of two innocent men,
appears to have made a deep impression on Arthur Griffith and
coloured his attitude to the use of physical force by men who,
however patriotic their motives, were responsible for their acts
to nobody but themselves. But Mallon had another version of
it,[31] and the State Papers present Poole as a mixed-up fellow
who, in custody, could offer to become an informer, and later, in

D*

a speech from the dock, call for cheers for the Irish Republic and to hell with English tyranny.[32]

6

Apart from the State Papers, few references to the INB have survived. Desmond Ryan in *Devoy's Post Bag* makes a passing reference to it. So does Maud Gonne in her autobiography. But neither she nor Yeats mention it by name, and Yeats's membership of it is confused in his letters with references to membership of the IRB. More remarkable still is the fact that Dr Mark Ryan in his *Fenian Memories* makes no reference at all to it, as if it never existed, or as if it was a bad dream that for one's peace of mind was better forgotten. George A. Lyons, himself an IRB man and the friend and biographer of Arthur Griffith, describes the movement with moderate accuracy in an article that appeared as late as 1950 and in an undated memorandum that the present writer has seen, but does not reproduce correctly either the name or objects of the organisation.[33]

7

Fred Allan and the *Irish Independent*

I

ALMOST FROM the beginning of the Parnell split it was evident
that those who stood by him, and against the alliance with the
Liberals, were fighting a hopeless battle; and the possibility of a
Liberal victory at the next general election and a third Home
Rule Bill did not improve their prospects. On the other hand
the anti-Parnellites in the Irish National Federation were under
attack from within, and the expulsion of the waspish Tim Healy
led to the formation by him of an organisation of his own. This
meant that by the end of 1895 there were three rival constitutional bodies of nationalists in the country—the Irish National
Federation led by John Dillon, who had succeeded Justin
McCarthy, the Irish National League led by John Redmond,
and Tim Healy's People's Rights Association. The schisms,
coupled with the failure of the Home Rule Bill of 1893, had a
depressing effect on American support. There was a considerable
falling off in subscriptions, which was a serious matter for Irish
members who could not support themselves at Westminster. For
a number of reasons, therefore, but most particularly because
there was no real difference of policy between them, the leaders
accepted the need for unity. Two things brought the matter to a
head. In January 1898 William O'Brien launched in the West
of Ireland an organisation with a strong agrarian base which he
called the United Irish League, and in February of the following
year John Dillon, who had been calling on the Parnellites to
come to terms, resigned from his chairmanship, enabling Parnellites and anti-Parnellites after almost a year of sparring, to agree
on a merger and to the election of Redmond, who was in direct
line of succession from Parnell, as the chairman of the reunited
Irish Parliamentary Party. This party could now represent the
mind of the United Irish League, which had become a great

power on the Irish landscape, could voice the national indignation at British imperialist policy in South Africa, and press for
more of the kind of social legislation the Unionists had been
giving them in the recent past.

Late in August 1900 Redmond's *Independent* papers, which
had been in low water for a long time, amalgamated with
Healy's mouthpiece the *Daily Nation*, which was controlled by
William Martin Murphy, a wealthy and strongly anti-Parnellite
Member of Parliament. Fred Allan had already ceased to be the
manager, and his departure had ended the use of the *Independent* offices as the IRB headquarters. A change in his relations
with Redmond had become observable as far back as February
1898 when he, for long on 'Dear Redmond' terms with the
Independent's chairman, sent him a 'Dear Mr Redmond' letter.
In this letter he said he had learned accidentally that some, if
not all, the members of the board had been told that in some
way he was neglecting his work in the office for the '98 movement. There was not the slightest foundation for the charge.
With the exception of writing a few letters and seeing a few
callers, all his work for the movement was done late at night.
He had never allowed anything outside to interfere with his work
for the papers. He continued :

> Of course, I cannot help feeling and regretting the change that
> has taken place of late as between the board and myself.
> Formerly they regularly sent for me for consultation if they
> were discussing commercial or mechanical business, but they
> have not done so four times during the past year, for whatever
> reason is best known to themselves. On account of this I
> welcomed heartily your presence in the office towards the end
> of last year, and greatly regret that you cannot be here all the
> year round.

Redmond sent a reassuring letter but made it known to Allan
that the directors thought that there was 'a looseness somewhere
in the business part of the concern'. To this Allan retorted that
if this was what the directors thought, it was their duty, apart
from any fairness to himself, to go fully into it. They would find
that the business side of the house was never running more
smoothly or more economically. Circulations were dribbling, but
this was not because of anything wrong on the mechanical work-

ing of the house. Theirs was the only Dublin morning paper which had not missed a train since the beginning of the year, but their sales were decreasing nevertheless. Redmond's regular presence was the only hope for the concern that had always lost money, which found it hard to obtain working capital, and to which the banks were not helpful.[1]

Mallon, who reported in detail on these developments, noted on 7 February 1899 that, unlike the *Freeman's Journal*, which had been able to pay a dividend of 8 per cent for the previous half-year, the *Independent* had never paid anything. In that respect it was like the *Daily Nation* which, with the *Freeman*, was sapping the *Independent*'s circulation. The *Irish Times* had a different sort of readership but was also 'giving way a little'. The situation of the *Independent* was crucial, and to meet it English newspaper magnates, the Harmsworth Brothers who, with the banks, held a lien on the paper, the extent of which was known only to Redmond, had sent over an official. He, after examining the accounts, showed how a saving of £3,000 a year could be effected. There was talk of Count Plunkett, Alderman Meade and some others coming to the rescue, offering to put in £5,000 a year each with which to pay off the creditors and work towards producing a dividend. A change in the tone of the paper was called for, and this was favoured by some Parnellites who favoured reunion with the anti-Parnellites and by others who did not.[2]

But, first and foremost, the paper's workforce had to be re-constructed, and this proved to be a painful process. Close on a hundred persons were fired from the various departments, and in some instances these were replaced by non-union men, some of them brought in from England. With satisfaction Mallon learned that John Merna, J. J. O'Kelly and John O'Mahony had gone and that Allan, J. W. O'Beirne and Michael Manning were likely to follow them. A strike was threatened, and to stave it off some of the large shareholders hurried to Dublin. The directors, taking fright, asked the Castle for 'police attention'. Some of them might be in danger of being assaulted. It was understood that the *Independent* was about to hand over the management to the Harmsworths, that there would be sweeping changes, and that attacks on property as a result were a real possibility. There were 'many ill-conditioned, drunken, idle fellows loafing about', and

Gosselin thought that the directors, if they could only see this description of the crowd they had cleared out, would put Mallon, its author, on the free list. The *Daily Nation*, relying, it was thought, on information supplied by Allan and company, painted a picture of despairing, disheartened men who had been discharged, standing outside the public houses. At missions, then being held in the city churches, the *Independent*, Parnellism and secret society men were relentlessly denounced. The weather was fine, and spring operations around Dublin and activity in the building trade left the poor literary hacks, the printers and compositors, as well as the professional politicians, severely alone. There was no money coming from America either.[3]

At a very stormy meeting of the directors on 2 March 1899 Allan, the manager, Michael Manning, the editor of the *Weekly Independent*, and P. J. O'Brien of the dispatch branch were dismissed. While the meeting was in progress from 150 to 200 members of the staff already discharged, with some sympathisers, lobbied about. There were rumours that 'something serious' would be attempted, but Mallon thought Allan too clever for that. Nevertheless, the English hands were becoming afraid of Merna and other fellows of his type, and John Redmond was also considered to be in danger of personal violence.[4] Nothing happened, however, and in a few days everything was quiet. Then Allan, with three months' salary in his pocket, opened a press agency in Dame Street, and some of his friends formed a committee, from which the 'hangers-on' at the *Independent* were excluded, to present him with a testimonial. The police view was that his star had set.[5]

By the end of April the agency had failed and Allan was in London looking for a job. He got a testimonial from Redmond, who was 'deeply pained' at the severance of their relations, retaining as he did the most friendly feeling for Allan.[6] In November Allan was in Dublin again and working on the commercial side of the *Freeman's Journal*, but a couple of months later he surprised everybody by becoming private secretary to Alderman Thomas Pile, the newly chosen Lord Mayor. According to Maud Gonne, Allan had helped to get Pile elected, coming to the '98 Centenary Committee with cheques from him and one of his henchmen. She had moved that the cheques be returned, as neither of the donors stood for Irish independence, but was outvoted on Allan declaring that he had converted both men to the national cause. Maud Gonne was no friend of Allan, and as she was active in the INB interest at the time, she would probably have been outvoted anyway.[7]

2

About the time of the Harmsworth reorganisation Allan gave a 'lecture' in the Nally Club on the spirit of the revolutionary movement, and the fact that among those who listened to him were Nolan and Merna caused Gosselin to remark that it was a curious sort of lecture. Mallon agreed. It was really an IRB meeting, he said, and they would likely know soon what had passed because 'a friend was at it'. Mallon had in fact no fewer than five 'friends' operating in that area at the time. Four of these he designated A ('Alpha'), B, C and D, and the fifth, whom he called 'Richmond', was a member of the Executive Council of the '98 Centenary Committee. Richmond's information, in Mallon's view, was the more valuable because it was given without reward. Richmond was at Allan's 'lecture', met Merna 'the Cardiff Lane murderer' there and had a drink with him afterwards in the Trades Hall in Capel Street. 'I could have known everything from him if I thought you wanted it,' he told his police go-between, Inspector Lynam. There was still dissension between the supporters of Tobin and Allan, a carry-over from the IRB–INB conflict. But people had become chary of joining secret societies. The game was played out, and there was no money around to sustain it. If crime was to be committed, it would be by one party upon the other. There was no longer any fear of harm being done to officials or buildings. The government was popular on account of the new Local Government Act and the prospect of a new university acceptable to Catholics.[8] Gosselin shared the Dublin Police Commissioner's enthusiasm for Richmond. They could do with a few more of the same kind, he said: his information, which ranged widely, had a most genuine ring.[9]

In March 1899 Richmond told Inspector Lynam, who was desperately anxious that no one but himself should question his 'friend', that for some time past very extensive inquiries had been carried out in the United Kingdom, and more searchingly still in America, by the leaders of the secret societies—presumably those of the IRB and the Clan na Gael—in order to ascertain to what extent the promoters of outrages had been in receipt of British government money. The brothers James and John Boland, it was said, had been behind the explosions at the *National Press* office, the Castle, the Four Courts and Exchange Court: James had made the plans for these outrages, and John had obtained the money from America to pay for them—and the inquiry established, Richmond said, that John Boland had been drawing £16 a month for a long time from a British consul in America while also receiving £30 a month from secret Irish-American sources. Both the Bolands were now dead. They had fallen under suspicion at home and, fearing assassination, which Mallon had for long thought was a possibility, James had attempted to commit suicide while a patient in the Richmond Hospital. John, coming home from America, carried poison with him to take should this become necessary. At Liverpool someone boarded the ship with the intention, he believed, of shooting him. He hurried down into the bowels of the ship and swallowed the poison.

A lesson had been learned over the Bolands, Richmond said. A completely new policy was on the way; in two or three weeks a meeting of the principal leaders of all the advanced sections would be held to form an organisation to secure every Local Government Act position such as aldermen, town councillors, county councillors and Poor Law Guardians, and the policy of crime, outrage and insurrection would be abandoned. There was no fear of the young generation doing anything on their own. They would consult the old men and were dead against any grouping that had for its object the commission of outrage.

J. J. Jones, the Dublin Police Commissioner, who was so enthusiastic about Richmond's stories, passed this statement to David Harrel, the Under-Secretary. 'This is a satisfactory report,' he commented, 'and as regards the past the facts set forth are correct. It is noteworthy that, since the deaths of the Bolands and Reeds [*sic*], outrages have ceased in Dublin. No person is in a better position than Richmond to know how secret society work goes on in this city, and what he declares is borne out from our other sources of information.' Things were quiet, and he hoped they would remain that way. On Jones's minute Harrel simply wrote: 'It is very interesting,' and Gerald Balfour, the Chief Secretary, concurred. Earl Cadogan, the Lord Lieutenant, added: 'Important if reliable,' to which Gosselin when he saw the file added: 'His Excellency has put the case in a nutshell.'[10]

3

Thomas Pile, whom Allan was said to have helped to become Lord Mayor, was a native of Grimsby who had built up an extensive fish and ice trade in Dublin and had acquired a considerable amount of house property in the city. He was a Methodist, a total abstainer, a Parnellite and a pronounced Home Ruler; Allan, as we noted earlier, had also a Methodist background, and there is reason to believe that family influence may have helped him to obtain the job as private secretary. In Mallon's eyes Allan was still 'a revolutionist, holding by physical-force doctrine; but he was very hard up, and his new job which carries a salary of £300 a year might modify his political views'.[11] With many enemies around, he was being accused of throwing over former associates to provide for himself, and in consequence, it was alleged, he was being threatened with violence, charged with misappropriation of money, and with having told a police officer that he was sorry he had not given up long ago.[12] The present writer has seen nothing to justify any of these statements. And if giving up meant leaving the IRB, this did not in fact happen.

Allan was soon in serious trouble, however, when Pile, with majority support in the Corporation, announced his intention to receive Queen Victoria when she visited Ireland in April 1900 and tender a 'loyal address' to her. The decision was bound to commit Allan to many public duties and appearances alongside the Lord Mayor, and the question was how he could do so consistently with his position as Secretary of the Supreme Council of the IRB? He went to his colleagues in the Council for a direction, and they, recognising that Allan's livelihood was at stake, concluded that his position was no different from that of another member, Peadar Macken, who ordinarily worked as a painter at the Viceregal Lodge and took his orders from the Lord Lieutenant. A minority thought otherwise. In their view the movement could not but be compromised if such a well-known republican appeared in the Lord Mayor's entourage at the reception of the Queen and organised a children's fete in her honour. His conduct did indeed cause misgivings among the rank and file, notwithstanding the Supreme Council's ruling, and was long remembered against Allan. Maud Gonne staged a children's party in opposition to Allan's, and James Connolly published criticisms of what he termed secret republicanism and open loyalty.[13] Some IRB men planned to blow up the artificial city gates where the Queen was to receive the keys from the Lord Mayor, but the plan miscarried as Fenian plans usually did. On the way back to the city the gilded coach, in which the Lord Mayor and his pure-souled revolutionist secretary sat—the description is Maud Gonne's—was sorely battered by the infuriated crowd, and its occupants, white and trembling, were barely saved by the police from a dip in the Liffey.[14]

James F. Egan, the City Sword-Bearer, by virtue of his office, was likely to appear even more prominently than Allan at functions connected with the royal visit, and this possibility caused Arthur Griffith and some associates of his to act rather threateningly. He brought Egan to what was called a private conference in the rooms of the Celtic Literary Society in Abbey Street and there made him face the issue. George A. Lyons, who was one of the party, recalled many years later what occurred at this confrontation:

> Griffith said: 'Mr Egan, what are you going to do about the Queen's visit?' 'I don't know,' replied Egan. 'What is Fred Allan going to do?' . . . 'Never mind anyone but yourself, just at present,' said Griffith. 'Your reputation is higher than any of us. You have spent ten years in the jails of Queen Victoria; you have a long life's record of service and sacrifice for Ireland. You will surely not undo all your work at the end of your career.' 'I am not responsible for what is taking place these times, and surely history will not judge of me for what I may have to do in the course of my daily employment or in my private capacity,' replied James Egan. 'A man like you has no private capacity,' said Griffith. 'If I don't act in accordance with orders,' replied James Egan, 'Pile will sack me.' 'Pile can't sack you,' one of us suggested. 'You are an employee of the Corporation.' 'Well, the Corporation will,'

protested James Egan. 'Look here,' said Griffith, 'if you really think the Corporation would have the cheek to dismiss you for your nationalism, we will guarantee to get up a public testimonial to you that will be worth twenty years' purchase of your present position.'[15]

Egan agreed to 'consult his friends' and next day he showed Griffith a draft letter he intended for the press. It was a mild document, full of polite excuses and apologies for his inability to be present at the state reception. Griffith altered it out of all countenance and got Egan to sign it. It appeared in the press in this most spirited form next day and Egan was covered with glory, while, wrote Lyons, some of his colleagues, including Fred Allan, were so covered with odium that they never quite forgave Griffith's interference when they learned the secret story of the case.

As a result of Allan's behaviour, a split developed within the IRB. John O'Leary, the President, and some members of the Supreme Council suggested to him that he should resign from the secretaryship, but others pressed him not to do so. The Council consequently was unable to meet, and the Circles were called upon by individual Centres and by some members of the Council to offer fealty to the Centres Board that governed each District.[16]

4

Early in November 1899 Jackie Nolan, Jack Merna, John Walsh and John Rowan left Dublin for America. Gosselin told the Inspector-General of the Royal Irish Constabulary that if they were bent on mischief they had gone about it in a peculiar manner, as they put up in Liverpool with a man who was suspected of giving information to the government. Five months later an attempt was made in Canada to blow up the gates of Lock 24 of the Welland Ship Canal which runs from Lake Erie to Lake Ontario, with the intention of restricting the movement of troops and supplies for the South African War. There were two explosions, but as the charges had been thrown in against the side rather than against the apex of each lock, little harm was done. That night two men on foot were arrested five miles away.

They were Nolan and Walsh; and the police, aware that they had earlier been in the company of a short-set smooth-faced man crossing and recrossing the canal bridge, set out and hauled in this third man, who proved to be Luke Dillon, *alias* Karl Dullman, a native of Leeds and one of the few Fenian campaigners of the 1880s to have carried out bombing operations in England. He had subsequently taken a very prominent part in the fight against the Triangle and Alexander Sullivan.[17] The three men were tried at Welland, convicted and sentenced to penal servitude for life. Walsh, a Dublin printer, died in prison in 1908. Dillon was released in July 1914 and Nolan in December 1915.

But what about Rowan and Merna—what had happened to them? All the police reported of Rowan was that he returned to Ireland in June 1900, flush with money, whatever that indicated. Merna had apparently committed suicide on or about 12 March, before crossing into Canada, and the manner of his 'horrible' death was conveyed by Nolan to William Crossin, a member of the reunited Clan na Gael. Crossin had been to Dublin once, secretly, as a delegate to the IRB and, on leaving for New York, had been followed by a detective. In a letter found on Nolan when he was arrested Crossin wrote: 'I am stunned by the act. His mind must have been affected. Poor Jack, I am sorry that he died in that way. . . . Allan will be shocked when he hears this.'

Also found on Nolan was another letter, from Dublin, giving news of Allan's appointment as private secretary to Lord Mayor Pile and reporting that Patsy Gregan had done thirty-one days for brawling with some soldiers and shouting for Kruger, the President of the Transvaal Republic who had distinguished himself in the Boer War against the British; the writer promised to send shamrocks for St Patrick's Day. Nolan had also had a letter from his wife Polly. A friend of theirs was sorry to hear that Jackie had had such a bad voyage, and he hoped the Boers would win; that was everyone's cry in Dublin. And Polly sent the best wishes of all the boys in Brady's [pub] and from Willie Coscreve [Cosgrave] and all friends. (The reference here is to W. T. Cosgrave, President of the Executive Council of the Irish Free State from 1922 to 1932.) On John Walsh was found a string of beads—a rosary perhaps—a compass, a key, an aluminium comb, and three verses of a poem, 'Irish Exile' by D. B. Regan, which conveyed to the Canadian police a hatred of England and a desire to see the Green Flag replace the Union Jack on Irish soil.[18]

5

Fifteen years is a long time to spend in jail: it was coming up to Christmas 1915 before Jackie Nolan returned to Dublin from his Canadian prison. He lost no time in looking up Fred Allan, his old IRB chief and patron. Jackie was by now a wizened old man, and the young clerk who waited on him in Allan's office on Cork Hill noticed his hard, gnarled hands. 'Tell him it's Nolan,' the caller said. The clerk gave the message and Allan, rushing to the door with outstretched hand, cried, 'Jackie!' He brought him into an inner room and there they talked for a long time. Jackie was in bad shape physically, but Polly nursed him back to health, and Allan again fixed him up with a job, this time on the Corporation's pay roll.

He died in October 1920 in the house in James's Street and was buried from the parish church nearby. His coffin, draped in the Irish tricolour, a custom then beginning, was borne to the hearse by former associates of his in the Nally Club—'the bad lot'—and a party of British military saluted the coffin as they went by. W. T. Cosgrave, Joseph McGrath, later a minister in Cosgrave's government, Fred Allan and P. T. Daly were among those who attended the funeral.[19]

8

Arthur Griffith, an I.R.B. Man?

I

THE QUESTION of the connection of Arthur Griffith, 'the father of Sinn Féin', with the IRB is often raised. The first official reference to him in this context that the present writer has seen occurs in a police report of a meeting held on 7 October 1891 in Trinity Street, Dublin, which 'men from England, Scotland and Ireland attended'. John O'Leary and Fred Allan were there among a recognisable group of IRB men; the occasion was 'private', and although pressmen from the Parnellite papers[1] were present, they were asked to treat it as such. There was a police agent in the company as usual, and from what he wrote Major Gosselin could not see why anybody should have worried about maintaining secrecy. The speeches by O'Leary, Allan, Bracken —Thomas Bracken, a Dublin tailor, not Joseph K. Bracken of Templemore—and an ex-MP named Nolan were peppered with allusions to 'the old feeling', 'freedom by the sword', 'amnesty', and 'No support for any *one* political party'. It might all have been safely published, but that, said Gosselin, would have rubbed the bloom off it. Reports from the country on the progress of Parnellism were said to be most encouraging, but underlying them was a strong wish for a revival of physical force as an adjunct to it. It was rumoured through the Dublin men at the meeting that Jackie Nolan and Merna were in town and that soon 'something' would happen.[2] This was, of course, long before the Welland Canal exploit that ended so disastrously for all concerned.

Griffith was then (1891) only twenty years of age. He had worked as a compositor on the *Daily Nation*, and later as a copy-reader on the *Irish Independent*, and had become, with Willie Rooney, another young Dublin man with similar background and ideas, the moving spirit in the Leinster and Celtic Literary Societies. The two men, according to George A. Lyons, who was well placed to know the facts, were appointed by Dr Mark Ryan as chief organiser and chief secretary respectively in Ireland for the INB, though, in Lyons's estimation, two men less suited for such positions could hardly have been found. They were both shy and retiring and quite unlikely to have been any good in approaching men to join a semi-secret society.[3] At the end of 1897, business in his craft being bad, Griffith went to South Africa and worked there for a couple of years in casual journalistic jobs. Before he came home he helped to start an Irish Society in Johannesburg which gave military support to the Boers when they went to war in October 1899. Two Irish brigades served in the war on the Boer side, one led by Colonel Arthur Lynch, the other by Colonel J. Y. F. Blake whose second-in-command was Griffith's friend John MacBride, who had left Ireland in 1896 within months of returning from the INB's Chicago convention and was considered by Michael Davitt to be one of the most reckless and daring of fighters. His command, with which an energetic Transvaal Committee at home kept in touch, supplying volunteers under cover of maintaining an ambulance for the Boer wounded and flooding the country with anti-recruiting pamphlets, was never very large, but they fought with distinction in the Dundee, Modderspruit and Colenso, and occupied one of the kopjes that surrounded Ladysmith during the siege. MacBride and his comrades would infinitely have preferred to have been fighting on Irish soil, but this was the next best thing. While resting at Ladysmith on Christmas Day one of the Irish company, Tom Byrne, who in later years was Captain of the Guard in Dáil Éireann, sang a song that Griffith had specially written for them. A verse ran :

> Oh mother of the wounded breast !
>   Oh mother of the tears !
> The sons you loved and trusted best
>   Have grasped their battle-spears;
> From Shannon, Lagan, Liffey, Lee,
>   On Afric's soil to-day
> We strike for Ireland, brave old Ireland
>   Ireland far away !
> We smite for Ireland, brave old Ireland
>   Ireland, boys, hurray !

When the Boers were finally subdued the Irish brigades disbanded and the Irish who were British subjects had to find shelter in foreign lands. The Boer government chartered a steamboat to take the Irishmen to Trieste, paid their passages from there to America, and gave each of them a small sum of money. MacBride went to Paris, however, and was met there by Griffith and Maud Gonne. They were reported to be seeking permission from the French government to form another Irish brigade which would attract young men who might otherwise enlist in the British army, and the Dublin police hoped that it might be found possible to obtain a conviction against Miss Gonne to stop her in her tracks.[4] In Paris Griffith sat down with MacBride to compose a series of lectures on his South African experiences to be given in the United States, the proceeds from which were to aid the anti-recruiting work in Ireland and Griffith's newspaper. Maud Gonne was to be employed on a similar mission. In the course of working together, on tours of American centres arranged for them by the Clan na Gael chief, John Devoy, and his assistant, T. J. Clarke, recently released from an English prison, their friendship ripened, and they married and had a son. The inevitable policeman looked in at the christening and noted that it had been intended that John O'Leary was to have shared the sponsorship with MacBride's mother but that his declaration of faith was not considered satisfactory.[5] (There is reason, however, to doubt the entire accuracy of this report.) As Griffith foresaw, knowing the temperaments of the two parties as intimately as he did, the marriage did not endure. It broke up in 1905 in a welter of charges and countercharges and was never resumed. MacBride, when he was able to return to Ireland, held a number of minor posts in the Dublin Corporation. He remained a close friend of the Allans, lived with them, and produced Mrs Allan as a witness at his court martial in 1916.

In March 1899 Griffith, back in Dublin, was editing the *United Irishman*, a four-page halfpenny paper, with Rooney as his assistant, and in October of that year he was catalogued by the police among Fenians of the worst type who had organised a meeting to further the aims of the Transvaal Committee which Mallon had directed his detectives to watch.[6] A consultation with Dr Mark Ryan was believed to be concerned with sending men out to the Transvaal.[7] In January 1900 he returned from a visit

to Paris flush with money,[8] and this was presumed to have paid
for anti-British posters that appeared throughout Dublin and
which the police were ordered to take down wherever they could
do so without attracting attention. These parodied the Beatitudes
and were noted by Mallon as akin to *Paudeen O'Rafferty's Ten
Commandments*, published in Land League Days.[9] Seen, as it
were, through Jingo and Co.'s new glasses, they began : *Blessed
are the big guns and their blessed lyddite children, for such is
the kingdom of heaven*, and they ended : *Ye are the saltpetre of
the earth*.[10]

Griffith was next mentioned in a minute of Mallon's (8 Feb.
1900) which reported the continuing decline in the fortunes of
the physical-force men. In recent municipal elections three candidates who had their solid support had been defeated. In a
parliamentary by-election in South Mayo a similar fate had
overtaken MacBride despite his reputation as a freedom-fighter
and the fact that Griffith had canvassed strenuously for him. A
pro-Boer resolution before the Dublin Corporation had fallen
through, the pro-Boer tone of the *Independent* had disappeared,
and it was rumoured that the paper was to be taken over by the
Freeman's Journal. If that happened, it would be the most
serious blow of all. There was evidence also, Mallon hinted, that
the physical-force men had begun to pay attention to their
personal positions, and he quoted a man who knew them well
as saying that the fire-eaters were trying to gobble up everything
for themselves. T. J. Clarke, was an unsuccessful candidate for
the post of superintendent of the Dublin abattoir, and Arthur
Griffith was trying to get a county council clerkship. Clancy, the
ex-sub-sheriff, seeing no prospect of being reappointed, had
tried every means of becoming the President of the Court of
Conscience and had failed.

Some of the men who carried out the outrages of the early
1880s were still meeting nightly in Mullett's pub in Lower Bridge
Street. Some dirty work might be afoot, a police watcher thought;
but Mallon, who knew better, said their purpose was in connection with a move to get a job for Mullett's son with the local
authority. Something might conceivably arise to make it necessary for the reunited Irish Parliamentary Party to make use of
the physical-force men, but he saw no reason for serious apprehension on that score because of the decline within the IRB

itself.[11] This view was supported by the RIC chiefs. The non-election of MacBride in Mayo bore out their opinion that the young men of that time were too well educated, and the distrust of leaders too pronounced for activist organisations to succeed.[12] And when an AOH man was stabbed by an IRB man in County Cavan, Gosselin said that, paradoxical though it might seem, those quarrels were a good sign. If there was anything serious afoot, there would be no quarrels.[13] It was generally agreed that the Transvaal Committee had reached its zenith, and that Maud Gonne was discredited all over Ireland outside Dublin.

2

Ramsey Colles of the *Irish Figaro* did not like Maud Gonne, and what she said about the Boer War particularly annoyed him : it was all so untrue. His feelings getting the better of him, he put together an article in which he likened her to Herodotus, the father of lies, though Herodotus, he insisted, was a lover of the plain, unvarnished truth compared with this lady, if a liar could be considered a lady. She had written in the French gutter press that the Irish soldiers were put on board the transports for South Africa with 'manacled wrists', and that the majority of them, when they got there, laid down their arms and refused to fight. The Transvaal Committee, with which Miss Gonne was connected, likewise made use of falsehood as a constant weapon.[14]

The immediate sequel to this outburst was the appearance of Arthur Griffith in the police court charged with unlawfully and wantonly assaulting Colles. Colles deposed that Griffith had entered the *Figaro*'s offices in Grafton Street and had struck him on the head, knocking off his hat. Colles closed with him and broke the stick. Griffith then said : 'You can have me arrested,' and at the police station he declared that it was because Colles had slandered Miss Gonne that he had attacked him. To the magistrate Griffith admitted the offence and asked for an adjournment so that the case could be gone into in detail—he was obviously anxious to exploit its publicity potential—but this was refused. The magistrate imposed a fine of £1 or fourteen days and directed Griffith to enter into bail in two sureties of £5 or go to jail for another fourteen days. Griffith, leaving the dock, said that he would not enter into any bail to keep the peace towards Mr Colles, and duly served the sentence.

The *Figaro*, full of fight, reported the court case and threatened that if Griffith, 'the maudlin youth', or any of the crowd of reptiles that constituted the Transvaal Committee dared to come to the offices again, they would get a reception they would long remember. It laughed at how the knocking off of a man's hat had become in Griffith's own *United Irishman* a horsewhipping and 'a sound thrashing'. It concentrated some of its fire on W. B. Yeats, who, it said, was an utter literary fraud laying claims to the laurels of the poet. When a person of such ignorant views laid aside 'his idiotic occupation of tinkering nonsense rhymes together' and proceeded to write letters to the press in which the Queen of England was referred to in terms which the reporter's pen refused to transcribe, 'it was high time that the persistent buzzing of such a noxious insect should be put an end to, even at the risk of soiling one's nails'.[15] The paper went on to express surprise that Maud Gonne could continue to accept at the hands of the government the sum of £300 a year as a pension in recognition of her father's services in an army which she had done her best by fair means and foul to vilify.

This led to further court proceedings, Maud alleging that a *Figaro* poster implied that she was nothing more than a spy in the employment of the British government. She had never received a government pension, she told the magistrate; such money as she had came out of her parents' savings. Griffith again rallied to her defence and submitted to a cross-examination which aimed at demonstrating that people in public life, like Maud Gonne and himself, should not be too thin-skinned, and should not be surprised to get as much in the way of vituperation as they were accustomed to give. Griffith admitted responsibility for having published in his paper that John Redmond, the leader of the Irish Parliamentary Party, had been 'appointed to a scullionship in Buckingham Palace'. In the same context he agreed that he had written that Ireland had been turned into a breeding-ground for human oxen—creatures with minds so degenerate and ignorant that they might be fitly compared to the beasts of the field. That, he told the magistrate, was unfortunately too true; and that was the sort of journalism he wrote. For her part, Maud Gonne conceded that for four years she had been proclaiming in public that the Irish soldiers of the Queen were traitors to their country, and that she had taken a hand in composing a leaflet to that effect. She had not heard it being said at a meeting at which she was present that the Irish soldiers should shoot their officers, but she would approve of it. She took full responsibility for an article she had written in which she said that the Queen, in the decrepitude of her eighty-one years, was after all a woman, and however vile and selfish and pitiless her soul might be, she must sometimes tremble as death approached. The Queen had always been ready to cover with her royal mantle the crimes and turpitude of her empire, and held the shamrock in her withered hand. Redmond was not a traitor, Miss Gonne thought.

When the evidence was completed, counsel for Colles observed, not unfairly, that he had seen many political farces in Ireland in his time, but had never seen a more screamingly funny one than Miss Gonne coming into a court of justice—'a British Court of Justice, mind you, not a Transvaal Court, or a French Court (laughter)'—and seeking the protection of the criminal law because a society journal said she had got a pension from the government. However, the magistrate was not impressed. He thought that the reasonable and only effect of the poster was to hold Miss Gonne up to hatred, contempt and ridicule, as nothing could be meaner than that she should be abusing the government and at the same time taking a pension from them. Mr Colles should have foreseen that when he distributed the poster. So, to applause from the gallery, he held that the case was one in which informations should be returned. Subsequently in the Recorder's Court Colles admitted that Miss Gonne had never been in receipt of a pension, and unreservedly withdrew the statement, apologising for the mistake and for any misconception as to her position. The apology was accepted and the matter allowed to drop, but Colles made it clear in the next issue of his paper that the apology did not imply a change in his attitude to Miss Gonne as a political agitator.

3

In May 1900, at the time of the announced mission to America of two recently released Invincibles—Joseph Mullett, the hunchback brother of James Mullett referred to elsewhere in this story, and James Fitzharris, otherwise 'Skin-the-Goat' (so called because of a tale about his selling the hide of a pet animal to pay his drinking debts)—Mallon came into possession of a 'very curious letter' which had been 'picked up on the floor of an office by a man who was struck by its contents, showed it to his brother and then brought it to me'. The letter by one J. F. McCarthy of 'Ormond Quay', a law clerk and member of the Transvaal Committee, was addressed 'Dear Arthur', which Mallon said was Arthur Griffith. It began :

> I could hardly credit my eyes when I saw about F. and M.'s proposed visit to the States. How in the name of common-sense did it creep into the papers? It might have upset our project completely and everything has been going on so smoothly lately. But [ ] I know for a fact have not taken any notice yet. I expected to see you at No. 32 [Lower Abbey Street] on Thursday night last. Everything is going on swimmingly for our children's feast. I have heard nothing further re Colles. . . .

On the back of the letter the following was written in pencil in what Mallon said was Griffith's hand :

> Bank of Ireland
> 24 ft. 2 in.
> Within 2 flags from wall
> ? ?
> Acknowledge same (him?)
> Meet McCarthy and McBride corner Essex Bridge,
> tobacconist's side, give the usual sign.
> Get Colles' address (private)

Mallon doubted if Fitzharris would travel to America. If he went he could only be used for a show, just like a bear. He had no intelligence and was nearly always drunk. Joe Mullett was a different proposition. He was a very well-educated fellow and a fluent speaker.

As to the mysterious letter and notes, were they genuine? Mallon was in no doubt that they were, and that they had not been planted, which was a possibility to which Gosselin adverted when Harrel, the Under-Secretary, sent them over to him to look

at. To Mallon, Griffith's pencillings suggested the likelihood of
dynamite attempts on the Bank of Ireland and on Colles's private
residence, and he arranged immediately that both places should
receive special attention from the police. Griffith, he said, had
been to South Africa and knew how to use dynamite. But what
did the letter mean? 'I am assured', he said, 'they are arranging
for some new movement, as they expect the war in South Africa
will soon be over and that then the Transvaal Committee will
dissolve. Just as the Amnesty Association did when the [Fenian]
prisoners were released.'

Gosselin, uncomfortable and alarmed, cabled his New York
agent about Fitzharris and Mullett, and this contributed to
having them both expelled from the United States, than which,
Gosselin said, secret societies had never received a worse blow.[16]
He believed that the letter and the notes were concerned with
some particular subject and not a general one such as the reorganisation of the IRB which he took Mallon to have in view.

4

The letter and notes ascribed to Griffith are more mysterious in
the light of the launching by him and Rooney in October of the
same year (1900) of a new constitutional political organisation,
Cumann na nGaedheal which Dublin Castle's translator ponder-
ously rendered as 'The Confederation of the Gaels'. Griffith had
come to the conclusion that Ireland at that stage was unable to
achieve victory against England's armed might. The new body
would work for Irish independence by cultivating a fraternal
spirit amongst Irishmen and promoting the objects to which
other groups were clearly committed, such as the support of Irish
industries, the study and teaching of Irish history, literature,
language, music and art, the cultivation of Irish games, resistance
to everything tending towards anglicisation, the nationalising of
public boards and the development of 'an Irish foreign policy'.
There was nothing here that pointed towards separatism in the
full sense of the term, and the choice of John O'Leary as its first
president was a gesture towards the past rather than the future.[17]
But whatever the intentions of its founders, Cumann na nGaedheal became largely an open propagandist cover for the IRB.[18]
It is well to remind ourselves that the police reports were

occasionally jaundiced. Mallon's unrestrained contempt for a certain class of nationalist became most evident when he read in Griffith's *United Irishman* the long list of individuals said to have been present at the first convention of Cumann na nGaedheal. He did not believe, he said, the representation was anything like as elaborate as was said; this was mere space-filling copy. All the Dublin men named had been seen at different places and at different times by the police on the day of the convention. The majority never put foot in Abbey Street where the convention was held in premises loaned by the Celtic Literary Society to the Transvaal Committee. Two of them were habitual drunkards, two were old Corporation scavengers who spoke Irish and were over sixty years old, two were schoolboys, the Emmet Guard man was a car driver and bandmaster of the Milltown Band. 'Egan, Griffith and Quinn were the only bad ones. Three of the parties were so drunk at 8 o'clock that they were groping their way about. One of them who, I suspect, wrote the article spent a quarter of an hour trying to find the letter box in the door of the publishing office of *The United Irishman*.' Among those who attended the convention and who were concerned to advance their views about reviving the Irish language and literature there was a majority of deranged faddists.

Maud Gonne, who had collaborated closely with Griffith in bringing Cumann na nGaedheal into being, had recently sent him three remittances of £10, £10 and £15.[19] Most of this money went to support the *United Irishman*, for which Griffith was both editor, manager and main contributor. The pressure on him was appalling. He told MacBride:

I am trying to get two papers out this week, and I am withered up. . . . I am . . . tired to death, and I feel now that I have asked and not received. I have gone to the very utmost limit of my duty to my country. Though I hate and loathe writing, I kept firing away because I believe it is only by dogged insistence on obvious truths we can get the hypnotised Irish sometime or other to realise them and make an effort to prevent their extinction. But I feel quite satisfied now that I have done my part when I offered to continue work that has become in itself detestable to me, and that only a sense of individual responsibility to this country has kept me so long at it.

Don't think I have grown pessimistic, because on the contrary, I have strong hopes, but the strain of three years' continuous writing has rather given me brain weariness and made me more querulous and abrupt and cynical than I used to be.[20]

In 1901 the most active associations in Dublin were said by the police to be the Celtic Literary Society, the Gaelic League and the Gaelic Athletic Association. The funds of the two latter bodies were being used by secret society men to visit country districts as delegates from Dublin and vice versa. J. F. Egan, F. B. Dineen, J. W. O'Beirne, Arthur Griffith, W. O'Leary Curtis and P. F. O'Loughlin of Tullamore were the most active channels of this propaganda, but the immediate results were not alarming. Towards the end of the year, however, little activity was observable in secret society circles, principally owing to want of funds. The energy generated when the '98 clubs sprang into existence in 1898 had in great measure subsided. Such clubs still existed, but a majority of them met irregularly, and their meetings were not well attended. In Dublin there were twenty-six of them, including the Executive Council of the '98 Centenary Committee, with a nominal membership of 800, but the real membership was down substantially in 1900 and consisted almost entirely of secret society men. Every effort was made to collect money but with little success, and most of what was collected was embezzled; for this and other causes a projected Wolfe Tone '98 memorial bazaar had to be abandoned.

Of the Dublin clubs considered by the police to be the most dangerous, the first was the Transvaal Club, which numbered about forty members and was led by Arthur Griffith. They met at 32 Lower Abbey Street twice a week. They were all secret society people and were connected either with the Celtic Literary Society or the Daughters of Erin (Inghinidhe na hÉireann), a separatist society for women formed by Maud Gonne in 1900. They carried on propaganda against enlistment in the British forces and distributed literature. The second most dangerous club was the Major MacBride Club, which had also about forty members, mostly youths, who met once a week at 18 High Street. It promised to be a good recruiting ground for the IRB. A 'Celtic literary class' was held—which we take to mean that the Irish language was taught—and the members attended public meetings to demonstrate for the things they believed in and to heckle speakers whose opinions they did not like. The third most dangerous centre was the Foresters' Hall, 41 Rutland Square. This had become the chief resort of secret society men since the National Club ceased to exist, and nine of the '98 clubs met there, held 'Celtic' classes, gave lectures on political subjects, and organised dances and reunions for IRB men and their confederates. Among the most notable figures to be seen in this building were Patrick Thomas Daly and Fred Allan. The fourth group on the most dangerous list were the Irish Socialist Republicans who met at 138 Upper Abbey Street, and their most prominent members were James Connolly, J. Stewart, D. O'Brien and T. J. and M. Lyng. This was not a secret society, but it was a most disloyal one, and was usually at one with the IRB in causing disturbances and promoting disloyalty. These organisations, one and all, were now turning their attention to the coming municipal elections and were expected to run candidates in five or six of the city wards. They were also endeavouring to pledge candidates not to support an address from the Corporation to the new king should he come to Dublin in 1902.

P. T. Daly, the man seen in Allan's company, was a compositor employed on the *Daily Independent*. He had been an active member of the Robert Emmet Club since its formation, and was secretary to the Wolfe Tone and '98 memorial bazaar committees. The police noted that he figured prominently in all secret society movements but was in some degree suspected by his confederates of dishonesty in money matters. At the end of 1902 he was the official organiser of Cumann na nGaedheal and in that capacity visited the South and West. By this time Cumann na nGaedheal's most prominent figures included John O'Leary as president, Major MacBride, Robert Johnston, John Daly, J. F. Egan, T. J. Clarke and Maud Gonne as vice-presidents, and Arthur Griffith leading the committee. The election of both MacBride and Maud Gonne among the vice-presidents of Cumann na nGaedheal arose out of a serious division of opinion. Following the divorce proceedings in Paris, an attempt was made by the IRB to have MacBride elected at the Cumann's annual convention and to exclude Maud Gonne. The women's organisation, Inghinidhe na hÉireann, opposed this move. P. T. Daly directed the IRB men present how to vote, but Hobson and

E

McCullough, as representatives of the Belfast executive of the Cumann, refused to follow his lead, and others may have done the same, hence the decision to compromise by electing both candidates. 'During the debate', said McCullough, 'I went to the foyer for a cigarette. MacBride followed me out and assured me that he was no party to the move on his behalf, and urged me to vote as I thought right. I treasured his friendship always afterwards.'[21]

With such leaders as these Cumann na nGaedheal looked increasingly to the police very much like an IRB front. P. T. Daly was closely watched, therefore, and reports on his movements began to accumulate. In September 1902 'Peter, an IRB organiser, known as Mr Daly' was shown as having visited a variety of places. He had recently shaved off his moustache and adopted other disguises. And Major Gosselin told the Under-Secretary that a file, containing a photographed copy of Daly's letter of instructions from Dr Mark Ryan, was in the hands of the London Metropolitan Police.[22]

9

The Castle in a Liberal Mood

I

THE IRISH were always fond of funerals and were particularly skilled at turning those of erstwhile advanced men to political account, as we saw when Terence Bellew MacManus, John O'Mahony and Charles Stewart Parnell were buried. The death of James Stephens in Blackrock, Co. Dublin, in March 1901 should, therefore, have been the signal for a great demonstration had circumstances been normal, but Stephens had lived since 1866 under a cloud, and all that could be agreed upon was to give him a public funeral with no graveside oration. There was little enthusiasm on the day, but a thousand 'tradesmen' walked with nine amateur bands in what the police saw as a personal tribute rather than anything political. Michael Davitt was a pallbearer, with C. G. Doran and other '67 men; Davitt also paid the funeral expenses, for Stephens had been badly off and an appeal by the IRB, over the signatures of Fred Allan and James Mullett, had met with a poor response. Through the instrumentality of Parnell Stephens had been allowed to return to Ireland in 1891 and went to live in Sutton, Co. Dublin, with the intention of keeping clear of politics. He had kept that resolve, his only appearance at a '98 procession in September 1898 creating some excitement. He was often visited by old comrades and by some of the younger men who wanted to meet the ex-Head Centre of the Fenian organisation which they were still endeavouring to keep alive.

The annual Parnell commemoration in October was seen as a complete failure by the police. The extremist element was altogether absent, only a few of the old and inactive men taking part, the younger and more active ones being of the opinion that Parnell and his parliamentary methods were principally responsible for the decline of their organisation. But when Father

Eugene O'Growney, a leading Gaelic Leaguer who had died in 1899, was reburied in Ireland early in 1902, his funeral was a colossal affair; the coffin was conveyed from California to Maynooth College, some fifteen miles outside Dublin, by easy stages, at each of which the Irish congregated in huge numbers to pay their respects. A police report believed that advantage was taken of the occasion to send delegates from America to assist in the reorganising of the I RB.

The police saw the Gaelic League as a variable quantity. Basically it appeared to be unobjectionable, but it was known that 'the extreme party' looked on it as the very best means at their disposal for implanting their ideas in the minds of the rising generation. The police also saw that politics, if introduced into the League, would be its undoing. In some places it was controlled by the IRB and was on the way to becoming a mere school for teaching Fenianism and hatred of the British government. It could be a source of danger. The Celtic Literary Society was more openly political. In it instruction was also given in the Irish language and in Irish history, but always with the object of giving its members a general aversion to everything English. Persons joining had to be of Irish descent and pro-Boers. An active branch in Tullamore was directed by P. F. O'Loughlin, whom Gosselin described as much more than 'a literary enthusiast'. He was, in fact, a dangerous villain whose name first came to Gosselin from America and who had been implicated in the explosions at Dublin Castle and the Four Courts and in the murder of Pat Reid.

Among some highlights about political suspects, the Dublin Police Commissioner mentioned an effort being made in 1902 to organise a testimonial to Michael Cusack who was 'broken down from drink'. He had formerly been a successful civil service tutor and had played a prominent part in founding the Gaelic Athletic Association and in promoting the Gaelic League. His last appearance had been at an election in Galway where he spoke in Irish in favour of the Unionist Horace Plunkett who had stood against the pro-Boer Colonel Lynch and was soundly beaten. A brother-in-law of Jackie Nolan now doing penal servitude in Canada, named Boothman, who worked as a telegraphist in the GPO, was trying to get recruits for the IRB. Maud Gonne was especially active at the second convention of

Cumann na nGaedheal and had taken part in some of the Irish plays in the Antient Concert Rooms given under the auspices of this organisation. The socialist James Connolly, who was going to America on a lecturing tour, was remembered in connection with the displays of black flags during the 1897 jubilee celebrations, and for having been an agent for Maud Gonne. His work in Ireland had failed, and he was unable to support his family on the pittance he received as an organiser for the Irish Socialist Republican Party. He was to remain eight years in America, returning in 1910 to work in uncomfortable harness with James Larkin, the demagogic founder of the Irish Transport and General Workers' Union.

The Anglo-Japanese alliance of 1902 which preluded the Russo-Japanese War had its repercussions in Irish-American circles. The British Foreign Office heard in June 1903 of a meeting held in New York at the instance of the Russian representative in Washington, who was said to have concluded some arrangement with the Irish organisations in the United States. Gosselin had no doubt that there was some 'philandering' between the two 'august' parties, but he did not attach any importance to it for the time being. Mr St John Gaffney, one of the leaders of the Irish societies in New York, was very intimate with Count Cassini; and Sir Percy Sanderson, the consul-general in New York, reported that Baron Schlippenbach, at one time Russian vice-consul at New York and now consul at Chicago, was constantly in touch with the Clan na Gael.[1] Sanderson tried to maintain contact with his Russian 'colleague'. On St Nicholas's Day 1905 (the Emperor's name day) he called upon him, and again when he got the news of the assassination of the Grand Duke Serge, but the Russian did not think fit to call or send his card in return. Anglo-Russian relations had been strained by the Dogger Bank incident. On the other hand, Sanderson had seen two of the Russian's letters addressed to St John Gaffney. In the first he referred to 'a systematic anti-Russian campaign inaugurated by the three enemies of Christian Ireland and Christian Russia—England, the Jews and, not least, Japan'. In the second letter, which was written on green paper and enclosed in an envelope having 'Imperial Russian Consulate-General' printed outside, he inquired tenderly as to 'the prospects of Irish Home Rule in connection with events in the British Parliament'. 'I am not at all sure', said Sanderson, 'that he is not writing more of these things with the view of their being brought to my notice.'[2]

2

From its inception the Fenian movement in Ireland had been harried and hunted by the Castle administration, aided prodigiously after 1874 by John Mallon, the head of the Detective Division of the DMP. The situation changed materially with Mallon's retirement at the end of 1901 and the appointment, at about the same time, of a very untraditional Under-Secretary in the person of Sir Antony MacDonnell. He was a Catholic. He had a brother in the Irish Parliamentary Party and was known to be generally sympathetic to Irish national aspirations. He had accepted appointment as the permanent head of the Irish administration in preference to taking a more exalted job in the Council of India where he had already worked with distinction and where he had been nicknamed 'the Bengal Tiger' because of his fierce, unrelenting character. It would appear that he either came to Dublin Castle under a misunderstanding with George Wyndham, the Conservative Chief Secretary, or was reneged upon by Wyndham when, with Lord Dunraven, he engaged actively in the formulation of a moderate scheme of political devolution for Ireland inside the United Kingdom which he believed had Wyndham's approval. That led ultimately to disaster for both of them; but MacDonnell remained long enough at the Castle to show a frank and independent outlook on matters of general administration submitted to him by a civil and police service which was stuffed with patronage appointments. Of what they had to say to him about the state of the country he was particularly suspicious. He was equally suspicious of his political chiefs, and they found him desperately hard to move. One of them once said that he had the obstinacy of ten thousand mules and could only be drawn back with oaths and violence from any position he assumed.[3]

In March 1903 Ivon H. Price, an Acting Divisional Inspector of the Royal Irish Constabulary, engaged on political work, or what was called Crime Special, summarised the reports of the Crime Special sergeants for the southern and eastern counties. These commented on 'the remarkable dullness in Secret Society work' and the fact that no efforts were being made to reorganise though this was, obviously, urgently necessary. The prime suspect at the time was P. T. Daly, who was in great demand as a speaker at branch meetings of the IRB. He usually cautioned his audiences against confiding in the clergy even in the confessional, and denounced the United Irish League (UIL) and all other organisations that were not bound by oath to take up arms.[4] But he surely was straying from his brief when in a lecture in County Tyrone he gave the procuring of employment as one of the advantages of joining 'the Organisation'.

P. N. Fitzgerald and J. K. Bracken were on the move, and J. F. O'Sullivan, Frank Dorr and Alderman James Nowlan of Kilkenny were mentioned in connection with the GAA, whose clubs were said to be almost invariably under IRB control. Every effort was being made to exclude soldiers and sailors from them, to decry Saxon games, and to work up hatred of the British government. There was, however, considerable jealousy and mistrust between the older and younger members of 'the Organisation'.

The IRB, though nothing but the shadow of a once terrifying name, was also endeavouring to encourage the Gaelic League, but as most of the branches were under the control of Roman Catholic clergymen, no countenance was given to secret society work, and priests frequently denounced such societies from the altar. Recruiting for the army, on the other hand, was good. On Price's summary of these matters MacDonnell wrote: 'I confess I am not much impressed; and the information I receive from other quarters does not invest the Gaelic movement at all events with malign and disloyal objects, though the objects are certainly "national".'[5] The Assistant Under-Secretary, J. B. Dougherty, an Ulster Presbyterian, thought there was no real ground for alarm when the Dublin police chiefs recommended special precautions in March for some occasion or other, and MacDonnell was similarly unimpressed, though he admitted that W. V. Harrel, the Assistant Commissioner, knew his business.[6]

3

There were other examples later of a growing critical, not to say cynical, attitude towards police reports. On an account of what appeared to be a revival of the INB MacDonnell wrote that time would settle the question, which, after all, did not seem of supreme importance. And he followed this up with the observation that since 1894 nothing had come out of all these reports and suspicions and there was less reason now than ever to consider them substantial.[7] There was some concern as to the sort of reception Edward VII would receive on his first visit to Ireland as King, but the authorities were somewhat relieved when John Redmond, the Irish constitutional leader, made a reassuring speech on the subject. He did stress, however, that the King represented a system of government that the Irish regarded as an usurpation,[8] and because of this remark the government's agents predicted trouble. The police were alerted, Mrs Maud Gonne MacBride was closely shadowed, and her associates carefully noted and watched.[9] It was far from easy to supervise Maud as she moved backwards and forwards between her homes in Dublin and Paris. In Dublin Arthur Griffith often visited her, and she came to meetings of his Celtic Literary Society. She assisted in forming a so-called People's Protection Association, later the National Council, whose chief object, it was said, was to prevent the King being cordially received. Griffith, who was closely involved in this exercise, was reported as saying that Cork needed special attention—it was 'the right place to make a dash'—because flunkeyism was more rife there than in Dublin.

The royal visit passed off quietly, however, and MacDonnell wrote, with some pleasure, it may be surmised, 'that the proceedings throughout Ireland during the King's visit contradicted every piece of "information" given to us by these secret reports. . . . I have not during nine months of close observation noticed a single tangible collaboration of any alarmist report submitted to government.'

Gosselin, when he read this, was provoked into a reply. The occasion was a great temptation to the police agents to paint a gloomy forecast and perhaps some of them had yielded, he said.

A policeman at these times is in a very unenviable position. If he hears alarming news and withholds it he undertakes a responsibility which the teaching and traditions of the RIC does not encourage. In extenuation I must state that for the past 20 years there have not been in Ireland so many prominent members of hostile Irish-American Societies. I was myself much concerned, tho' I never deviated from a full conviction that the king would be as safe in Ireland as in England and have given voice to this with no uncertain sound. You can see in the American newspaper extracts which I send to Dublin . . . a reflex—tho' exaggerated—of my views on secret societies in America. What I think of them in Great Britain is best shewn by my having advised government that the time has come for doing away with my office.[10] [Gosselin was about to retire on pension.]

In November 1904 some of the civil servants in the Castle, taking a cue from what their superiors had said in previous years, ventured to add that there was nothing in the précis of police reports of sufficient importance to trouble the Lord Lieutenant or the Chief Secretary with, but Dougherty saw to it that they were forwarded as usual. They were of value, he thought, as showing the low ebb to which secret societies had fallen.[11] But MacDonnell remained as disapproving as ever. In March 1905 he wrote: 'During $2\frac{1}{2}$ years of careful observation I have not seen a particle of substantial evidence to shew that there is in Ireland any secret political activity of which the Government need have the smallest apprehension.' And he added that this too had been the opinion of Major Gosselin, the experienced Chief of the Intelligence Department of Ireland in England.

This continually critical attitude towards police reports and counter-secret society activities must have had a depressing effect on the men engaged in this work, and it appeared to C. A. Wilkins, who succeeded Gosselin, when he saw MacDonnell's latest spiel, that the abolition of his post was a possibility. He hastened to enter a caveat.

So far as my limited experience goes, [he wrote on the file] I think that there is little activity amongst the secret societies in America at present. But I am of opinion that it would be a great mistake to abandon all supervision over them, for they are quite a potential for harm, and there are amongst them undoubtedly individuals who advocate violent measures, and who would not hesitate to resort to such measures if they had their way and saw their chance. With only a couple of months' experience of the work, I still think that the withdrawal of all supervision would tend to encourage these more unscrupulous

E*

spirits; they must know that they are watched, and they fear the consequence of being found out. In this opinion I am confirmed by the greater experience of other officers with whom I have discussed the subject.[12]

And there the matter seems to have rested.

MacDonnell had earlier intervened to correct again the attitude of the Irish police to the movement for the revival of the Irish language. 'The Gaelic League', he wrote, 'is a respectable society, and is not to be confused with suspicious associations.' At that time the League conducted an annual procession through the streets of Dublin in order to publicise its aims and collect money, and in the organisation of this and in the actual procession itself other kindred national societies collaborated. The police were quick to notice the presence of any IRB men or leaders of Cumann na nGaedheal who shared the League's concern to save the Irish language from extinction but who had more advanced views respecting an Irish Ireland and separation from England and who also worked hard to prevent enlistment in the army and navy.[13] The trouble was that some people were members of both organisations, and members of both sometimes joined together to oppose developments they did not like. Thus in March 1904 a citizens' meeting to support an international exhibition, which it was believed would lead to the widespread purchase of foreign goods, had to be abandoned because of hooting and hissing and the expulsion of disturbers. Among the demonstrators were P. T. Daly, Edward Martyn, John Sweetman, John MacNeill (Eóin Mac Néill, a vice-president of the Gaelic League) and Arthur Griffith. Daly by this time had become a member of the Dublin Corporation; in his election campaign he had been supported by every secret society man and extremist in the city, his principal opponent being a nominee of the United Irish League. His success, which elated the IRB, did not promise well for good government in Dublin, it was thought.

4

Cumann na nGaedheal was greatly stimulated during 1904 by the appearance in its paper, the *United Irishman,* of a series of articles by Griffith which were subsequently published in pamphlet form under the title *The Resurrection of Hungary*. In these Griffith drew a parallel with the policy which had won for the Hungarians their independence from Austria and propounded a programme which included the withdrawal of the Irish MPs from Westminster and passive resistance to British government. The police sensed a certain exhilaration among these Confederated Gaels. They had become 'the extreme party'.

The police reports for May 1905 also mentioned activity in the Ancient Order of Hibernians, to which many IRB men belonged, though the Order on the whole adhered to the United Irish League and was claiming considerable success in local elections. The IRB itself, by contrast, was generally inactive, though the leading suspects in it maintained contact with one another. Corroboration was being sought for an informant's report that rifles had been distributed in Tyrone. By contrast, the GAA, whose council was mainly composed of IRB men, was very active; it was a strong anti-recruiting body. The Gaelic League was progressing and was becoming a rather formidable organisation in the country. It was being quietly watched. Many extremists were deeply interested in it, and the *United Irishman* continued its strenuous advocacy of it. Its editor, Arthur Griffith, and the suspect W. P. Ryan were on the industrial committee of the League. Cumann na nGaedheal (it ceased at this stage to be called the Confederation of the Gaels by the police) was active and in close touch with the IRB and the Gaelic League.[14]

In the summer of 1905 the IRB was 'rather dormant' or 'very dormant'. Funds were lacking and the rank and file were apathetic. The Wolfe Tone demonstration at Bodenstown had been a miserable failure. The setback in erecting the Wolfe Tone memorial in Dublin and the squandering of the funds were serious obstacles to further successful collection of money. The anti-recruiting, anti-British movement, under cover of Cumann na nGaedheal, the GAA and the Gaelic League, was attracting public attention and controversy in the press. The development was being carefully watched with a view to securing legal evidence against the guilty parties. There was no doubt that extremists prominent in the Gaelic League were using that organisation for disloyal purposes. Seditious leaflets, for example, were being distributed by IRB suspects at Gaelic League *feiseanna* and outings.[15]

In September it was reported that the Clan na Gael in America was advocating the Sinn Féin policy of calling for strong support for the Gaelic League which, it said, was 'preparing the way for the work of the Clan'. (This may have been the first appearance of the words 'Sinn Féin' in a police document, and the policy referred to was Griffith's Hungarian policy.) The IRB man P. T. Daly appeared to have a strong following in Dublin. In addition to being a member of the Dublin Corporation, he was president of the Dublin Trades Council. He had addressed a meeting of the newly formed Dungannon Club (No. 1) in Belfast—a second had been started in Derry—that had the same general objects as Cumann na nGaedheal. (These Dungannon Clubs owed their inception to the two Ulster IRB men Denis McCullough and Bulmer Hobson. As the name indicated the clubs looked back to the Volunteer Convention held in Dungannon which led to the winning of the constitution of 1782.) The appointment of O'Donovan Rossa as assistant secretary of Cork City Council was an indication of the strength of disloyal influence in that body. Rossa told a Young Ireland Society meeting in Cork that the Clan na Gael had decided to revive the physical-force party in Ireland, and that plenty of money for that purpose would be forthcoming from America.[16]

Dougherty, the Assistant Under-Secretary, was unimpressed, and on the report for March 1906 he wrote that it showed 'the nakedness of the land' so far as secret society work was concerned, and on that for April he repeated that there was nothing in it in the least worthy of notice. During that month the *United Irishman* had ceased publication, as the result apparently of a verdict obtained by a Father Dolan at the Limerick assizes, but a prospectus had been issued for a paper to be called *Sinn Féin*, which was to be the organ of the National Council which existed in parallel with Cumann na nGaedheal and which since 1904 was giving effect to Griffith's policy. (Cumann na nGaedheal was a loosely co-ordinating body to which other nationally-minded societies might be affiliated. The National Council, which was formed to organise protests against the visit of King Edward VII, had no constitution but was open to all those who believed in the freedom of their country.) The National Council fused with the Sinn Féin League (itself an amalgamation of Cumann na nGaedheal and the Dungannon Clubs) in September 1908 to form the body simply known as Sinn Féin, whose grand object was the re-establishment of the independence of Ireland. Dougherty noted that the report for May again showed secret society work at low-water mark. Apart from the appearance of the first issue of *Sinn Féin*, the only item of interest was the visit paid by the old Fenian Captain John McClure to the grave of his comrade Peter O'Neill Crowley and to the scene of their joint exploit at Kilclooney Wood in 1867.[17]

In June Douglas Hyde, the president of the Gaelic League, returned from America and was escorted to his headquarters by a procession of some four to five thousand people and nine bands. The police recognised in the demonstration contingents from Cumann na nGaedheal, the GAA, the Wolfe Tone Memorial Fund Committee, the Old Guard Union, Gaelic League branches, and members of the Dublin Corporation. In a speech Hyde was alleged to have said that the Sinn Féin movement was to receive help from the £10,000 he had brought back; but this was denied by the officials in Dublin Castle. In a longer than usual comment Dougherty again said that the value of these reports was very small so long as the police could obtain no information regarding the real nature of the business of Clan na Gael men like Daniel F. Cohalan who were among Hyde's helpers in the United States. He suspected, however, that that business, if revealed, would prove to be of small importance—probably blood-and-thunder talk over flowing bowls of whiskey punch. Dr Hyde had been in doubtful company, admittedly, but as far as Dougherty could judge by his speeches his attitude throughout had been scrupulously correct. As for the Sinn Féin policy in which the police saw the danger of the future, he was in no way alarmed. The policy of passive resistance would not commend itself to Irishmen.[18]

5

Cohalan was in Ireland in August 1906, and among those he visited were John O'Leary, now in the last year of his long life, J. B. Yeats, the painter father of W. B. Yeats, and Fred Allan. Otherwise the month was so uneventful and so much of a pattern with what had gone before that the principal officers in the Castle ventured to say to Dougherty that manifestly no secret criminal society was at work, or even in existence, in Ireland. This explained, they suggested, why the Crime Special sergeants were devoting their attention to open associations like the Gaelic League, the GAA, the AOH, etc. Even the advocates of the Sinn Féin policy worked in the open. The time would therefore appear to have come when the Crime Special Branch might be abolished without loss to the government, and with benefit to the police. The services of the men employed under it were wasted. MacDonnell, the Under-Secretary, was very much inclined to agree with this recommendation. The National Council could hardly be termed a secret society and it was absurd to regard the Gaelic League as one, but the moment, he thought, was not opportune for such a departure. James Bryce, who had been the Chief Secretary since the Liberals took office in December 1905, likewise thought that there was much to be said for disbandment, but directed that the matter deserved to be further considered. There is no evidence that it was. Pollard in *The Secret Societies of Ireland* (a useful book, but one that has to be read with great discrimination) says that in 1910 Bryce broke up the remains of the Irish political secret service. Bryce was not the Chief Secretary in 1910, but a question lingers as to whether the reference applies to Augustine Birrell's handling of the matter in his term.

John O'Leary's funeral in March 1907 testified to the IRB's reduced condition. In comparison with the great Fenian occasions of the past, it was of modest size only and was inefficiently organised. The traditions were observed, however. The coffin, covered with a flag, was carried by four comrades, James O'Connor, P. T. Daly, John MacBride and John O'Hanlon; and elsewhere in the cortège Fred Allan, John Daly and Arthur Griffith forgathered with an American representative of John Devoy who, as always, was keeping his eye on things. At the cemetery there were a few hundred men carrying hurleys, but no oration was given. The torrential rain had stopped that perhaps. 'The Organisation' was coming to the end of a long inactive chapter of its history and might not have survived without the transfusions that were on the way.

Bryce went as ambassador to the United States in January 1907 and was replaced as Chief Secretary by Augustine Birrell, to whom MacDonnell poured out his criticism of the Crime

Special reports. More important by far than anything that occurred in Ireland in 1907, he said, was the action of the American Clan na Gael and the German societies in uniting to make trouble for Bryce among United States senators. In Ireland the reports had become a 'monstrous record of inactivity' on the part of the secret societies. They had recently been telling of the movements of Major MacBride as he organised on behalf of the IRB or simply looked for a job—he was said to be in straitened circumstances and had failed to obtain an appointment as a Corporation markets inspector—and of P. T. Daly, the Secretary of the Supreme Council, now a traveller for Dollard's printing house, who had been to England and Scotland giving rosy accounts of what was happening at home and advising his listeners to spread the Sinn Féin movement, which since its formation had strengthened the IRB beyond all expectation. It was being taken up by younger hands. He also went to New York at the end of February 1908 to a Clan na Gael convention and on his return was seen in the company of Fred Allan. But J. B. Dougherty, who had just replaced MacDonnell as Under-Secretary in the Castle, did not think there was much intelligence shown in these reports and nothing of interest.

He had not, of course, the foresight to recognise the importance of the news that T. J. Clarke had returned from America with his wife, who was a niece of John Daly of Limerick, and child. After looking at some vacant shops in Dublin Clarke had settled down at 58 Amiens Street as a tobacconist and newsagent; he moved subsequently to 75A Parnell Street which became a focal point for the IRB men. The likelihood that he would begin to travel as the sole agent for Colonel Everard's Irish tobacco was an excuse for placing him on the B list of suspects whose names were telegraphed as they went from place to place. Sinn Féin had put up C. J. Dolan, a former Irish Parliamentary Party MP, as their candidate for a parliamentary vacancy in Leitrim, and Arthur Griffith had travelled backwards and forwards to the constituency to help him. New names—some of them of future great importance—began to appear in the reports. John (Séan) MacDermott, for instance, who had been a principal speaker at a Sinn Féin demonstration in the Rotunda, was seen accompanying Dolan on a visit to Dublin. They were met on arrival by one of the younger men, Bulmer Hobson, who had been unsuccessfully seeking employment in the city. The advanced members of the Sinn Féin League proposed appointing him as an organiser of cottage industries.

In the summer of 1908 Dougherty conceded that there had been some activity among the IRB suspects but claimed that little importance was to be attached to the movements of these people and their friends of the Clan na Gael. The usual result, he maintained, was an increased consumption of porter and whiskey. Sinn Féin showed signs of weakening. He quipped again that 'passive resistance' did not suit the genius of the Irish people. Money had come from the Clan na Gael, but this would be duly 'liquidated' as usual. Anyhow, £300 was hardly sufficient to finance a successful insurrection![19]

The sum of £300 was normally sent each year by the Clan na Gael to the IRB for organisation and general purposes. For a few years it was temporarily increased to £600, the extra money being for recruiting and for winning back old members who, for one reason or another, including the INB diversion, had fallen away from the fold. The £600 was paid in two moieties in the spring and autumn. In 1908 the second £300 was not received, and, on an investigation which dragged on till 1910, it was found that the money had been paid to P. T. Daly during his visit to America and used by him for his own family expenses. Daly threw himself on the mercy of the Supreme Council, who were loth to treat him harshly. For three or four years he had travelled wherever in Ireland, England or Scotland there was a Circle or remnant of the IRB. He was known to the Centres and to large numbers of the rank and file as one of the leaders of 'the Organisation'. He had neglected his own work and had lost his job; and Fred Allan and Jack O'Hanlon, the two Dublin members of the Council, confirmed that he was in bad circumstances and that while he was in America his family had suffered a great deal of illness. For these reasons, and in view of the possible reaction of the organisation to the blacklisting of one of its best known leaders, it was decided to regard the £300 as voted to Daly exceptionally, but to remove him from the Council. It was also decided to co-opt Tom (T. J.) Clarke in his place, so that if the Clan had any suspicion of looseness in connection with the £300, they would be reassured.

At the following meeting Allan and O'Hanlon reported that

Daly did not appreciate the leniency that had been shown him, and had failed to co-operate with Allan, who had been appointed Secretary in his place. He had not handed over all the property of the organisation—a typewriter was specifically mentioned— nor supplied certain information in his possession. They later reported that Daly was making trouble in the organisation, alleging that he was a victim of a plot. The Council thereupon decided that he should be expelled, blacklisted, and the full story released; and this was done.[20] The Castle reacted by taking Daly off the B list of suspects: he was no longer a danger to them.[21] At or about this time Daly fell from grace in another respect. He, who was understood to be a temperance advocate, was arrested for being drunk and disorderly while attending a technical congress in Sligo. A leaflet was found on him dealing with the raising of funds to enable James Connolly to tour Ireland in the interests of the Irish socialist movement. Connolly had been in America for seven years and had published there a small socialist magazine called *The Harp*. An effort was being made to revive the paper in Dublin with James Larkin as its editor, and copies had been sold at socialist gatherings.

After Daly's disgrace, Fred Allan 'got most things on to a business footing'. From December 1910, however, his communications to the Clan na Gael were left unanswered, and a report went into circulation that the reason was American dissatisfaction with him because of his identification years before with Lord Mayor Pile and the reception of Queen Victoria. Allan was deeply upset because, as he told John Devoy, any enemies he had in Ireland were due to the bad feeling created against him over the Triangle crisis and the INB. That feeling had never been allowed to die out. He, who had carried the IRB over many sterile years, accordingly resigned from 'the Organisation', but he stressed, in doing so, that his political faith remained unaltered.[22] There was another reason for his resignation, which we shall examine shortly, connected with the identification of the Clan na Gael with the rising young men within the IRB. This was why Allan's letters to America had been ignored.

It was about this time too, apparently, that Arthur Griffith severed his connection with the IRB. He did so, George A. Lyons tells us, in protest against encroachment by the Dublin Centres Board on freedom of choice in the election of a particular

Centre. No disagreement on political principle was involved, nor did Griffith rule out the use of physical force in certain circumstances.[23] P. S. O'Hegarty insisted, however, that Griffith left because, having launched the Sinn Féin policy and established the Sinn Féin organisation, he found irksome the IRB rule that gave the Supreme Council the right to dictate a policy to members of the Brotherhood in public organisations. Nevertheless, the IRB continued, as always, to work with him, recognising him for what he was, the greatest separatist force in the country,[24] and it financed some of his periodicals.

6

Towards the end of 1909 Dougherty again told Birrell, the Chief Secretary, that there was nothing of interest in the police reports and that money spent on obtaining 'that sort of information' was wasted.[25] The reports, nevertheless, occasionally contained points on which he found it desirable to comment. One was the identification of a murder club in Craughwell, Co. Galway, with the IRB: this he described as a libel on the IRB, which had never been associated with agrarian murders. Another was the honour paid by the GAA to Tom Kenny, the 'ruffian' who led the Craughwell band, which was a significant illustration of the spirit and temper of the GAA itself. A third point was a story that the Sinn Féiners were ready, on certain terms, to coalesce with William O'Brien, who had withdrawn from the main constitutional grouping led by Redmond and Dillon of the United Irish League. The terms appeared to include the repudiation of the principal plank in the Sinn Féin platform, which did not sound a likely proposition; but poverty, said Dougherty, made strange bedfellows.[26]

Griffith continued to be watched as a suspect, along with some old-timers such as T. J. Clarke, Major MacBride and Jack O'Hanlon, and some new ones, Bulmer Hobson, Seán MacDermott, Denis McCullough, T. S. Cuffe and George A. Lyons. Lyons, 'an active member of the Sinn Féin League and other kindred associations', reported to the police one evening in July 1909 that he had accidentally killed a friend. The police on going to Lyons's room saw a young man on the floor with a bullet through his head. Two revolvers and several rounds of ammunition were found nearby as well as some anti-enlistment papers and other Sinn Féin literature. Lyons was charged with murder but got off scot-free, though the fatality had obviously occurred when two IRB men were practising the use of weapons.

Dougherty drew Birrell's attention to a report in which, as he put it, 'the "Countess" Markievicz blossoms out as a full-blown physical force revolutionist. She is a sister of Sir Jocelyn Gore-Booth of Co. Sligo. I noticed her husband the "Count" at a Castle function the other evening!' That was in April 1910. By the end of the year she was asking a Belfast audience, mostly young boys aged under seventeen, for a show of hands of those who were willing to suffer for their country as the Manchester Martyrs had done in 1867. All in the room responded. She then asked the boys to prepare to be ready in case they were required, and to be true to the teaching of their leader, Mr Hobson. From another source the police learned that Mr Hobson had recently been appointed the IRB secretary for Ulster. His name was being associated with a new monthly called *Irish Freedom*.[27] Another colourful lady, Maud Gonne, was said to have interested herself on behalf of her estranged husband, Major John Mac-Bride, who was a candidate for a position as water-bailiff in the Dublin Corporation. This did not appear to have brought about a reconciliation between them : on the contrary, the Major was said to have resented her interference in the matter.[28]

In January 1911 the toast of the King was removed from a list of those to be drunk in Belfast at the annual dinner of the Association of Irish Post Office Clerks. This was the result of pressure from certain delegates of extreme political views, among them John O'Hegarty of Cork, brother of P. S. O'Hegarty, who threatened to make a scene if the toast was proposed. A split in the Association was probable.[29] There was a bad atmosphere abroad, and Dougherty now admitted that secret societies were spreading in some parts of the country. The reaction, however, against Kenny and the Craughwell gang, and the vigorous de-nunciation of clandestine movements by Bishop O'Dea of Galway were healthy signs. The Bishop had appealed to young men at Ballinderreen not to allow themselves to be trapped by the designing men who attempted to swear them into these societies at hurling matches and porter sprees. He had expressed the utmost admiration for members of the national organisations who were making a stand against these machinations.[30] In the same consoling category Dougherty placed the failure of Sinn Féin to work up any effective opposition to the royal visit that was planned to follow the coronation of George V. Under the auspices of what were described as the 'United National Societies' a meeting had been called for Beresford Place, Dublin, on Coronation Day.[31] Dougherty thought this should be allowed to take place : to proclaim it would give a much needed advertisement to a party that was badly in need of funds and out of touch with decent nationalist opinion. Moreover, a proclamation would probably lead to the holding of three or four meetings instead of one. The Chief Secretary entirely agreed. 'To advertise these semi-ridiculous persons would be to meet their wishes. On the other hand,' Birrell said, 'they must not be allowed to form a procession which can clash with the great concourse of people who will be in the main streets on the occasion. The Police Acts give all necessary powers to regulate the traffic on particular occasions. As to ribald utterances the police must exercise a wise discretion and *if possible* turn a deaf ear.'[32] Both the Coronation Day celebrations and the royal visit, from the viewpoint of the authorities, were resounding successes.

In 1912 the Liberal government produced a Home Rule Bill against which the Ulster Unionists mounted a fierce agitation. Birrell and Dougherty were worried. The police reports, as usual, contained nothing of importance, Dougherty told his chief, for the reason that the Crime Special men were giving all their attention to secret societies of one colouring. 'It might be well', he said, 'if they gave a little more attention to Secret Societies of another shade.' Birrell could not have agreed more. He had read for more than five years these reports about secret societies and their goings on in different parts of Ireland and had occasionally succeeded in extracting useful information from them as to the state of feeling and habits of life in one or two affected areas. The reports were necessarily largely concerned, he said, with the local intrigues and dissensions of a number of ruffians and bullies whom he wished could be forcibly deported to some distant land. It was most important that a watchful eye should continue to be kept upon those suspects and known ill-doers and breeders of outrage. But, he added, taking Dougherty's point,

I think the time has come when the same microscope should be employed in another part of Ireland, if that be possible; and information collected as to the 'goings on' in parts of Ulster of Clubs and Organisations who have been lately supplied with arms and are being drilled to prepare for eventualities. Those 'Secret Societies' are for the moment at all events of greater importance than these whose movements are recorded in these reports.[33]

Birrell, in his autobiography, written many years later, confessed that the developments in Irish literature and drama were of greater significance to him than the RIC reports; and it has been appositely commented that while it was natural that as a man of letters Birrell would have been captivated by what the Irish poets and playwrights were writing, as a politician he should have realised that the themes on which they were engaged made the study of the police reports all the more imperative.

As for Dougherty, he was of the opinion that the resuscitation of the IRB, of which they had heard in the Castle, was, in the circumstances of 1912, 'a hopeless proposal'.[34] He could not have been farther off the mark. He had not sufficiently taken into account the likelihood that circumstances would change under the threat of Ulster resistance to Home Rule and the involvement of Britain in a major war, nor the effect of the continuing encouragement that came to Ireland from the United States, particularly through John Devoy. He could hardly have been blamed for underestimating the revolutionary potential of Devoy's disciple, Tom Clarke, or of two other younger Irishmen, Bulmer Hobson and Seán MacDermott.

10

The Rising of 1916

I

IT IS NOT unfair to say that at this stage, after more than half a century of existence, the IRB had achieved no practical result whatever. The suggestion that it could lay claim to having brought about the disestablishment of the Church of Ireland in 1869 and the passing of the Land Act of 1870 is hardly worth considering. It certainly never showed interest in either of these issues. The most that could be said for the theory is that Gladstone recognised Fenianism as a feature of the disturbed political landscape of the country he set out to pacify on forming his first administration. 'The Organisation' had survived, diminished in numbers—there were only 1,660 members in Ireland and 367 in Great Britain in 1912—and improved in the quality of its members, but it was a comparatively insignificant body that depended for stimulation and financial support on its American counterpart. John Devoy summarised its history before 1916 in terms that accord pretty well with the story that has come to us through the police reports. It had suffered many vicissitudes, he said, and at times had a hard struggle for existence. It was at some periods very strong, and at others it dwindled to small proportions. From 1871 to 1916 it was maintained almost entirely by moral and material support from the Clan na Gael. In 1879, when he had conducted a personal inspection of 'the Organisation', there was a compact body of 35,000 men which continued to grow during the Land League agitations. Later the numbers fell off considerably, mainly through the manipulation of the parliamentary leaders who overthrew Parnell, until finally it was reduced to a mere skeleton. A revival set in when Tom Clarke returned to Ireland in 1907. Inspired by his resoluteness and singleness of purpose, 'the Organisation' began to assume new life and vigour.[1]

If we look for an achievement, it can only be that 'the Organisation' always managed somehow to promote the separatist ideal and to keep alive the expectation that, in circumstances such as the involvement of England in a major war, Ireland might secure its freedom by the exercise of physical force. That was as much as could be said for it; and little more could be said for the response to Griffith's allied Sinn Féin, whose basic idea was to withdraw the Irish members from Westminster and set up a legislative Council for Ireland. In fact, every 'advanced' grouping in the country was completely overshadowed by the United Irish League, the popular constitutional movement led by John Redmond and John Dillon, which, in alliance with the English Liberals under Asquith, was set fair on the road to achieving Home Rule, a form of self-government within the United Kingdom.

Despite Devoy's opinion to the contrary, it is clear that the revival in the fortunes of the IRB to which he alludes had begun before Clarke returned to Ireland in 1907. This primarily was the result of the work of Bulmer Hobson. Hobson was a very unusual man. His name was unusual: it rang and still rings strange on Irish ears. Stranger still, and very unusual, was the fact that he, an Ulsterman of Cromwellian stock, and a Quaker to boot, should have anything to do with Irish nationalism— and physical-force nationalism at that. He became a republican at school under the impetus of the 1798 centenary demonstrations, and even before he left school he was saving up his pennies to subscribe to the *Shan Van Vocht*. He made the acquaintance of Ethna Carbery (Anna Johnston) and in her house he met Douglas Hyde of the Gaelic League, Maud Gonne and John O'Leary. Independently he began to engage in a number of youth activities connected with the Gaelic League and the Gaelic Athletic Association and he joined Cumann na nGaedheal in Belfast, the body which, as we saw, was founded by Arthur Griffith in Dublin in 1900, and was supplemented subsequently by the so-called National Council.

Hobson, himself a fruitful begetter of societies, called into being in 1902, at the age of nineteen, an association of junior hurlers, and when the local county board of the GAA refused it recognition he started Na Fianna Éireann ('The Warriors of Ireland'), whose purpose was to study the Irish language and to give its young members a sound national formation. In 1909 a boys' national organisation was started in Dublin on the same lines and under the same name by Hobson and Countess Constance Markievicz, and this body, senior members of which were sworn into the IRB, was to play a significant role in the history of the next decade. The development of Hobson's own political ideas is evident in the constitution of the Fianna. Its object was to re-establish the independence of Ireland; and 'military exercises' were among the means by which this was to be achieved. He had joined the IRB in 1904, being introduced by Denis McCullough, who had himself been sworn into the movement by his father, a Belfast publican, at the age of seventeen. There were at that time in Belfast three Circles of the IRB which were being run as a 'sort of tontine society'.[2]

The first thing McCullough, with the newcomer Hobson, did was to make a clean break with the older generation, some of whom were inactive politically—the counterparts of Dublin's 'tinpikemen' and 'armchair republicans'—and some who drank too much to be good either for themselves or for an ostensibly secret society. There was nothing new in this attitude to drinking: the heavy drinker was always recognised to be a serious risk to the integrity of 'the Organisation', but it was not easy to control him. It had been laid down in black and white as far back as the 1870s that 'no habitual drunkard, no man of bad character, dissipated habits, or dishonest occupation' was to be enlisted; but a document containing this injunction 'printed at the IRB Steam Press Office, Dublin' was found by the police on the person of a drunken bargee. They would have seen the humour in the situation.[3]

The Belfast reformers, affected by the puritanism they found in the Gaelic League and Gaelic Athletic Association, formed a new IRB Circle of their own and recruited into it picked young men with whom they set out to organise Ulster. Their influence spread in time to Dublin and other parts of Ireland. Nor did they miss any chance of changing the image of the movement on their own doorstep. McCullough induced his father to retire from the ranks. Hobson got an agreement from Neil John O'Boyle, an old man who for years had represented Ulster on the Supreme Council, to cede his place to McCullough. Most importantly for the future of Irish republicanism, a Paddy Carberry, who frequently came to meetings heavily under the influence of drink, was told he would have to quit the organisation.

He pleaded to be allowed to stay and was given a final chance. He was soon as bad as ever, and McCullough spoke sternly to him. 'Very well,' said Carberry regretfully; 'but if I have to go, will you take a good man in my place?' 'Who is he?' McCullough asked. 'He is a chap called Seán MacDermott.' The deal was completed, and within a decade this MacDermott, 'the rawest bloody recruit you could imagine', 'engineered a rising'.[4] He had begun his career as a pupil teacher in his native parish but, following a row with a priest, he went to Glasgow and worked in a public house. He was later a conductor on the Belfast trams. When McCullough first met him he was an enthusiastic member of the Ancient Order of Hibernians, 'a fresh, frightened young fellow whose mother had warned him against secret societies. . . . He could not speak for nuts, but he could curse like forty men, calling on God to paralyse any girl who would speak to a policeman. . . . He was a weird bird.'[5] Hobson, writing of him after the 1916 affair, said that MacDermott never got over the AOH's habits of intrigue and wire-pulling behind the scenes. He was doubtless feeling that he had suffered from them. However, that was in the future. Hobson, himself never well off—he was dismissed from places of employment because of his open association with the Gaelic League and Sinn Féin—raised a small fund, mostly subscribed by men who could only afford a few pence a week, and put MacDermott on the road organising Dungannon Clubs, whose policy of abstention from the British parliament was on the same lines as Griffith's.

In 1906 Hobson founded and edited a weekly paper called *The Republic*, to which Robert Lynd ('Y.Y.'), the essayist, contributed; and in 1907 Devoy brought him to New York to introduce what was about to become the Sinn Féin movement through the amalgamation of the Sinn Féin League (i.e. Cumann na nGaedheal and the Dungannon Clubs) and the National Council, whose membership overlapped a good deal. When the merger occurred Edward Martyn, and shortly afterwards John Sweetman, became President of Sinn Féin, and Griffith and Hobson its Vice-Presidents. The latter pair did not get on well together. Griffith had left the IRB and was concentrating on the repeal of the Union and the re-establishment of the King, Lords and Commons of Ireland, whereas Hobson was wedded to the idea of an Irish Republic, though he did not define it narrowly or exclusively. In a few years Hobson pulled out of Sinn Féin altogether and devoted his time to the IRB, the Fianna, and to the formation of Freedom Clubs. His weekly *Republic* disappeared, but, nothing daunted, he started another paper.

He came to Dublin in 1908 and worked for a year on the *Irish Peasant*, a weekly edited by W. P. Ryan. When that paper got into financial difficulties towards the end of 1909 he returned to Belfast but was back in Dublin again in 1911 and joined the Teeling Circle of the IRB whose Centre was a bank clerk, Michael Cowley. At that time the total membership of 'the Organisation' was not much above 1,500, of whom at least half were in Dublin. On Cowley's resignation over a dispute about control, Hobson became the Centre. He automatically became a member of the Dublin Centres Board and, after a short time, was elected its Chairman. He also became, in succession, a member of the Leinster provincial executive, chairman of that body, and its representative on the Supreme Council. Now at the very heart of things, he was able to employ his great energy in what he saw as 'the usual conflict between the younger generation who wanted to press on and the older who wanted to hold back'. In Dublin, when he came to know the IRB there intimately, he found 'the Organisation' practically controlled by three members of the Supreme Council—Jack O'Hanlon, Fred Allan and P. T. Daly—and he alleges, in a book he dictated towards the end of his life, that their influence had almost stifled all activity.

Other members of the Supreme Council at this time included P. S. O'Hegarty, a British Post Office official, representing the South of England, Denis McCullough from Ulster, John Mac-Bride for Connacht, later to be succeeded by Seán Mac-Dermott, and the co-opted Tom Clarke who, though older than most of the others, always demanded an active policy and supported the younger men. He stood against Allan and O'Hanlon when, towards the end of 1910, Hobson proposed that the IRB should publish the monthly *Irish Freedom* as a frankly republican paper; this appeared for the first time in November of that year and kept going until it was suppressed by the government in December 1914. The paper was financed by a monthly subscription of one shilling collected from every IRB man. When the decision to produce it was taken, Allan and O'Hanlon objected to Hobson becoming its editor, and, in an attempt to meet the difficulty, Dr Patrick McCartan became the nominal editor with Hobson doing the work. The breach between the older and younger men widened over the control of the paper and its editorial policy, and towards the end of 1911 Allan and O'Hanlon actually seized one issue on the eve of publication. The younger men promptly retaliated by issuing another edition as 'edited by Dr Pat McCartan', so that for the month of December 1911 there were two distinct versions of *Irish Freedom*. This development brought matters to a head. The Supreme Council met and debated the issue in the presence of Hobson, with the result that Allan and O'Hanlon resigned from the Council and subsequently from the organisation : they got little support, even in Dublin where they had thought their lead would be followed. The 'progressives' were now in control, and they sent as their delegate to the Clan na Gael convention, held in Atlantic City, New Jersey, in September 1912, 'one of the finest young fellows of the young school'. This was Seán MacDermott, and the description was Tom Clarke's. MacDermott, reporting to the convention, set out 'the blocks in the way' of the development of the IRB : these were his own old organisation, the Hibernians; the Irish Parliamentary Party; the clergy; the spy system; and a lack of funds.[6]

Fred Allan's resignation from the IRB did not end his long connection with the national movement. In later years he was associated with the Irish Volunteers. He was joint trustee with Michael Collins and George Nesbitt of the Irish National Aid and Volunteer Dependants' Fund after the 1916 rising. He worked in Sinn Féin and in the Republican Courts. He served three months in Mountjoy Prison, declining to give bail, for having in his possession or under his control certain documents likely to cause disaffection; he told the magistrate : 'I have been a republican for forty years, and I am not going to change by a rule of this court.'[7] He was later arrested when presiding over a Republican arbitration court and was interned in a military detention camp until the end of 1921. He was subsequently politically active and served on the executive of Cumann na nGaedheal, the resurrected title of the pro-Treaty organisation. He was a senior official in the service of the government of the Irish Free State at the time of his retirement. He died in March 1937.

2

The playwright Seán O'Casey was a very active member of the Teeling Circle that Bulmer Hobson joined, and as the years went by he conjured up a poisonous dislike for Hobson, whom he described as the 'protestant secretary of the IRB, editor of *Irish Freedom*, and head bottlewasher of all Nationalist activities'. He pictured him with his moony face, half-covered by a mutton-pie hat, a rapt look on his features and moving about mysteriously; and he complained to Tom Clarke in his little tobacconist's shop about the dullness of the articles Hobson was writing and claimed that they were being read by members of the IRB only out of a sense of duty. Clarke, mightily offended, ordered O'Casey out of the shop. He would listen to nothing against Hobson, whom he said he loved as his own son.

Apart from his post as the secretary of the Wolfe Tone Memorial Fund Committee, the IRB was O'Casey's main interest at this time, and he sought to serve it by recruiting members from the ranks of the Gaelic League, to which he also belonged, and by trying, unsuccessfully as it proved, to forge a link between the IRB and the militant labour movement. From his youth he had been a socialist. He had in fact been everything but what one would expect an Irish Protestant to be. He may even have thought of becoming a Catholic!

One recruit he brought into the IRB was the Ulsterman Ernest Blythe, who has described how O'Casey, later to become a dramatist of international repute, had at that time no interest whatever in the theatre. Blythe, on the other hand, was a regular theatregoer, wrote reviews of plays for the *Irish Peasant*, and subsidised the Abbey Theatre when he became Minister for Finance in the government of the Irish Free State. He was, for many years, the theatre's managing director. O'Casey and Blythe were fast friends, disagreeing only when religion was discussed. O'Casey had a predilection for the ultra-Catholic features of High Church Protestantism, whereas Blythe remained immovable in his inherited Low Church position. He was once assailed as a 'Presbyterian bastard' and was able to retort that the accusation was 'wrong on both counts'. What he and O'Casey had in common was membership of the Gaelic League and an unconcealed admiration for the teacher of Irish who became the wife of Éamon de Valera.

In his book *Trasna na Boinne* ('Across the Boyne') Blythe describes how O'Casey drew him into the secret movement at the age of seventeen, using a variation of what was apparently the traditional method. He waited for an opportunity, which came when Blythe expressed regret that, under pressure from the Catholic Church, the formidable military organisation the Fenians had created had gone out of existence. O'Casey promptly replied that the Fenians had not died; they were very much alive; he was one of them himself; and he suggested that Blythe should become one. Blythe had recently read Tynan's book *The Irish National Invincibles*, and he told O'Casey that he personally could have nothing to do with an organisation that engaged in murder, to which O'Casey replied that the IRB had nothing whatever to do with murder; that they existed to engage in open warfare with the English and were preparing to do so. Blythe spent that night thinking and praying about the matter and next day told O'Casey that he was ready to take the Fenian oath and play his part in whatever activities that would involve him in. He wanted to join right away, but O'Casey told him he would have to wait. He was now an 'applicant'; he would be observed for a while to ensure that he was fully satisfactory on all counts. Blythe surmised later that Seán had not followed the usual procedure of first mentioning him to the Circle as a suitable person for admission before approaching him. Had he done so, and had 'the Organisation' been prepared to admit him, there would have been no delay once he had accepted an invitation to join. Blythe, being so young and his background unknown, it took somewhat longer than usual to clear the lines for his admission.

When word came through that everything was in order, O'Casey took Blythe one night to a house on the west side of Parnell Square—No. 41, probably—and introduced him to the Centre, Michael Cowley. Cowley took him into a darkened back room, where Blythe, his right hand raised, repeated the words of the oath. Cowley then shook hands with him and, outside the door, handed him back to O'Casey, who led the neophyte into a crowded front room and introduced him to his friends. (This ritual was not always followed. Peadar Kearney, the author of the Irish national anthem, was sworn in as he walked down a city street.[8] The man who brought Richard Mulcahy into the movement simply took a paper out of his waistcoat pocket and told Mulcahy that that was the oath he was to take.) Blythe—to return to him—recognised some Gaelic Leaguers—one of them Seán T. O'Kelly, who in 1945 became President of Ireland —but he noted also that apparently little had been done to recruit among the members of his own Central Branch. Cowley called the meeting to order in the name of the Irish Republican Brotherhood, a roll was called and answered in Irish, and Blythe discovered that the Circle had a pseudonym, the Bartholomew Teeling Literary and Debating Society. False minutes were in evidence designed to show that everything was above board should the police look in. These described a debate that had never taken place, and were signed by the Centre as chairman of the society.

The work proper of the 'Teelings' was mainly concerned with recruitment, and this was so successfully done that the Circle had to be divided in three. In Blythe's experience little else transpired at the meetings apart from the collection of subscriptions and a talk from a visiting Centre on behalf of the Dublin Centres Board. This was how policy announcements were usually made, it probably being thought that more attention would be paid to what a stranger said than anything coming from somebody they knew too well. The visits had the additional advantage of maintaining contact with the rest of 'the Organisation' in the event of the Centre's sudden demise or similar occurrences; but, these visitors apart, the members of the Circle could only discover by accident who else belonged to the IRB.

Blythe mentions the organisation's strong opposition to admitting anybody who indulged in alcoholic liquor. If a candidate was spotted coming out of a pub, that was usually the end of his chances of being elected. There had been too many cases of betrayal from that cause in the past. Candidates related to policemen or to active supporters of the Irish Parliamentary Party were similarly rejected. On the other hand, Blythe remembered the enthusiastic acceptance by his Circle of a fellow who had rioted in the Abbey Theatre against Synge's *Playboy of the Western World*. Seán O'Casey's own *Plough and the Stars* was to suffer a similar fate sixteen years later.

Protests of this kind, as we saw earlier, were not unknown to the IRB, and, indeed, the only public activity in which Blythe says he was involved as an IRB man was a fruitless attempt to wreck a meeting in the Mansion House at which John Redmond and Joe Devlin, the leader of the Ulster Nationalists, were the principal speakers. This was held after the failure of the Irish Council Bill of 1907 which P. H. Pearse, who had not yet become a republican, openly supported. That apart, the impression that emerges is that the IRB, in Dublin at any rate, was now a rather respectable, middle-class organisation, and that O'Casey, in his muffler and cloth cap, was probably an exception. Almost entirely composed of practising Catholics, it was perturbed by the Church's attitude to secret societies, which at this time caused some resignations, threatened many more, and inhibited recruiting. 'Often when after tedious investigation a man was deemed fit in every respect the inquisitor found himself up against a stone wall, that of religious scruples.'[9] In an effort to deal with the problem in Dublin, the most unusual step was taken of calling all the members to a meeting in the Town Hall, Clontarf, where they were addressed by Father Denis O'Sullivan, a native of Valentia, who had just returned from the American mission and who argued that the IRB was not banned by the Church: he himself was a member of the sister oath-bound organisation, the Clan na Gael, and had no scruples about it.

The Church's prohibition on membership of secret societies continued to be applied down through the years, but not uniformly. One of Dublin's diocesan clergy refused absolution to Emmet Dalton in 1921 on the eve of the daring operation to rescue Seán Mac Eóin from Mountjoy Prison when, recognising that his prospects of survival were decidedly slim, Dalton knelt before him in the confessional and acknowledged that he was in the IRB. He fared better afterwards on presenting himself to a Jesuit.[10] There is no reason to think that that particular Jesuit had IRB leanings; but the one who figured in an earlier story definitely had. When Paddy O'Daly, an up-and-coming man in the movement, went to work in Galway he was told by Seán MacDermott to go and see an old Jesuit priest there, Father Henry Foley, who encouraged him to persist in the IRB and to have nothing to do with lukewarm members. The IRB at this time was glad to find itself sharing a common policy with the Church on cattle-driving; and, in Galway, where the IRB was divided on the issue, O'Daly was directed to speak out strongly against the practice and did so.[11]

Incidentally, the choice of venue for the Clontarf meeting confirms that the Dublin membership was not at that time very large. It also gave the Dublin men an opportunity of seeing who was and who was not in 'the Organisation'. Ernest Blythe discovered his own civil service chief in the crowd and that Arthur Griffith was an absentee, which made him think that maybe the man whose writings they all read regularly in *Sinn Féin* was not, and perhaps never had been, an IRB man at all.[12] The question had been posed and answered in a letter that Dr P. McCartan sent to Joe McGarrity, a leading Clan na Gael figure, sometime in 1910. 'Griffith', he wrote, 'resigned from the family because he would not confer with his brothers to discuss the course to be taken on certain things as they turned up publicly.'[13] We have quoted a variant of this, and another explanation, earlier. A different point of view was expressed in 1964 by Patrick O'Keeffe, one-time secretary of Sinn Féin. Griffith, he said, never left the IRB at all. 'He was never put out and never went out. There are all kinds of fellows like that.' Apparently he just ceased to attend meetings. The IRB people wanted to squeeze Griffith, O'Keeffe said, so that the paper he was editing would become their official organ, but Griffith was determined that he was not going to be tied by anyone. 'That was the whole business,' O'Keeffe insisted, 'and let nobody tell you anything different.' Probably up to 1904–05 Griffith used to attend an IRB Circle. The publication of his *Resurrection of Hungary* in 1904 marked some kind of a chasm between the IRB outlook and Griffith's. Some doctrinaire republicans went so far as to call him a traitor for promulgating his idea of a King, Lords and Commons of Ireland.[14]

3

The Irish Parliamentary Party's alliance with the English Liberals secured the enactment in 1911 of the Parliament Bill, which deprived the House of Lords of its fearsome power of preventing a public measure from becoming law. A Home Rule Bill had fallen under this veto in 1893; now it was virtually certain that nothing could stop a similar bill from going to the statute book.

The immediate violent reaction of Ulster Unionists was the clearest proof that this was the reality. They stridently voiced their alarm and turned for help to the English Conservative opposition. They were convinced that Home Rule would not only bring absolute ruin to Ireland but was a serious threat to the survival of the British Empire. Religion, they insisted, was the prime issue. They were fully determined not to be under the rule of a Roman Catholic parliament. They wanted to stay as they were, permanently linked to what they saw as British Protestant parliamentary institutions. Home Rule in any shape or form was abhorrent to them, and if it was to be forced through parliament, Ireland would have to be truncated by excluding the Ulster counties. And to make sure that their view would prevail, they made arrangements to convene a provisional provincial parliament, and simultaneously organised an Ulster Volunteer Force which proceeded to train in the open with arms imported surreptitiously from Germany. Their slogan was that Ulster would fight and Ulster would be right; and one of their leaders declared that Germany and the German Emperor, then emerging as the great threat to the British Empire, would be preferred in Ulster to the rule of John Redmond.

How extravagant this behaviour was can be seen from the fact that the Home Rule Bill, when it saw the light in 1912, offered a meagre measure of autonomy. Even control of the police force was not immediately to pass to the new Irish government, and the supreme authority of the United Kingdom parliament 'over all persons, matters and things in Ireland' was specifically retained. However, the Nationalists, for the time being, were in a mood to be easily satisfied. At a convention in Dublin they expressed their solemn conviction that Home Rule on these terms would link the people of Ireland to the people of Great Britain by a union infinitely closer than that which then existed, and by so doing would add immeasurably to the strength of the Empire. The Sinn Féin leaders, of course, condemned the bill as hopelessly inadequate, but the vast majority of nationalist people, long taught to regard Home Rule as the panacea for Ireland's ills, and untroubled by constitutional detail, gave Redmond their uncritical support.[15] Home Rule monopolised the mind of the nation.[16]

Redmond was under enormous pressure, as indeed was his

F

Liberal ally Asquith, to come to terms with the Conservative and Unionist opposition on the Ulster question. There were endless comings and goings toward that end before Redmond, who had always made it clear that he was prepared to support any reasonable attempt to settle the question by agreement, very reluctantly and as the price of peace, consented to a six years' exclusion of the counties of Ulster on an optional basis. This concession was announced on 9 March 1914 on the second reading of the Home Rule Bill on one of its circuits of the House of Commons under the provisions of the Parliament Act. The terms of the announcement were received in nationalist Ulster with bitter disappointment, and with a sense of betrayal, and yet the Orangemen were not satisfied. Their parliamentary representatives rejected the idea of a time-limited exclusion. They did not want a sentence of death with a stay of execution.

By this time an extremely important event had occurred in nationalist Ireland without Redmond's prior knowledge or approval. Professor Eóin Mac Néill, a co-founder of the Gaelic League and a historian of considerable repute, had written an article, under the inspiration of what had happened in the North, advocating the formation of a force of Irish Volunteers. It appeared, he wrote, that the British army could not be used to prevent the enrolment, drilling and reviewing of volunteers in Ulster. There was nothing, therefore, to stop the rest of Ireland from following suit. Mac Néill's article was enthusiastically welcomed in IRB circles where, at the instigation of Bulmer Hobson, secret drilling had again begun. Indeed, as P. S. O'Hegarty, a member of the Supreme Council at that time, has written, before ever there had been so much as a public whisper of a volunteer force, the Council had discussed it. Any such force started by physical-force men or by advanced nationalists would be suppressed, but the existence of the Ulster Volunteers made it difficult to suppress a southern force sponsored by unsuspectable people. That was, says O'Hegarty, how Eóin Mac Néill and other unsuspectable people started the Irish Volunteers. They thought they were acting on impulse when they were really acting on suggestion. Everything they did, then and afterwards, was supervised by the IRB.[17]

This strongly suggests that Mac Néill was a mere puppet for the IRB; but F. X. Martin, a considerable authority on the history of the period, argues otherwise. According to him, the IRB and Mac Néill understood but underestimated their respective positions, the full implications of which only became clear a couple of years later. In November 1913, as the Volunteer idea took root, the IRB and Mac Néill stood in mutual need of each other.[18]

In collaboration with The O'Rahilly, the honorary editor of the Gaelic League paper, Hobson secured Mac Néill's agreement to preside at a committee meeting to discuss the formation of a Volunteer body. This committee, largely IRB in character, convened a public meeting in the Rotunda in Dublin to which some seven thousand people turned up, and at this meeting a manifesto written by Mac Néill was read declaring the object of the Volunteers to be the securing and maintaining of the rights and liberties common to all the people of Ireland. The duties were to be defensive and protective: neither aggression nor domination was contemplated. Two of the speakers were Eóin Mac Néill and P. H. Pearse. Hobson did not speak. Pearse, as to whom more anon, had warned Mac Néill of the danger of allowing extremists like Hobson to gain control. However, Hobson was soon considered by the IRB Directory not to be extreme enough. The IRB had taken steps to secure and keep control of the Volunteers at points that were considered vital, but Hobson felt it to be very important that in the Volunteers there should be genuine co-operation between men of all parties. So when Redmond, alarmed by the rapid growth of the movement, demanded representation on the Volunteer executive, Hobson agreed with Mac Néill and Sir Roger Casement to concede this in the interests of unity and in the belief that in any event real power would continue to rest with them. 'I decided, if we opposed Redmond's demands,' he said, 'that the whole Volunteer movement would disintegrate in a political faction fight. My view was that we must accept Redmond's nominees in order to save the Volunteers.'[19] The decision was not at all to the liking of Clarke and MacDermott, who had for some time been increasingly critical of Hobson because of his friendship with men like Mac Néill and Casement, who belonged intellectually and socially to a different world from theirs. Clarke was sure that Casement was a British spy.

James Deakin and Denis McCullough, successive Presidents of the IRB between 1913 and 1916, constituted with Clarke, the

Treasurer, and MacDermott, the Secretary, the Directory or Standing Executive that acted for the Supreme Council in between meetings, but as Deakin was a busy businessman and McCullough lived in Belfast, Clarke and MacDermott were effectively in control at the centre of affairs in Dublin and appear to have acted very much as they liked. After the decision to admit Redmond's nominees they called Hobson to a meeting and subjected him to a shower of abuse and accusations of having betrayed the cause. They went so far as to ask him how much he had been paid by Redmond for selling the Volunteers. The upshot was that Hobson broke with Clarke and Mac-Dermott and resigned the editorship of *Irish Freedom* and his place on the Supreme Council. He continued, however, to be the Centre of the Teeling Circle and Chairman of the Dublin Centres Board. Clarke, as always, was in very close touch with Devoy in New York, and as a result of what passed between them at this time, Devoy dismissed Hobson as the Irish correspondent of the *Gaelic American*. He changed his attitude subsequently, but Hobson never wrote for the paper again.

4

In the six months preceding the outbreak of the Great War in August 1914 three startling events occurred in Ireland. The first was the near-mutinous incident at the Curragh Camp when fifty-eight British cavalry officers made it known that they would prefer dismissal rather than be involved in a military operation designed to deal with threatened action by the Ulster Volunteers against local military arms depots. The trouble was quickly patched up, but to the detriment of the Liberal government; and the Ulster Unionists were left with the strong conviction that in an emergency they could rely upon the support of the army. A still more dramatic event occurred a few weeks later when some hundreds of Ulster Volunteers threw a cordon round the harbour at Larne, excluded the police and customs officers, disrupted the telegraph and telephone communications, and proceeded to take on shore the contents of two steamers that had simultaneously arrived from Germany. What they unloaded was 35,000 rifles and 5 million rounds of ammunition, and this substantial cargo of mischief they then rapidly dispatched to Volunteer units through the province or hid away near at hand in places where the police would not find it. The government was horrified by this development and debated what should be done, but did precious little. That was in April. In the following July small harbours at Howth and Kilcoole outside Dublin were the scenes of similar landings of arms, but on a much smaller scale, and this time in favour of the Irish Volunteers. The landings were devised and directed by a group in which Hobson was prominent, and the money for the arms, again imported from Germany, was advanced by some liberally-minded English and Anglo-Irish men and women. The Howth landing ended in a confrontation on the streets of Dublin between soldiers and a crowd of people, three of whom were killed and thirty-eight wounded. This caused a tremendous hullaballoo in political circles because of the obvious contrast, between the North and South, in the treatment of gun-runners and their admirers.

By the time the war began no agreement had been reached on the question of Ulster's position in a Home Rule settlement; so, in order to maintain a front of unity before the German enemy, the Home Rule Bill as it stood was passed into law along with a short measure which postponed Home Rule for the duration of the war and ensured that parliament would then have another look at the knotty Ulster problem. The Irish Volunteers as an united force did not survive the first weeks of hostilities. They split towards the end of September, following a speech by Redmond in which he exhorted them to prove on the continental fields of battle the gallantry and courage which had distinguished the Irish race all through history. Redmond had not consulted the Volunteer executive before making his appeal; and with little ado Mac Néill and Hobson and a majority of the original members brought their connection with him to an end. But only about 11,000 men followed their lead, retaining the title of Irish Volunteers; the vast majority—about 184,000— went with Redmond and were subsequently · known as the National or Redmondite Volunteers. Incidentally, there were in Ireland at about this time some 1,660 'paying members' of the IRB: 850 in Leinster, 300 in Ulster, 260 in Munster and 250 in Connacht. In Scotland there were 250 'paying members', and in England 117.[20]

In the autumn of 1914, according to Hobson, the Supreme

Council of the IRB decided to embark on an insurrection before the war came to an end. Some members demurred, Hobson said, but ceased to oppose the proposition when they saw they were outnumbered.

> None of them apparently remembered that such action was forbidden by the [IRB] Constitution they had all sworn to obey. No time was fixed; just a decision to act before the end of the war. A small committee, of which MacDermott and Clarke were the effective members, was appointed with instructions to examine the project and to report back to the Supreme Council. They never reported back. The Supreme Council met seldom after this and they were never informed what their committee was doing. The Supreme Council was, in effect, superseded and ceased to count. The committee proceeded to co-opt whom they pleased and to consult whom they pleased, and they were very careful to conceal their proceedings from any members of the Supreme Council who could not be counted on to approve of their actions. Even the President of the Supreme Council, Denis McCullough, was not allowed to know of their proceedings and the fact that he did not then live in Dublin made it easier to keep him in the dark. This secrecy was maintained until a few days before the insurrection.[21]

Consulting, as Hobson says, whom they pleased, Clarke and MacDermott in September 1914 revealed their intentions to a meeting held in the library of the Gaelic League headquarters in Parnell Square to which they invited the labour leaders James Connolly and William O'Brien; Major John MacBride; Arthur Griffith, Seán T. O'Kelly; Seán McGarry, who was later to become President of the Supreme Council; and a group of younger men that included Patrick Henry Pearse, Thomas Mac-Donagh, Éamonn Ceannt and Joseph Plunkett. The intention to rise before the war ended can only have come as a surprise to Connolly, O'Brien, Griffith and possibly MacBride. The others were already involved in the preliminaries. The labour men were expected to speak for the Citizen Army, a body of a few hundred men which had come into being during the cataclysmic industrial disorders of 1913 to protect workers against the baton-happy Dublin police. Seán O'Casey had been secretary of this microscopic army, and in weekly articles for the *Irish Worker* he had poured scorn on the Irish Volunteers and managed to generate an atmosphere of opposition to them that lasted right up to the eve of the Easter Rising. By that time he had resigned from both the Citizen Army and the IRB because he could not have his way. He left the IRB during the 1913 lockout when Hobson, arguing that their organisation was a democratic one, caring equally for all its citizens, which should not commit itself to class warfare, swayed a mass meeting of the IRB against intervention on the side of the workers. O'Casey on that occasion criticised the IRB, alleging that it appealed only to clerks and artisans, few of whom knew how to use a pick or shovel! His remarks got some support, but the majority of those present tried to howl him down, and in an atmosphere of pandemonium Hobson on the platform drew a gun.[22]

Some of the younger men who attended the meeting in the Gaelic League library had relatively recently joined the IRB, and one of their number, Pearse, had already begun to assume a leading position in it. By October he was warning the American Clan na Gael not to entrust to Mac Néill and company the expenditure of the money they were sending over. He did not doubt their honesty, he said, but 'they are not of our counsels, and they are not formally pledged to strike, if the chance comes, for the complete thing'.[23] He had already made up his mind that a *coup d'état* was the thing, once arms were available.[24]

Pearse was a protégé of Clarke's, and Clarke's biographer suggests that the greatest service perhaps that Clarke rendered to Ireland was 'to encourage against heavy odds and guide Patrick Pearse on the road to the redemption of Ireland'. The heavy odds were apparently the opposition of men who made no secret of their dislike of Pearse, whom they suspected of political ambition. 'They went so far, it was said, as to form a cabal which for over four years barred Pearse's admission to the IRB. Twice his name was put down for nomination at the Teelings, Dublin, and twice he was rejected,' on both occasions because of his attitude to British proposals for modest self-government. Clarke was impressed by the work Pearse was doing in his school, turning out 'Irish Irelanders' by the score, and by his having written in advocacy of the thesis that the liberty of a people can be guaranteed only by its readiness and ability to vindicate it in arms. In May 1913 Clarke overcame objections to Pearse being allowed to give the annual oration at Wolfe Tone's grave, and was rewarded by hearing him in an oratorical flight describing Bodenstown as the holiest place in Ireland, holier even than where Patrick slept in Down, for, as he said, Patrick brought us light, but Tone died for us. And he urged his listeners to pledge themselves to follow in the steps of Tone and never to rest by day or by night until his work was accomplished. Before the year was out Pearse was co-opted a member of the IRB by order of the Executive, and the oath was administered to him by Hobson. This procedure was rarely adopted; it became necessary in Pearse's case because of the refusal of the Teeling Circle to accept him as a member in the ordinary way, and to show appreciation of Pearse's genuine acceptance of the IRB doctrine, and of his acknowledged value to the movement.[25]

The meeting at the Gaelic League headquarters appears to have followed two others, namely the meeting of the Supreme Council at which the decision was taken to embark on an insurrection before the war ended, and a meeting that took place in New York between a special committee of the Clan na Gael and the German ambassador, Count von Bernstorff. Devoy places the latter meeting in August 1914,[26] and, if his date be correct, it means that the Germans were approached before the Supreme Council of the IRB took their decision. That decision was taken in the *autumn* of 1914 according to Hobson.[27] Some time subsequently in September the meeting in the Gaelic League premises was held. The meeting with the Germans was planned by the Clan na Gael, but when it took place it did so in the most casual circumstances, that is to say, during a reception at the German Club and in the presence of Bernstorff's military attaché, von Papen, and other officials, with guests hovering about at what Devoy called a respectful distance.

> Our spokesman [Devoy wrote in later times] told the Ambassador that our friends in Ireland intended to use the opportunity presented by the war to make an effort to overthrow English rule in Ireland and set up an independent government; that they had not an adequate supply of arms, had no trained officers, and wanted Germany to supply the arms and a sufficient number of capable officers to make a good start,

but that we wanted no money. . . . The point was stressed
that a rebellion in Ireland would necessarily divert a large part
of the British army from the fighting front on the Continent
and that therefore it would be in Germany's interest to help
Ireland in her fight for freedom. Count Bernstorff listened
attentively and with evident sympathy, asked many questions,
so as to be sure he fully understood our position, and he
promised to send our application to Berlin. We took our
departure and went to work at once to prepare for the arduous
work before us. The Home Organisation was informed at the
earliest possible moment, through Tom Clarke, of what had
occurred, and we were empowered to do the best we could
and keep the Supreme Council informed of our progress as
far as it could be done with safety.[28]

All the members of the Clan na Gael Executive also put their
names, after Devoy's, to an address to the Kaiser, dated 25
August 1914, which had been drafted by Sir Roger Casement.
This prayed for Germany's triumph over Ireland's traditional
enemy and hoped that Ireland, contributing towards that
triumph, would be freed from British control.

The approach to the Germans effectively disregarded the pre-
vailing political circumstances in Ireland, which were that the
vast majority of the nationalist population supported Redmond's
constitutional policy, that the Volunteer movement had divided
in the proportions of seventeen to one in favour of Redmond,
and that thousands of Irishmen had begun voluntarily to join
the British forces for the purpose of overthrowing the IRB's
German friends. It was in keeping with the traditional Fenian
policy of exploiting actual or anticipated English difficulties in
order to advance the cause of Irish independence. The Fenians
had turned to the Spaniards in 1877, to the Russians in 1878,
to the Boers in 1899; now their prospective formidable allies
were the Germans. Britain's break with. Germany was long
anticipated and entered into the calculations of the Clan na Gael
leaders as they corresponded with the IRB, sent help to enable
the Irish Volunteers to be trained and armed, and discussed
possibilities with the IRB envoys who crossed the Atlantic to
attend the biennial Clan conventions. MacDermott was in
America for this purpose in 1912, and Diarmuid Lynch in 1914.

F*

The September 1914 meeting at the Gaelic League headquarters is the only evidence of an effort by the IRB to bring
together the diverse Irish elements to whom Irish emancipation
through the success of the German arms was a likely prospect.
We do not know the trend of the discussions, but those present
at the meeting are said to have agreed (*a*) to strengthen the Irish
Volunteers, the Citizen Army, Fianna Éireann (the boy scout
organisation Hobson had founded) and Cumann na mBan (a
women's auxiliary body); (*b*) to assist German forces landing in
Ireland, conditional on their help being available to win Irish
freedom; (*c*) to oppose with all their strength the imposition of
conscription or an attempt to disarm the Volunteers; and (*d*) if
the war showed signs of ending without an effort having been
made to stage a rising, that such a rising should be organised and
the freedom of Ireland proclaimed to the world. They believed
that action along these lines would confer some sort of entitle-
ment on them to advance the national cause after the war,
though they had little hope that the rising would be successful.[29]
The meeting was to reassemble sometime but never did; and the
ultimate decision to stage a rising on a fixed date, taken later in
circumstances to be described below, was not communicated at
all to those who had been called into consultation in the first
instance. Arthur Griffith, notably, was not informed. The late
Liam Ó Briain was told by Griffith that he had been asked to
resume membership of the IRB and to join the Supreme
Council. He declined to do so because he wanted to be completely free to comment and write as he thought fit. This he
would not be able to do in the IRB.[30]

From September 1914 onwards there was a discernible growth
of pro-German propaganda, an increase in recruiting activity on
behalf of the Irish Volunteers, and a corresponding push to
counter recruiting for the British forces. The spread of the Irish
Volunteers was largely the result of the work of full-time organisers—Ernest Blythe was one of them—who saw to it that
wherever possible the officers were IRB men like themselves.
This was an important factor in planning for the rising when the
IRB leaders had not yet ensured the agreement of Mac Néill
and others on the Volunteer executive.

In July 1915 O'Donovan Rossa, who had died in America,
was brought home for burial in Dublin, and the propaganda

potential of the occasion was as fully exploited as ever before. He was kept lying in state for days in the City Hall, and on the day of the funeral thousands of Volunteers, including many Redmondites, marched to the graveside and fired a parting volley. Since John O'Leary's funeral only eight years before rifles had replaced hurleys, and a uniformed Pearse, his hands resting on a sword, delivered the oration. He called on Irishmen to renew the vows they had taken on being re-baptised in the Fenian faith. He mocked the British, the Defenders of the Realm, who thought they had foreseen everything, provided against everything, but, fools that they were, they had left Ireland her Fenian dead, and while Ireland held these graves, Ireland unfree would never be at peace. In the weeks following, Volunteers marched openly with arms in the streets of Dublin and Connolly and the Countess Markievicz together led the Citizen Army in a sham attack on Dublin Castle.

On the evening of the O'Donovan Rossa funeral the Supreme Council held a meeting in Parnell Square. Those eligible to attend were Seán Tobin (Leinster), Diarmuid Lynch (Munster), Alec McCabe (Connacht), Denis McCullough (Ulster), Joe Gleeson (North England), Dick Connolly (South England), Pat McCormick (Scotland), but McCormick, who was attending for the first time, does not remember seeing McCullough or Tobin there. The main purpose of the meeting, he says, was the co-option of four members as provided for in the Constitution. Those co-opted were Thomas Clarke, Seán MacDermott, Patrick Pearse and Dr Patrick McCartan.[31]

5

The IRB was making itself felt, and yet not uniformly throughout the country. Some old-timers in 'the Organisation' were apathetic and doing little or nothing to promote the Irish Volunteers. The experience of Alec McCabe, the representative of Connacht on the Supreme Council, was probably typical. He spent his week-ends and every evening after he had closed his school visiting country parishes on his bicycle and swore in a few reliable men here and there. He avoided the towns because all the shopkeepers were 'on the side of the establishment'. He was told there was a Circle in Sligo, but he failed to find it. It was evidently of the cloak-and-dagger variety which believed in keeping itself dark. Men who he suspected belonged to it went to the other side of the street when they saw him coming.[32]

This was also the experience of Desmond FitzGerald, recruited in Kerry in 1914 by Ernest Blythe when, excluded by the government from certain areas under the Defence of the Realm regulations, he went to live in Bray, Co. Wicklow. Officers of the IRB there had been apprised of his coming, and two of them came to his house. FitzGerald recalled :

> I was, of course, delighted to see them, and only regretted that they came accompanied by such a strong odour of alcohol. I wanted to talk business with them, but they seemed only to want to tell me of the veneration amounting to awe with which they looked upon a patriot against whom the ever-perfidious enemy had struck with all his venom. . . . I asked when and where the Circle met. They seemed rather vague about that, but told me to lift up my heart, for they and the other members were all united in their admiration of me. I said I required to know, as I supposed that I should attend the meeting. That proposal seemed rather to shock them. They said there was certainly no need for me to attend. Everybody knew that I was staunch. . . . As I seemed to be getting nowhere, I asked how many members they had. They both replied at once naming a number, but they did not name the same number. But that was unimportant, except as I pointed out to them, that I was starting a company of Volunteers in that district, and as they knew the Supreme Council had issued an order that all members of the Organisation should join the Volunteers, it would be useful for me to know so that I could be guaranteed that their full membership would come to the meeting that I would call. They did not seem to be quite sure as to whether they had heard of any such order. I said in any case it didn't matter whether or not the order had been received by their Circle, obviously every member would recognise it as his duty to join the company that I proposed to form. They did not seem very convinced about that, but agreed rather inarticulately, and went on to assert the enormous respect they felt for a man like me and what an honour it was to them to be in my presence.

Later FitzGerald met a man whose name carried great weight in the area as a great patriotic leader. He expressed the most extreme sentiments, referred to the fact that he had been an IRB man all his life but only put difficulties in FitzGerald's way.[33] Blythe introduced FitzGerald to Hobson, but FitzGerald was not impressed by this man of whom he had heard so much. He was too much of a know-all, FitzGerald thought, too determined to make an impression. He spoke as if he knew all about the war and how it was going to develop, and he was apparently so deep in the confidence of the German leaders that FitzGerald thought it would look as if he was asking Hobson to betray a confidence if he pushed his questioning any further.[34] Hobson, it is hardly necessary to say, had no contact whatever with the Germans. That business, unknown to him, was in other hands. FitzGerald says, however, that Hobson told him that it was definitely decided that the Irish should rise while the war was on : there was no fear that the war would end suddenly and unexpectedly before the Irish had struck a blow.

6

The IRB, as we saw earlier, had used the Gaelic League as a recruiting ground and had injected much of its revolutionary and anti-British ideas into the branches. Hobson recalls the voice of a teacher ringing through a room in Belfast as he described Queen Elizabeth I as 'that woman with bowels of brass'.[35] They had also managed to have some members elected to the League's executive committee.

Éamon de Valera noticed some such influence at work at the Árd-Fheis in 1911 and considered that his own defeat for election to the executive committee was due to this 'hidden hand'. He did not know at the time that the IRB even existed, but he sensed that the election had been rigged. He wrongly put the blame on Sinn Féin and vowed that he would never have anything to do with it.[36] In 1916 he joined the IRB for the odd reason that he had discovered that subordinate officers of his, who were already members, knew more about the Volunteers' plans than he did. This suggested to him that the Volunteer movement was subject to dual control, and he complained about it. He was then assured by Thomas MacDonagh that this was

not the case, that the Volunteer executive was controlled by the
IRB and that whatever orders were given would be those
initiated by the IRB. De Valera scrupled about the oath, but
MacDonagh assured him that it involved nothing more than
accepting the orders of the Volunteer executive.[37] De Valera
had earlier been appointed a battalion commander by Pearse on
getting a satisfactory answer as to what he would do in the
event of a rising.[38]

In 1915, as it prepared to give O'Donovan Rossa a national
funeral, the IRB secured control of the Gaelic League executive,
winning acceptance of a free as well as a Gaelic Ireland as the
League's objective. In doing so they overreached themselves. Dr
Douglas Hyde, a great national figure in the Anglo-Irish Protestant tradition who had striven to keep the League non-political,
was forced out of the presidency, and the general secretary left
with him. Hyde in his early days had held extreme views, cursing
the English, toasting O'Donovan Rossa, taking Parnell's side
against 'the scoundrel Tim Healy'. But, as time went on, he
became convinced that cultural regeneration was more important
than political independence, and it was strangely ironic that his
removal from the headship of the League should have been
contrived by men whose Fenian forebears he had formerly held in
high esteem. Hyde foresaw the destruction of the Gaelic movement by what he called the politics of the moment and warned
against the danger, but his words were lost on the men of the
IRB.[39]

What particularly upset Hyde was the news that Seán Ó
Muirthile, one of the League's organisers who was also a member
of the IRB, had received fifty proxies which, instead of being
distributed to Irish speakers as would have been proper, were
given to politically motivated people who did not know Irish
and cared little for it.[40] The IRB then saw to it that the vacan-
cies they had created were filled by men of their choosing. Eóin
Mac Néill became president. He was not an IRB man, nor
indeed a republican, but since he was President and Chief of
Staff of the Irish Volunteers, the IRB played along with him in
the hope that ultimately they would win him over to their
insurrectionary ideas. Mac Néill, like Hyde, lived to regret the
introduction of politics into the Gaelic League. He believed that
it had turned many people away from what had been a genuinely

national movement, and that it had made the prospect of Ireland becoming Irish-speaking much more difficult.

When it came to appointing a new general secretary Ó Muirthile, who believed he had a claim to the job in preference to Seán T. O'Kelly, another IRB candidate, was grievously disappointed. A meeting of the IRB members of the governing body of the Gaelic League was held at the instigation of Tom Clarke and presided over by him, and this meeting decided that Ó Muirthile was to stand down and leave the way open for the appointment of O'Kelly.[41] This was a truly bizarre situation. The IRB were determined that no one outside their ranks, however qualified, was to get the job; and, in choosing one of their own men, competence in Irish was a secondary consideration. Ó Muirthile undoubtedly knew Irish better than O'Kelly did, while Clarke, who directed the choice, knew no Irish at all. He was interested primarily in the Gaelic League as an instrument for promoting the separatist policy to which he was so fanatically devoted.

7

Denis McCullough has left on record a detailed account of the sequence of events summarised by Hobson in a paragraph we have quoted earlier. McCullough had been for some years the Ulster representative on the Supreme Council when, at the bi-annual meeting in December 1915 or somewhat earlier,[42] he agreed with much reluctance to become President. The meeting was held in Clontarf Town Hall in a room provided by the caretaker, Michael Maginn, a former member of the Council; and, as the members forgathered, McCullough mentioned to MacDermott that one of the things they had to do that day was to choose a President in succession to John Mulholland, who had resigned 'as a result of whatever happened at the Council meeting' at which, following the outbreak of war, the possibility of a rising was discussed. He later tendered his resignation to the Scottish Division which he represented on the Council, and left the organisation. McCullough said that he intended to propose Pearse in his place. 'Oh, for the love of God, don't be stupid, don't be foolish,' MacDermott said. 'Why?' McCullough asked. 'Isn't he an excellent man?' 'We never could control that bloody fellow,' MacDermott replied. ('And, of course,' said McCullough in an aside, 'in the IRB that was the important thing, to control men.') 'And who are you going to have?' he then asked. 'Now leave that to Tom [Clarke] and myself,' MacDermott said. 'We will get all that fixed.' 'And then he came along', recalled Mc-Cullough, 'and proposed me. They probably thought they could control me. I never pushed myself. I said that's absurd. I couldn't do this. I couldn't take that job. I live in Belfast and you people are in Dublin here, and things are going to happen here and how could I possibly be of any value.' 'That's all right,' said MacDermott. 'We can fix that. You must take it,' and under pressure, McCullough agreed to take it: 'Very well, if I must take it, I'll make myself available on an hour's notice if you send me a wire any time you want me.' 'That's how I became President,' McCullough commented later. 'I shouldn't have been President at all. . . .'

The Constitution provided for an Executive of the Supreme Council, composed of the President, Secretary and Treasurer of that body, and that the decision of any two of these was binding on all. McCullough, Clarke and MacDermott filled these three posts at this time, and in theory, therefore, jointly ruled the IRB, but McCullough asserted that his presidency was hardly more than nominal and that Seán MacDermott was effectively the Executive. It was through him that the IRB exercised control over practically all the key Volunteers throughout the country, the policy being to get an IRB man always appointed to the key position. If this failed, the person appointed was to be induced to join 'the Organisation'. 'We regarded Mac Néill and everyone else like Mac Néill as instruments we could use for our purpose.'[43]

The next meeting of the Council after McCullough's appointment was in January 1916. McCullough described what took place:

Pat McCartan [a co-opted member] was there, Dick Connolly a post office man from London [representing the South of England], [Joseph] Gleeson [representing the North of England] and Diarmuid Lynch [representing Munster]. So the question came up that we would have to have a Rising [meaning presumably an early implementation of the decision taken at the outbreak of the war], and it was discussed very seriously.

Pat McCartan fought hard. He said 'Who are we like the Three Tailors of Tooley Street to call a Rising? Before you commit a nation to war, you should have the support of the people. We haven't the support of the people. We should gain that first.' I was in the chair and I said, 'Well, what are we organised for? 'Tis obvious the country will never do it unless we start it. It's our job to start it,' I said, 'to organise for it and trust the people afterwards.' And he [McCartan] was violently opposed by Dick Connolly and Gleeson. I said Mc-Cartan must get a hearing. They wouldn't listen to him. . . . It was agreed then. That was the meeting (lasting three hours) at which it was decided that a Rising would be held.

The next step was to appoint a military committee, 'people who could run a Rising. We hadn't the knowledge or the mentality.' MacDermott and Pearse were accordingly appointed to represent the Supreme Council in the committee, with power to co-opt. The committee took charge of all the arrangements. 'As far as Tom Clarke and myself were concerned,' continued Mc-Cullough, 'we abdicated. . . . The Supreme Council lost volition and the military committee took over. . . . Although I presided at the meeting at which it was decided to have a Rising, I was never told a further word about it.'[44]

McCullough complained later that there had been a good deal of deceit. He apparently did not know that a military committee (later known as the Military Council) consisting of Pearse, Joseph Plunkett and Éamonn Ceannt had been in existence since May 1915, that Clarke and MacDermott joined the committee later that year and approved the detailed military plans the other three had worked out, and that Plunkett, reputedly the military expert, had been to Germany and had arranged that a cargo of guns and ammunition would be delivered in Ireland by Easter 1916.[45]

McCullough detected deceit when MacDermott failed to carry out a promise to give him a fortnight's notice of the Rising. On the Saturday before Holy Week he picked up a clue that the fatal date had been fixed and hurried to Dublin. 'MacDermott dodged me on the Saturday and the Sunday. On Sunday night I was in Tom Clarke's house and I said to Tom: "What in the name of God is going to happen?" He said, "I declare to God I know nothing more than you do. All I know is I have orders to report to Ned Daly on [Easter] Sunday morning and have my arms and equipment and I have them ready." He brought out an old revolver that would have killed him if he had fired it.' On the Monday McCullough went to the office in D'Olier Street and found MacDermott there. McCullough's account of their conversation is as follows:

'I'll see you in a minute', MacDermott told me. 'You'll see me in a minute, will you? You'll see me now. You have been avoiding me for the last two days. I want to know what's happening, and I'm entitled to know,' and I turned the key in the door. 'Now', says I, 'you've got to tell me.' 'Alright,' says he, 'I'll tell you what's going to happen,' and he told me what had been arranged. He told me a cock and bull story of probably a German submarine coming up the Liffey, and that the Germans were going to send us at least 250 officers, and other things . . . and to me, says he, 'What are *you* going to do? What do you think of it?' and I said, 'Well, Seán, in truth,' I said, 'it looks to me like murder and suicide.' 'But what are you going to do?' he said. 'Well,' I said, 'if you are going to turn out, what can I do but turn out my men and do my best. But', I said, 'if I live through this, Seán, I'll have something to say to you and Tom Clarke.' And he laughed and threw his head back and said, 'I don't think you need bother about that because probably neither of us will live through it. . . .' I left Seán on that note. As a matter of fact we embraced each other, a most unmanly thing to do. He put his arm around my neck and kissed me. 'Good-bye, Denis,' he said. 'Probably we will never see each other again.' When I saw him next he was going out to his trial in Richmond Barracks.[46]

8

The government, of course, knew all this time that the IRB was still alive and that it represented the most advanced section of the conglomerate element they incorrectly described as Sinn Féiners; but, in their view, 'the Organisation' had little current importance, though Circle meetings were occasionally held, mostly in the North of Ireland. At one time its membership had been estimated at nearly 40,000, but now it could not exceed 1,000.[47] Hobson's impression was that it had an overall strength on the eve of the Rising of about 2,000, of whom there were about 700 in Dublin, 150 in Cork, a few hundred more in Limerick, Kilkenny, Waterford and Wexford, and some considerable groups in London, Liverpool and Newcastle-on-Tyne.[48]

The prime object of government policy at this time was to keep Ireland quiet so that recruiting for the war could proceed and the way prepared for the transfer of functions under the Home Rule project. This meant looking at sedition less sternly than they otherwise would have done. They had their list of suspects but this was out of date. The Head of Military Intelligence regarded Hobson as the most dangerous man in Ireland, the intellect of militant republicanism, but, as we saw, Hobson had been side-tracked and the initiative now rested with other men. To one of them, Tom Clarke, the government paid particular attention, but they did not know that detailed plans for a rising had been worked out by the Military Council (or Committee) of the IRB consisting of three high-ranking officers in the Irish Volunteers, working in close concert with Clarke and Mac-Dermott. In January 1916 James Connolly, the socialist and Citizen Army leader, was brought into the Military Council in order to prevent him from taking the independent action he had begun to threaten, and, later still, Thomas MacDonagh was added to the group. All of these seven men—six of them members of the IRB—signed a Proclamation of the Republic in Easter Week of that year and paid for doing so with their lives. Other IRB men, commanders of areas in the Rising, suffered the same fate. So did John MacBride, though why is somewhat of a mystery. He was not in the counsels of the leaders, and appears to have known little or nothing about the Rising until it began. Then, true to form, he left the veteran Fred Allan's house where he had been lodging and joined in, becoming a deputy to Mac-Donagh, who commanded one of the Dublin areas. In his death he was remembered by Yeats as 'a drunken vainglorious lout' who had done most bitter harm to one near his heart, but who had been transformed by the 'terrible beauty' of the Rising. When she could do so, Maud Gonne, who had been so long separated from MacBride and was otherwise out of the national picture, returned to Ireland in widow's weeds and never afterwards cast them off. John MacBride, after all, was her husband and had died for his country. She was in what Yeats described as a joyous and self-forgetting condition of political hate the like of which he had never encountered.

9

Mac Néill and Hobson, when they stumbled upon evidence that a rising was about to take place, did their best to have it called off but only partially succeeded. Their opposition to a rising was based on a number of grounds, one of which was their belief in its impracticability. The only reason that could justify it, they thought, would be a reasonable prospect of success, and that was out of the question. England had more than ample power to crush the Volunteer movement and had only refrained from doing so because no open revolt had taken place. The situation might be different after the war, when the disillusioned remnant of the 150,000 Irishmen who had fought abroad returned and asked for the Home Rule that had been promised.[49] And if a fight were forced on them to resist disarmament or conscription, for example, they thought it should take a guerrilla form throughout the country rather than that adopted at Easter 1916 when groups of insurgents locked themselves up in public buildings and invited the British, as it were, to eject them.

Mac Néill was strongly opposed on moral grounds to a rising. In a memorandum, written in February 1916,[50] he unsuccessfully counselled his IRB colleagues on the Volunteer executive to recognise that the conditions for a morally defensible revolt did not exist: to enter deliberately on a course of action which was morally wrong was to incur the guilt not only of that action but of all its direct consequences; and to kill any person in carrying out such a course of action was murder. Hobson had an argument which he felt should have made a greater appeal to IRB men, namely that their own Constitution prescribed that they should await the decision of the Irish nation, as expressed by a majority of the Irish people, as to the fit hour of inaugurating a war against England. This provision, as we saw earlier, had been inserted in the Constitution following the débâcle of 1867, and Hobson, after the event, relied on it to defend his opposition to the Rising. He added that it was not the

Supreme Council of the IRB in any event who had organised the Rising, but a small junta acting with the utmost secrecy and without the knowledge of the President and most other members of the Council.[51]

Another critic of the Rising was Douglas Hyde. 'My work for 22 years was to restore to Ireland her intellectual independence,' he wrote to a friend. 'I would have completed it, if I had been let. These people [the IRB] "queered the pitch" on me, mixed the physical and the intellectual together, interpreted my teaching into terms of bullets and swords—*before the time*, and have reduced me to impotence.' He had been asked to return to the Gaelic League, but 'Why on earth', he asked, 'should I be browbeaten and outvoted on every question of politics, and then be held responsible by the public for acts of flaming indiscretion which I had striven against in vain. I know I would be a nice figurehead for them, to be thrown over like John MacNeill when it suited them.'[52] Mac Néill had argued against the sacrificing of lives in order to produce an ultimate effect on the national mind. Apart from the questionable morality of so doing, he shared Hobson's view that the national spirit at the time was good and steadily on the upgrade and did not need an act of redemption to save it.[53]

The 'junta' were not deterred by such arguments. They were committed to a rising, to their German allies, to their American friends, and some of them were imbued with the notion of making a blood sacrifice, of saving Ireland by offering their lives for her. In a manifesto that bears the imprint of Pearse's style they proclaimed a republic and asserted that Ireland spoke through them; and, to the surprise of most people who had never heard of them, including men who were about to follow them into battle, they revealed themselves as Ireland's secret revolutionary organisation, the Irish Republican Brotherhood. One of their followers said in later years: 'Just inside the door [of the General Post Office, the insurgents' headquarters] I leaned back against a small table on which was spread a bundle of posters. They were copies of the Proclamation of Easter Week and I was dumbfounded to learn for the first time of the existence and the activity of the secret society, the Irish Republican Brotherhood.'[54] The 'junta' claimed that the Irish Volunteers and the Irish Citizen Army were their 'open military organisations', but this claim was repudiated by Mac Néill in so far as the Volunteers were concerned. Appointing Pearse President of the Republic, presumably meaning to replace McCullough at the head of the IRB, though it is extremely doubtful if they had authority to do this, they went out on Easter Monday 1916 with as many of the IRB-controlled units as they were able to mobilise. Their original intention was to begin action on the previous day, but in this they were frustrated by Mac Néill when he discovered what was afoot. They then pretended to accept his countermand but did so only in respect of 'manoeuvres' announced for Easter Sunday. On the Monday they attempted to re-jig the operation, but confusion and conflicting loyalties so affected the mobilisation of the Volunteers that in most places outside Dublin nothing happened. And the solitary boat containing guns and ammunition from the Germans went to the bottom of Cork harbour.

The status of President of the Republic conferred on Pearse did not prevent him, during a lull in the fighting, from discussing the possibility of a German prince being installed as king of an independent Ireland.[55] It was not the first time the idea had been heard of. At a meeting of IRB organisers before the Rising, Joseph Plunkett, who had recently visited Germany, propounded and won general acceptance for the notion of an independent Irish kingdom headed by a German Catholic prince.[56] A German victory in the war was anticipated, and the link with Germany through a German king was seen as the best way of averting any future aggression from Britain. The Constitution of the IRB and the declaration of a Republic on Easter Monday were seemingly irrelevant.[57]

The Rising, doomed to failure from the beginning, was speedily quelled. The British were fighting for survival in a world war and were not in a mood to tolerate a major act of treachery, as they conceived it, at their back door. Their army pushed into the centre of Dublin and, using artillery freely, set fire to the General Post Office, the insurgents' headquarters, and forced a surrender. All the other posts followed suit.

The popular reaction was unmistakable; and Redmond, the Irish parliamentary leader, gave expression to it in the House of Commons when he spoke of a feeling of detestation and horror. The nation had been let down, the scores of thousands of Irishmen and women serving in the war insulted. 'If Ireland as a whole', said P. S. O'Hegarty, 'could have got hold of Tom Clarke and his comrades during that week it would have torn them to pieces.'[58] The National Volunteers were at this time engaged in some places on Home Defence duties in order to enable regular soldiers to be released for war service, and Redmond was pressing the GOC in Ireland to employ them more extensively.[59]

Hobson, for different reasons, shared in the general disgust. On the Good Friday evening, while still Chairman of the Dublin Centres Board of the IRB and secretary of the Irish Volunteers, he had been called to a meeting of the Leinster executive of the Brotherhood to be held at Martin Conlon's house in Phibsboro, a Dublin suburb. He arrived to receive the surprise of his life.

> The rest of the members of the Leinster Executive produced guns [he related later] and said I was detained. I laughed and said 'You are a lot of damn fools.' There was nothing I could do, so I sat back and accepted the situation. I felt I had done my best to stop the Rising. There was nothing more I could do, and I felt almost a sense of relief that the matter was off my hands. They were very nice to me. I remained under detention until Monday evening and spent the time reading. I did not talk to my guards because any conversation would have been in disapproval of what they were committed to. Then Seán T. O'Kelly came with orders for my release.[60]

After the event, some people wondered why other important IRB men—like Séamus O'Connor, who was also a member of the Volunteer executive and who disapproved of the Rising—had not also been arrested. 'It would have been drastic no doubt,' said Ó Muirthile, 'but if the only way of preserving a united front . . . it might have been a practical step to take. . . . To prevent MacNeill from issuing his orders would have meant that the whole country would have supported the handful of insurgents who had to bear the brunt of the battle alone in Dublin.'[61]

A very different point of view was expressed in later years by P. S. O'Hegarty:

> I thought what they would do would be to call out the Circles, which of course they were entitled to do, and put those of them who had been trained as Volunteers in command. That,

I suppose, was very simple of me, but for years I had been singing about 'Righteous men shall make our land. . . .' at the close of at least one meeting every week, and it never occurred to me that they would use the Volunteers without the knowledge of the Executive of that body, or that chaps would be called out for a route march and then given the alternative of insurrection.[62]

Hobson would have agreed with O'Hegarty. As he passed the GPO on that Easter Monday, on his way into comparative obscurity, his mind was doubtless full of the impending disaster for which he held Pearse personally responsible. He saw him as a sentimental egotist, full of curious Old Testament theories about being the scapegoat for the people, a man who had not contributed greatly to the hard grinding toil of building up the movement, but who, capitalising on the work of others, had seized the opportunity provided by the existence of a small organisation and a handful of arms to make his blood sacrifice.[63]

The initial popular reaction did not long endure. The protracted executions of the leaders and others—the wounded Connolly strapped to a chair; the sentencing of many men to penal servitude; the dissemination of the writings of the executed men, including some poetry of a religious or quasi-mystical character; these developments provoked a chauvinist backlash. By midsummer Sir John Maxwell, the GOC of the British forces, was greatly disturbed by the change in people's attitudes. In May prisoners on their way to British jails and internment camps had been hooted in the streets and had been condemned publicly by politicians, clergy and press. Now a great recrudescence of what Maxwell called Sinn Féinism was evident. Mourning badges, Sinn Féin flags, demonstrations at Requiem Masses, and the resolutions of public bodies were all signs of a profound shift of opinion. The prisoners were being looked after too, and their dependants succoured by a National Aid Association. Nevertheless it was Ocober 1917, and following by-election defeats in South Armagh, Waterford and East Tyrone, before the renunciation of the Irish Parliamentary Party policy of representation in the British House of Commons became widely acceptable. In South Armagh the abstentionist candidate, Dr McCartan of the IRB, lost by over a thousand votes.

Michael Collins

I

WITHIN THREE months of the Rising the IRB had begun to stir again. 'As far as can be ascertained,' Maxwell told the government, 'no secret meetings are being held but there are some signs of revival.'[1] He opposed the unconditional release of Sinn Féin leaders of importance, and considered it desirable to encourage the emigration of such of them as were let out. But, not for the first time, Maxwell was wrong in thinking that secret meetings were not taking place. In Frongoch camp some IRB internees came together to discuss what the future might have in store. Among them was Michael Collins, a young man of tireless energy, unusual intelligence and unlimited courage, who had been recruited into the IRB in 1909 by Sam Maguire while working in the Post Office in London, and who was to cause the British enormous concern in a relatively short time. He was, in fact, to outdo Hobson (and MacDermott) completely as the most dangerous man the government had encountered. He had been in the GPO in Easter Week, had acted as Joseph Plunkett's *aide de camp*, and was seen by Desmond FitzGerald as 'the most active and efficient officer in the place'.

In August 1916 John Archdeacon Murphy of Buffalo was sent to Ireland by the Clan na Gael with a large sum of money that had been collected in the United States for the prisoners' dependants; he was also instructed to ascertain what was being done to re-create the republican movement on a physical-force basis. In the same month and under cover of a much depleted Oireachtas held by the Gaelic League in the Minerva Hotel on Parnell Square in Dublin, a meeting to reorganise the IRB was attended by Dr Patrick McCartan, Diarmuid O'Hegarty, Martin Conlon, Peadar Kearney, Luke Kennedy, Seán Ó Muirthile and 'a patriotic young priest from the North' whose presence was an agreeable surprise to the others in view of the avowed attitude of the Church to secret societies. All the laymen in this group, with the exception of Diarmuid O'Hegarty, who had been released in error from prison, had escaped arrest.[2] At this meeting a Provisional Governing Body was appointed which functioned until the bulk of the prisoners were released.[3] Afterwards O'Hegarty with Ó Muirthile interviewed a messenger from America who brought news that the Germans were ready for another effort, but O'Hegarty and Ó Muirthile rejected this out of hand and never found out whether the proposal had any substance.[4] They assumed that the Clan na Gael were well enough aware of the weakness of the position at home and would not, therefore, have given the idea any serious consideration.[5] In any event, they were unhappy about the messenger, who was a Volunteer who had left Dublin during the progress of the Rising. But it looks as if the initiative for a second rising was in fact taken by the Revolutionary Directorate of the Clan. The Germans had reacted favourably to a suggestion and were prepared to land arms, but no troops, in February or March 1917. Their offer was declined. Without troops 'it would be useless'.[6]

The bulk of the prisoners were released in December 1916, and before the following summer the Provisional Governing Body, which had distinguished itself in its own estimation by sending greetings to the new Russian regime, was replaced by a Supreme Council whose members included Thomas Ashe, Seán Ó Muirthile, Seán McGarry, Diarmuid Lynch, Alec McCabe, Joe Gleeson, Pat McCormick and Michael Collins, and whose first Executive comprised Ashe as President, Ó Muirthile as Secretary and Lynch as Treasurer. They operated under a revised Constitution which had been drafted by Ashe, Lynch, Con Collins and Michael Collins and which aimed at bringing 'the Organisation' into accord with the situation that had developed as a result of the Easter Rising.[7] (The full document is reprinted in H. B. C. Pollard's *The Secret Societies of Ireland*, but is wrongly stated to derive from 1914.)

The first object of the IRB now was to establish *and maintain* a free and independent republican government in Ireland; the second was the training and equipping of members as a military body for the purpose of securing that independence by force of arms. It was required of the IRB to work in co-operation with all Irish military bodies (this was an acknowledgement of the 1916 alliances); and consistent with its own integrity it was to continue to support every movement calculated to advance the cause of independence. An understandable change from the previous Constitution was the omission of any reference to the organisation's policy in time of peace; and more significant still was the deletion of the earlier provision requiring the IRB to await the majority decision of the Irish people as to the fit hour for inaugurating a war against England. That provision, as it had stood since 1873, made the dynamite campaign of the 1880s and the Easter Rising itself unlawful. Consistent, too, with its idiosyncratic view of itself as a government, 'the Organisation' empowered the Supreme Council to inflict a sentence of death for treason, though one does not need to be a moralist to question its right to take the life of even the most miserable informer.

The new Constitution also introduced some structural or organisational changes. The Supreme Council was to consist of eleven members with authority to co-opt four others, that is to say fifteen in all compared with the previous total of eleven— the 'Black Fifteen', as they were subsequently called by the *Daily Mail*. The enlargement was achieved by having eleven electoral divisions, each of the four geographical provinces of Ireland being divided into two and leaving the South and North of England and Scotland unchanged. Specific provision was made for a Military Council, possibly because of the prominent part played by the *ad hoc* Military Council or Committee in promoting the 1916 Rising. But it was now emphasised—very significantly—that this organ was at all times to be subject to the Supreme Council and was to have no power to direct or interfere with the policy of the government of the Irish Republic nor in any way to alter the Constitution of the IRB.

Ashe, the newly elected President, was arrested in August 1917 for making a speech calculated to cause disaffection and died in Mountjoy Prison in September following a hunger strike in which he was forcibly fed. The funeral was used to denote a revival of militancy. Three volleys were fired over his grave, the 'last post' was sounded by a bugler, and Michael Collins, in Volunteer uniform, declared that nothing further remained to be said : 'That volley which we have just heard is the only speech which it is proper to make above the grave of an old Fenian.'[8]

Ashe was succeeded in the presidency by Seán McGarry, who thus became, in accordance with the IRB Constitution, the head of the Irish Republic; and Collins functioned for a while as Secretary.[9]

The convicted prisoners had been released in June 1917 in order to secure a favourable atmosphere for the deliberations of a Convention which the government had set up to discuss a possible settlement of the Irish Question. The Convention failed, and was boycotted by Sinn Féin which had now begun to win seats from the Irish Parliamentary Party in by-elections.

With 350 Circles claiming a total membership of 3,000, and with each Circle forming the nucleus of a Volunteer company, the claim was made in time that ninety per cent of the best Volunteer officers in the country were in the IRB. 'The Organisation' was obviously thriving, the drive coming particularly from Collins, Diarmuid Lynch, Harry Boland, and Seán Ó Muirthile. Collins said the IRB at this stage was 'a force organised on practical lines and headed by realists', which, we may take it, was an implicit criticism of the IRB at the time of the Rising, for whose leadership and military capacity he had not too high an opinion. Of 1916 he said : 'I think the Rising was bungled terribly costing many a good life. It seemed at first to be well organised, but afterwards became subjected to panic decisions and a great lack of very essential organisation and co-operation.' In the same letter Collins compared Connolly and Pearse. 'There was an air of earthy directness about Connolly. It impressed me. I would have followed him through hell had such action been necessary. But I honestly doubt very much if I would have followed Pearse—not without some thought anyway.'[10] The drive for new members was, as always, directed towards national bodies, which, in the post-Rising euphoria, were also enjoying a revival. Sinn Féin was an obvious mark. Indeed, the question was raised as to whether the IRB should not disappear and leave the way open for Sinn Féin. But Collins would have none of this. 'There are many things to be said in favour of Sinn Féin,' he wrote, 'many of whose ideals are but the re-weighed ideals of the IRB. But the things to be said in favour of Sinn Féin do not outweigh the uses of the IRB which is respected and acknowledged by many who will think twice about the prospects of Sinn Féin.'[11]

Sinn Féin had in fact already begun to be taken over by men who brought with them the aura of 1916.[12] The aims of Sinn Féin were also henceforth declared to be the securing of international recognition of Ireland as an independent Irish Republic, and in the takeover the IRB, as we shall see, played a major part. However, some former members of the IRB dropped out because they believed that the necessity for a secret oathbound society had passed in the light of what had happened at and since Easter 1916, or because the IRB continued to be condemned by the Catholic hierarchy. Among these were Éamon de Valera, Seán T. O'Kelly, Ernest Blythe and Desmond Fitz-Gerald.

De Valera's membership had never been more than nominal, and he had avoided being used by the Brotherhood other than as an officer of the Volunteers. He determined now to cease all connection with the IRB and tried—unsuccessfully—to persuade close associates, including Harry Boland, to withdraw from it. He and Cathal Brugha maintained that the movement ought henceforth to be an open one and that no one who accepted responsibility as an elected representative, as he himself now was, ought to be subject to secret control.[13] The contradictory orders at Easter also exemplified for de Valera the problems that arose between a public and secret organisation, and he also disliked swearing to obey an executive of unidentified members.[14] Brugha was bitterly critical because the IRB membership had not participated in the Rising in force.

Bulmer Hobson, for other reasons, had no further connection with the IRB, but Denis McCullough might have continued to be a member were it not for the reception he got when, following his release from prison, he went to a meeting in Dublin which was attended by, among others, Seán Ó Muirthile and Séamus O'Doherty. 'I was kept in the outer darkness', he told his brother-in-law Richard Mulcahy later, 'while these people were inside, until I got fed up and I opened the door and I said "What authority have you to meet here or who the hell are you? As far as I'm concerned you can meet as often as you like. I'm through; there's no more use for the IRB. There is an authoritative body here and they will take charge." I was referring to the Volunteers.'[15] This meeting may have been connected with inquiries made at this time by the IRB and the Volunteers separately as to what went wrong with the call-out for the Rising, or, more likely, it may have been due to the fact those who had responded to the call had begun to behave as if it was the other fellows, not they, who had broken the rules.

Robert Brennan's autobiography shows the IRB machine at work in 1917 and the growing dominance of Michael Collins at both the Sinn Féin Árd-Fheis and the Volunteer convention. 'Before I went to Dublin for the Árd-Fheis', he says, 'I got an order from the IRB to see Collins before the meeting. In one of the houses on the west side of Parnell Square, I found a regular queue of men from all part of the country. Mick, sitting at a table, handed me a typed list. It was the ticket the Wexfordmen were to support for the National Executive.' A trial of strength was expected between de Valera, whom the IRB were backing, and Griffith, whose programme was not advanced enough for them, but the struggle did not materialise. Behind the scenes a compromise was worked out involving the international recognition of the Irish Republic as an aim to be worked for, and Griffith made way for de Valera to become the President of the organisation that Griffith had founded and headed for many years. In the election of the executive, however, most of the persons on the IRB list were beaten; but things went differently at the Volunteer convention held later in the year. On this occasion the IRB captured nearly all the seats on the Volunteer executive.[16] Thus Collins became Director of Organisation, Diarmuid Lynch, Director of Communications and Seán Mc-Garry, General Secretary. This was a repeat of what the IRB had done on the original Volunteer headquarters staff.

Having done this, the IRB employed extraordinary vigour in the recruiting, training and arming of Volunteers, so much so that by the early days of November 1918 Dublin Castle was rather alarmed. In a Commons debate on the government of Ireland Edward Shortt, the Chief Secretary, admitted that the question of the activities of the Irish Volunteers, dominated as they were by the Irish Republican Brotherhood, had arisen once more. They had made preparations for fresh acts of violence of the most serious description; the previous week at one of their headquarters there was seized a sufficient quantity of high explosives, with fuses all prepared, to have blown up the whole of Belfast and Dublin. The IRB element was still there. Their numbers might be small but they were extremely dangerous, and unfortunately they to a certain extent controlled the proceedings of the Sinn Féin party and added to the government's distrust of it.[17]

2

The Great War ended on 11 November 1918, and on 14 December a general election was held in which the Sinn Féin candidates —a majority of them in jail for alleged involvement in a 'German Plot'—won 73 of the 105 Irish seats at Westminster. The candidates, according to Patrick O'Keeffe, the Secretary of Sinn Féin, were selected by Michael Collins, Harry Boland and Diarmuid O'Hegarty of the secret organisation,[18] a cynical example of democracy in practice, as P. S. O'Hegarty sarcastically observed in *The Victory of Sinn Féin*. In April 1919, at another Sinn Féin convention, Collins and Boland were again in their element, 'seeing with artless candour to its constitution'. The phrase is Frank O'Connor's, who says that what had gone on at previous conventions was only child's play compared to this. 'It was packed with Volunteers and members of the Irish Republican Brotherhood. Many of them did not even know what areas they were supposed to represent until they arrived at the Mansion House, where they were taken into a separate room and provided with suitable credentials. Young soldiers and conspirators, who regarded the political movement in much the same way as Collins himself, voted for men they had never met merely because of their good national record.' That evening, quiet men with good national records opened the papers to discover with a mild start of astonishment that without their own consent they had been elected members of the governing body of Sinn Féin.[19]

On 21 January 1919 the successful candidates in the general election who were free convened the first meeting in Dublin's Mansion House of an Irish parliament, which they called Dáil Éireann. The subsequent history of this body is too well known to require restatement. Its republican character, however, its determination to legislate for Irish affairs, its search for international recognition, and more particularly its election of a President and government, created a problem for the IRB, whose current Constitution declared the Supreme Council to be in fact, as well as by right, the sole government of the Irish Republic, that the President of the IRB was the President of the Republic, and that the enactments of the IRB were the laws of the Republic until such time as Ireland secured national independence and a permanent republican government was established.

Seán Ó Muirthile, who was the Secretary of the Supreme Council at this time, describes in an unpublished memoir, of which there is a copy in the late Seán Mac Eóin's papers, the steps taken to meet the situation. Many of the deputies, deemed to have been elected to Dáil Éireann as a result of the British general election, were, of course, IRB members. So too were members of the Dáil cabinet, notably Michael Collins, and officials of the secretariat, like Diarmuid O'Hegarty. Their natural concern was to reconcile conflicting positions, not to maintain two bodies in conditions likely to cause difficulties. The possibility of this happening may have been seen at the beginning of 1919, when the two Presidents of the Republic, McGarry of the IRB and de Valera of Dáil Éireann, found themselves in Lincoln Prison together and were both rescued by Michael Collins and Harry Boland, two of the vital new generation of IRB men. The situation became acute when Dáil Éireann required from all servants and soldiers of the Irish Republic an oath of allegiance to the Republic and to its government, Dáil Éireann.

There was no question, of course, that the IRB would go out of business, which was what some former members, like Cathal Brugha, the Minister of Defence in the government of the Dáil, believed the situation demanded, for Collins and other members of the Supreme Council were convinced that 'the Organisation' had still important work to do. Instead of disbanding they added to the relevant part of the Constitution of 1917 a couple of clauses which they prefaced by a statement that what they were doing was necessary because the policy of the IRB had succeeded in establishing a duly elected public authority that was competent to declare the will and give expression to the desire of the Irish people to secure the international recognition of the Irish Republic. The first of these clauses declared that members might in accordance with the spirit of their own IRB inception oath loyally accept and obey Dáil Éireann; and the second clause substituted for the concept of the President of the Irish Republican Brotherhood being in fact as well as by right the President of the Irish Republic a new provision which declared that the President of the IRB would direct the working of the Brotherhood, subject to the control of the Supreme Council or its Executive, of which he was one of three members. In this fashion, Ó Muirthile says, the IRB, cautiously safeguarding its rights pending the establishment of a freely functioning republican government, readily gave its allegiance to the Dáil. This seems to have meant that the governmental powers of the Supreme Council were ceded to Dáil Éireann and that the problem of the joint presidency of the Republic was disposed of. The changes were shown as 'Addenda to Constitution, September 1919' in a document published by the IRB and described as 'Constitution as revised to date 1920', but which otherwise does not differ from that of 1917.

By this time the first shots had been fired in a guerrilla campaign in which ambushes, raids on police barracks and planned assassination on the Irish side were answered by the British with internment camps, the shooting-up and burning of towns, executions and general terrorising. This was something very different from the honourable open warfare that Kickham, O'Leary and company had extolled in the old days. And yet, in the strange Irish way in which piety and xenophobia intertwine, people could sing exultantly 'Let me carry Your Cross for Ireland, Lord', which Ashe, IRB President and hunger striker, had composed.

The IRB through Harry Boland, its man in America, supported de Valera when unexpectedly, during his campaign in that country for the international recognition of the Republic and the raising of funds for the struggle at home, the Clan na Gael leaders John Devoy and Judge Daniel Cohalan refrained for reasons of domestic politics from according their support. The ensuing conflict must have greatly alarmed the IRB, to whom for more than fifty years the Clan had given the moral and financial sustenance which enabled it to propagate its republican ideas. It had provided the initiative and the means for the Easter Rising. It had also supplied the money with which the IRB was reorganised after the Rising, enabling it, as it had recently claimed when changing its Constitution, to establish Dáil Éireann, and was the chief agency in sending to Ireland a Relief Fund of $350,000 for the families of the executed and

G

imprisoned men. Naturally, Seán Ó Muirthile says, the proud leaders of a movement with such a record were slow to take dictation from any source. The position was that for ten years or so the Supreme Council of the IRB had felt that the Clan ought to be a subsidiary body of theirs, having its policy dictated from Ireland, whereas the Clan felt that they should be free to deal with matters affecting Ireland in the United States without interference from Ireland. They certainly were not content to hold the ladder for de Valera as he climbed to fame in America. The phrase is Ó Muirthile's. He, looking back on the rift that occurred, suggests that it might have been avoided if, on the one hand, de Valera and his companion Harry Boland had not suffered from an 'over-observance' of their own importance and a tendency to ignore the influence of Devoy and Cohalan, and if, on the other hand, Devoy and Cohalan had a more ample appreciation of the position de Valera then occupied. Boland and Patrick Moylett successively had replaced McGarry as President of the Supreme Council of the IRB—when is not clear —and Collins had replaced Moylett about the time Boland went to the United States. Collins and Boland were the closest of friends: more than that, they were to a lot of people the IRB.[20]

Being President of the IRB was only one of the many hats Collins wore at this period; but that particular post placed him in an intriguing situation in November 1920 when de Valera was in America and Arthur Griffith was in prison. At that point Collins became Acting President of the Republic in succession to Griffith. But as head of the IRB he was, or had recently been, in the terms of 'the Organisation', the real head of the whole movement and of the revolutionary government, and was thus merely succeeding openly to a position accorded him secretly and symbolically by the IRB.[21] He was also Minister for Finance, and from time to time he occupied simultaneously or consecutively a number of military roles, the most influential being that of Director of Intelligence. Through his IRB agents in the ports and on the ships he practically controlled all activities abroad. Almost every gun, every pound of ammunition, every ton of coke for the bomb factories, passed through his hands. Yet this did not by any means exhaust the total of his activities. He looked after the defence of court-martialled prisoners and the needs of their relatives, kept in touch with them through the warders, and organised and maintained his own secret lines of communication. It is not an exaggeration to say that this man Collins, having established through the IRB, and with startling suddenness, an ascendancy over the whole revolutionary movement, carried the war against the British on his shoulders.[22]

Two from a number of contemporary descriptions of Collins at the heart of things may be quoted in confirmation of this judgment. It fell to the lot of Tom Barry, an outstanding IRB officer, to see Collins at close quarters day by day for a week in the spring of 1921. Barry had been ordered to Dublin to discuss the progress of the war in the South with the cabinet and GHQ, and Collins arranged his programme.

> Indeed, [Barry later recalled] it was he who had arranged my billeting and briefing. During that time I stayed at some of his hide-outs and I visited four of his offices from which he conducted his IRA and Dáil Éireann business. At one he would meet some of his colleagues of GHQ for a discussion on army matters, then he would drive to another rendezvous to meet some sailors or dockers who were bringing in some arms or ammunition from Britain, then to another office to meet people from the country with collections for the Dáil Loan; from these I saw him go to another meeting place to meet Brigade Officers from country units. . . . And so he went on from early morning until late at night, working and plotting, striving against the forces of occupation. During all this period he had many hair-breadth escapes. Had he been captured and recognised, he would not have got an easy death.[23]

Piaras Béaslaí calls up a picture of a typical night at Vaughan's Hotel on Parnell Square in the city of Dublin :

> Around the table in the centre of the large smoke-room a group of us are seated, conversing in low tones, seriously but with an occasional laugh or frivolous remark. The regular frequenters of the place have a vocabulary of their own, a number of catchwords not intelligible to the uninitiated. Here are Dick McKee, Dublin Brigadier; Diarmuid O'Hegarty; Gearóid O'Sullivan, Adjutant-General; Rory O'Connor; Eamonn Fleming (Leinster Organiser of the Dáil Loan); Liam Tobin and Tom Cullen (Chief Intelligence Officers) and one

or two other intimates of the group such as Seán Ó Muirthile. 'Mick' has not yet arrived.

Sitting back against the wall in silence are six men, from different parts of the country, each waiting to see the Big Man. . . . Suddenly quick footsteps are heard bounding up the stairs.

The strange men start, almost fearing a raid by Black and Tans. The door is swung open and Mick strides rapidly into the room. He looks around, and all the men at the back rise and make a gesture to attract his attention. He scans them all rapidly, selects one, beckons to him, and calls him aside. In about three minutes he has got the gist of the man's business, made a decision, and scribbled a line on a sheet which he tears out of his notebook and places in his sock.

Then he calls the next man and quickly grasps his problem. He makes an appointment for that man at a certain spot at a certain hour next day—and woe betide that man if he comes a minute late!

With amazing speed he disposes of all the problems, and sends the men away contented. So thoroughly does he enter into each matter that each man has the impression that it is one of his greatest concerns.

Then he turns to those left around the table, calls the very reliable and trusted [porter] Christy Harte, and orders a round of drinks for the party. . . . He enters into the conversation of the others, picking up almost immediately the thread and interposing a relevant remark. He does not at first sit down. His restless energy finds vent in various sudden movements, which a chair would hamper.

His face continually changes its expression, as he speaks or listens. He looks now grim, now jovial, now angrily impatient, now deadly serious, now impishly mischievous. When he encounters serious opposition he thrusts out his chin doggedly and turns his head round till it is nearly in a line with his shoulder.

Frank Thornton arrives with a report of enemy activity and Collins goes aside to discuss the matter with him, Tobin and Cullen, and quickly determines what is to be done. The Intelligence Officers disappear for a time, and Collins returns and announces he will stay in the hotel for the night. He asks to be called at seven in the morning. Gearóid O'Sullivan and Seán Ó Muirthile are also staying, and when he rises in the morning and finds they are still asleep in bed, he enters their room to waken them with a fire extinguisher![24]

As Director of Intelligence Collins put into reverse the plan by which the British for decades had disposed of the Fenian men. The Royal Irish Constabulary and the Dublin Metropolitan Police had always been the government's eyes and ears. Collins, by infiltrating these forces, turned their intelligence capacities to his own use so that they enabled him, with utter ruthlessness, to destroy British agents and informers as they came on the scene, and with them the old G (Detective) Division of the Dublin police which for so many years had frustrated the activities of the IRB. John Mallon, Samuel Lee and Robert Anderson, and Nicholas Gosselin surely turned in their graves at the sight of this unbelievable transformation of the security scene, which Collins was further able to exploit through his agents in the Post Office, in the prisons and on the railways. His most daring personal coup was to visit the detective headquarters of the Dublin Metropolitan Police late one night in the company of a G-man, Ned Broy. They crept up the stairs together, past the dormitory in which Broy had locked his sleeping colleagues, and into the record room, where Collins worked into the early hours, turning over the secret files, one of them about himself, and making notes for future reference.

His *chef d'oeuvre*, on 'Bloody Sunday', 21 November 1920, was a simultaneous attack on officers living in various parts of Dublin who, though apparently ordinary civilians, were attached to a force of British Intelligence specialists formed in London under Major C. A. Cameron. Eleven of these were shot, some of them in front of their wives, and Collins excused this utterly cold-blooded business on the ground that if he had not got his blow in first, he and his men would have been eliminated. He certainly had good reason to fear this eventuality. In a letter to Dublin Castle that had come into his possession, the Commissioner for the Munster No. 1 Division of the augmented Royal Irish Constabulary mentioned that he had learned from Major-General H. H. Tudor of a new policy and plan to stamp out terrorism by secret murder.[25] The policy had already been imple-

mented. On the eve of 'Bloody Sunday' three Volunteers, two
of them senior officers, were shot dead in Dublin Castle, allegedly
while trying to escape. And, in reaction to the shooting of their
Intelligence Officers, some lorry loads of British Auxiliaries drove
that Sunday afternoon into Croke Park where a football match
was being played and fired on the crowd, killing fourteen people
and wounding another sixty or so.

A few individuals privately protested against the turn the war
on the Irish side had taken since a group of Tipperary Volunteers, entirely on their own initiative, had at Soloheadbeg am-
bushed police escorting a load of gelignite for quarrying. Deputy
Liam de Roiste complained at a private meeting of Dáil Éireann
on 25 January 1921 that there were many indisciplined forces
committing acts which had bad effects, and this was not the
sort of thing the movement should tolerate.[26] Another deputy,
Roger Sweetman, raised the subject in a letter to the press and
again at the same private meeting of the Dáil. He was quite
certain, he said, that a number of things like the events of that
Bloody Sunday would bring destruction to the Irish cause; he
wanted nothing done which they as moderate men could not
stand over. But though Sweetman was praised for his moral
courage, his protest received no support from his colleagues, and
he felt obliged to resign the next day. In a personal memoir,
written in later years, he enlarged considerably on the official
report of what took place at that meeting of the Dáil, which he
alleges was a sort of an IRA occasion, as most of the moderates
were in prison. De Valera, who had just returned from America,
made a statement suggesting that activities which savoured of
murder should be given up. Sweetman records the reaction in
the Dáil:

> Man after man of the IRA got up when he had finished and
> turned him down, saying that far from these activities being
> abolished or reduced they should be greatly increased. Where-
> upon he [de Valera] gathered up his papers and left, saying
> he had an appointment elsewhere. But either before or after
> his statement, but while he was there, I read him the memo,
> which I told him I had prepared for my interview with him
> which he had invited but shirked. The sequel was curious.
> De Valera made no considered reply [to the debate]. . . . Two

resolutions were then passed, I alone dissenting: (i) that all British Ministers should be shot and (ii) on a day to be fixed, all men in British uniform in the streets of Dublin should be shot.

But two men who were present at the meeting deny both the substance and detail of Sweetman's statement.[27]

Collins achieved much of his military success with the help of a small group of well-placed members of the DMP who passed out fundamental information to him, a small 'Squad' of carefully chosen gunmen sometimes called the 'Guard', and a larger Active Service Unit—these latter two elements comprising in all about 120 men. When the Squad was being formed in September 1919, with the authority of the Dáil government, Collins emphasised its selective character. They were not to discuss their movements or actions with Volunteer officers or anybody else. 'He gave us a short talk,' said one of them who had come through the IRB, the Fianna, the Volunteers and had participated in the 1916 Rising, 'the gist of which was that any of us who had read Irish history would know that no organisation in the past had an Intelligence system through which spies and informers could be dealt with effectively. That position would be rectified by the Squad which would take orders directly from himself.' He said this in the presence of Mulcahy, the Chief of Staff; the place in which he said it was, interestingly enough, the Keating Branch of the Gaelic League at 46 Parnell Square, where much more than Irish language had been taught.[28] This was the branch where, according to Mulcahy, 'they were all IRB people',[29] as indeed all or nearly all the members of the Squad and Active Service Unit were. Collins would have seen to that.

At this time some Circles were meeting less regularly than they were formally required to do. Speaking of those he was in a position to know about, Mulcahy said that they probably held no meetings at all after 1917: he, at any rate, attended none. Maurice ('Moss') Twomey, a noted IRA leader, in conversation with the present writer, confirmed this from his own experience in North Cork. On the other hand, Liam O'Doherty, the commandant of a Dublin battalion of the IRA, told the present writer that the Jemmy Hope Circle, consisting almost entirely of grocers' assistants, to which he had belonged since 1911, held a monthly meeting until he left it in April 1922. Mulcahy, of course, did not mean that by not holding regular meetings the IRB generally was inactive. He emphasised that Collins's spectacularly successful Intelligence machinery was built upon it. Without it de Valera could not have been brought to America, nor could military supplies have been imported through English and Scottish ports.[30] In some of these ports the IRB took a hand with the local Volunteers in destroying warehouses and timber yards, and elsewhere in England they made it hot for the families of Black and Tans and Auxiliaries who formed the spearhead of the government's attempt to break the Volunteers, now increasingly referred to as the IRA.

After Christmas 1919 Collins, in a communication about the current relationship of the two Fenian-connected organisations, the IRB itself and the American Clan na Gael, thanked the Clan for the financial and other assistance which had enabled weapons to be placed in the hands of Irishmen. He reiterated that the Rising of 1916 was the outcome of their joint work, and when he heard of a truce between Devoy and de Valera he wrote again 'welcoming the sanity and better feelings likely to accrue'. But when the Supreme Council raised, through Boland, the question as to whether the Clan regarded itself as a subsidiary body to the home organisation or as independent no reply was received. The Clan was in a bad way as a result of the clash which, Ó Muirthile too briefly explains, arose when de Valera, brushing aside suggestions from Devoy and Cohalan, insisted on bringing the Irish Question to the notice in turn of the two big American political parties. In so doing he obtained plenty of sympathy but no recognition for the Irish Republic. In July 1920 Diarmuid Lynch, a former member of the Supreme Council of the IRB, resigned his Dáil seat, basing his decision to do so, he said, upon an intimate knowledge of conditions in America and upon his general agreement with Devoy and Cohalan.

Boland returned to Dublin the following September. He asked for no fresh powers from the Supreme Council, nor were they given to him; neither had he any suggestion to offer other than that Devoy should be called to order. He returned to America and almost immediately took what Ó Muirthile terms the preposterous step of severing the Clan na Gael from the IRB, using the public press as the unprecedented means of announcing what he had done. The shocked Supreme Council met when they heard the news, but a suggestion that Boland should be recalled and his authority withdrawn was turned down. The Council next heard that he had begun forming a 'reorganised' Clan na Gael with Joe McGarrity of Philadelphia as its leading figure, and that de Valera had announced plans for a new open organisation, the Association for the Recognition of the Irish Republic, which thereafter coexisted with the Friends of Irish Freedom, the open organisation founded by the Clan some weeks before the Easter Rising. The rapid spread of the 'reorganised' Clan enabled supplies of money and some arms to be sent speedily to Ireland; but recognition of this new body, whose secretary was the old Fenian Luke Dillon who had been with Jackie Nolan in the attempt on the Welland Canal, was withheld by the IRB.[31] Collins regretted intensely that John Devoy should have suffered a certain ostracism as a result of the clashes with de Valera and Boland and never lost sight of the need to reunite the Irish forces in the United States.

3

During the struggle, which ended with a truce with the British in July 1921, the IRB became 'a rather remote, unreal and shadowy kind of organisation' to the rank-and-file member who was caught up in the activities of the Volunteers. 'It was a vague force far away in the distance, which very rarely affected one's actions, but which one felt might materialise some time in a more definite form.' This was the view of the historian James Hogan, who was in the IRB as well as being an active Volunteer; he was later to become a Director of Intelligence and Head of Inspection in the army of the Provisional Government and the Irish Free State.

I was in action with the IRA [he wrote] and was continually meeting senior and junior officers, and in all that time I only heard an odd passing reference to the IRB. In effect the IRB did not seem to cross the horizon of the ordinary IRA officer except very seldom. . . . Being a member was like being vaccinated—something that happened once, and that was all about it.

No member of the IRB in those pre-Truce days could fail
G*

to see that, as the Volunteer movement was growing strong and taking the whole burden of the national fight on its back, it was absorbing and assimilating the IRB . . . the secret organisation was losing itself in the open organisation. . . . In fact, I remember non-IRB members of the Volunteers referring contemptuously to the IRB men in a particular county and explaining the county's inactivity by the fact that all the senior Volunteer officers there were IRB men. I also remember how on one occasion two diverse orders were given to a Volunteer officer who was a member of the IRB, and as one order emanated from an IRB Volunteer officer, and the other came from a non-IRB Volunteer officer, the question was which order should be obeyed. It was decided that an IRA order over-ruled an IRB order. When the IRB ceased to be in a position to act, it was ceasing to exist, and I would say that on the eve of the Truce the IRB was semi-moribund beneath, and alive only on top or in its upper levels.[32]

Florrie O'Donoghue, the former adjutant of a Cork brigade of the IRA and an authority on the history of the period, confirmed that in the last six months before the Truce the activities of the IRB in a large area of the South were nominal. Nevertheless, 'the Organisation' had vitality and significance in that it bound a group of men into an historic and respected brotherhood which evoked loyalty of a high order, without undermining in any way the discipline of the IRA. At this time the total IRB membership for the counties of Cork, Kerry and Waterford was 1,170 compared with an IRA strength of 31,000.[33]

This is also what Liam Deasy, the adjutant of Cork's 3rd Brigade, thought. In his experience the IRA profited from IRB stimulation through the whole course of the fight with the British. He very appositely describes a visit to Dublin at Easter 1921 of brigade officers for discussions with the general staff. They met *first* in their IRB capacity, with Collins in the chair, before reassembling later as IRA men.[34] The IRB meeting was concerned with the recruitment of serving IRA men in order to keep the IRB ideal to the fore, and to strengthen incidentally the IRB's grip on the fighting men.[35]

'On top or in its upper levels' the IRB was certainly active. Frequent meetings of the Supreme Council and still more frequent meetings of the Executive (Collins, O'Hegarty and Ó Muirthile) were held during the whole of the period from January 1919 till the Truce. They were held in circumstances of great difficulty. Ó Muirthile describes one of his own experiences as follows :

> I was going from Parnell Square to Barry's Hotel with two packets of IRB papers for a meeting of the Supreme Council one Saturday evening. I had purchased a couple of evening papers, and loosely wrapped them around the documents, and when passing through Temple Street I was held up and searched by British Military who, while I held both hands aloft with a bundle of papers in each of them that would, as the saying goes in Ireland, 'hang the country', searched my pockets and let me go. Mick was sitting in a private room at the Hotel when I arrived, and when I told him my story he just laughed at me.[36]

The British realised the continuing need to check the movements of IRB men and, towards that end, considered at a Prime Minister's conference in July 1920 a proposal from Tudor, the head of the Irish police, to make passports necessary for entry into Ireland.[37]

The Truce prepared the way for negotiations with the British on the great question of how the association of Ireland with the community of nations known as the British Empire could best be reconciled with Irish national aspirations.

> At a meeting of the Executive, held shortly before the declaration of the Truce [Ó Muirthile says] we decided to call the whole Council and put the matter before them. Of all the bodies contributing to the War I think the Supreme Council had perhaps the best knowledge of the actual strength or weakness of the forces operating under Dáil Éireann, because secrets that were not always available to other bodies were from time to time before the Supreme Council. In other words, a good deal of the 'bluff' that was essential in public was shed in the IRB Council meetings, and realities were discussed. Collins and others who were high in the Volunteer councils were always present. The Supreme Council on this occasion unanimously agreed that the ends of the Organisation would be advanced by the representatives of Ireland entering

into the proposed conference and that the influence of the Organisation should be directed towards that end.[38]

No obstacles were placed in the way of Collins going to London as one of the Irish plenipotentiaries, though some members thought there was something sinister behind the suggestion and had the temerity to tell him that he was likely to become a scapegoat. There was an argument which Collins ended by saying: 'Let them make a scapegoat or anything they wish of me. We have accepted the situation as it is, and some one must go.'[39]

Bluff is, of course, an important element in military strategy, and it was employed by the IRA to cover their deficiencies in men and material. The Truce, when it came, brought considerable relief to the flying columns and active service units. From the South a deputation of IRA officers had gone to GHQ to explain that, owing to the shortage of arms and ammunition and enemy pressure, they were unable to continue the fight.[40] That any such suggestion was made has been denied, but there can be no doubt about the shortage of material. It was almost a *sine qua non* in some areas that weapons had to be won from the enemy to enable further activity to take place. The historian F. S. L. Lyons quotes the statement of Mulcahy, the IRA's Chief of Staff, to Dáil Éireann that because the IRA had to rely on rifles, machine-guns and home-made bombs they were unable to drive the British forces from anything more substantial than a police barracks; and a statement said to have been made by Collins to the Chief Secretary, in the aftermath of the negotiations with the British, admitted that the Irish resistance could not have lasted more than another three weeks.[41] 'The Truce was agreed to', Ó Muirthile said, 'because it was felt that the military campaign against the British could have no further success, and that perhaps terms could be obtained that would put Ireland in a position from which she could develop on lines that would enable her to achieve complete independence. In this matter the IRB was consulted and approval given to the Truce.'[42]

For their part, the British had good reasons for welcoming a truce. The coalition cabinet had failed to produce a properly structured system of co-ordinated action between the civil, police and military authorities and, in the light of political and public opinion, they were loth to convert a struggle with what some of them saw as a 'murder gang' into an outright war against the Irish people until the possibility of reaching some form of agreement in discussions with Sinn Féin could be explored.[43] Their most serious deficiency was a dependable Intelligence service. The police service, as we have seen, had been demoralised in the first instance by the actions of ministers and public servants as far back as the 1900s, and its morale was not boosted by the withdrawal in 1919 of the extra allowance for members of the RIC Special Branch.[44] The Rising of 1916 had been permitted to take place in circumstances that were no credit whatever to British intelligence and administration and involved an incredible misuse of information that became available from *outside* Ireland.[45] Three worsening factors operated thereafter: the internal demoralisation of the police forces, the militarising of the RIC and the introduction into it of non-Irish elements, Black and Tans and Auxiliaries, and, of course, Collins's robust countermethods. Spontaneous informers, so plentiful in earlier times, had become a rare breed: it was only through what they picked up in raids or sweeps or through the exercise of terror on individuals that the Castle authorities learned anything of value.

In the closing stages of the fight, the burning of the Dublin Custom House was a gigantic measure of defiance which paid political dividends, but it led to six men being killed, twelve wounded and about seventy captured, among them some of the best fighting material in the country. And the IRA were so thin on the ground that a diversion enabling the captured men to escape could not be improvised. 'We could not find a single man,' Emmet Dalton told the present writer. The 'Big Fellow' was understandably greatly concerned, for among those captured were a number of men from his own entourage, some of whom were 'wanted' for the Bloody Sunday shootings. The Truce saved their lives. That apart, Collins would not have disagreed altogether with the claim made in a British report he intercepted during the Truce that three months earlier the rebel organisation throughout the country was in a precarious condition.[46]

4

The Treaty which emerged from the London Conference on the 6 December 1921 gave Ireland an Irish Free State with essentially the same expanding status as Canada and Australia. It was debated by the Supreme Council, Ó Muirthile says, in the light of the article in the IRB Constitution which provided that the organisation would support every movement calculated to advance the cause of Irish national independence consistent with the preservation of its own integrity. It would perhaps have been more relevant for Ó Muirthile to have spoken of the deviations in the 1870s and 1880s from the straight and narrow republican path in order the sooner to reach the desired goal. Collins, Ó Muirthile tells us, had kept the Council informed week by week of the progress of the negotiations, and the Council in turn had placed Collins quickly in possession of their opinions. At one stage he produced to a Council meeting, attended by ten of the fifteen members, the draft Treaty. Dissatisfaction was expressed about the form of the Oath to be taken by deputies of the Irish Free State parliament on which the British insisted, and three of those present—all high-ranking Volunteer officers—prepared an alternative draft which they thought would satisfy the Volunteer mind. This first dealt with allegiance to the Irish Free State and contained mention of the King in a supplementary paragraph. When Ó Muirthile saw the Treaty in its final form he recognised that the Oath had assumed the change suggested by the Supreme Council. However, it was the Oath in this form which was the cause of most of the subsequent divisions in the IRB, in Dáil Éireann and throughout the country, though in all of those areas majorities were found in favour of the Treaty. In the Supreme Council the voting was eleven for and four against.

Shortly after the agreement with the British, Collins told a meeting of the IRB Circle of which he was Centre how the Treaty position had arisen. He thought it necessary to do this because, as he said, his first duty was to the IRB and he cared nothing for any other opinion. He explained that in the previous June the total number of men in active service units all over Ireland was 1,617, that they had but one weapon per man, that they had not as much as one cartridge per gun, that their ammunition supply route had just been discovered by the British, and that they had not been able to organise another. To that situation the Truce came as a godsend. Concerning the negotiations, he had told de Valera that he was not the person to go to London, that de Valera could get a better settlement if he left him at home as a sort of dark horse. He would be able to say in a crisis: 'We cannot accept that. Collins and the IRB would not stand for it.' The IRB could be played up as a last card.[47]

In America Devoy and Cohalan reacted to the Treaty in the same way as the Supreme Council of the IRB did. They, like others in the Fenian tradition, were impressed by the 'stepping-stone' argument, the argument that the settlement with Britain gave Ireland the freedom to achieve freedom. In the previous July Collins and Ó Muirthile had had several interviews with an envoy from the old Clan na Gael, who were concerned to redress the grievances they had suffered as the result of 'Harry Boland's high-handed attitude': Devoy particularly felt that he had been unjustly dealt with. The envoy took back to America a memorandum asking for information regarding the Clan's position *vis-à-vis* the United States and suggesting the appointment of a delegation to come to Ireland for talks to which 'the other body' was also being invited. Devoy's reply was to reject the proposal of a delegate conference and simply to ask for a resumption of the old relations, 'each body [the old Clan and the IRB] yielding to the other the fullest measure of confidence and co-operation, each supreme in its own field and working for a common end against the enemy of both'. Collins was disappointed. With some other members of the Supreme Council he was anxious to undo whatever wrong had been done without entirely alienating the support of the new Clan; but as no further progress seemed possible it was decided to leave the matter in abeyance until the outcome of the negotiations with the British was known. But 'Collins never lost sight of the matter and stuck to the desire to put things right'.[48] In a cable to Devoy in February 1922 he said: 'Our idea was to have some sort of a world-wide Irish federation, each separate part working through the government and in accordance with the laws of the country where it had its being, but all joined by common ties of blood and race. Unfortunately some of those we sent to America did not understand the vital principle of that idea, and more unfortunately still we were not aware of this until it was too late.'[49]

In March 1922 Denis McCullough went out to the United States as a Special Commissioner from Dáil Éireann to co-operate with the Dáil's newly appointed Envoy Extraordinary, Professor T. A. Smiddy, in an effort to bring about unity among Irish-

Americans on the principle of acquiescence by them in the wishes of the Irish people as constitutionally expressed. This would have involved supporting the Irish government for the time being, and abstention from taking sides as between Irish political parties.[50] McCullough was Collins's selection for this delicate mission. Not having resumed his membership of the IRB after 1916, he had had nothing whatever to do with the circumstances that brought about the American dissensions. He was, moreover, well known and highly thought of in separatist circles on both sides of the Atlantic, so that Collins and the other members of the IRB Executive, when they appraised the situation, saw him as a likely peacemaker, if peace among the Irish in America was at all possible.

Before McCullough left Dublin Seán Ó Muirthile gave him a letter outlining the plan of action he was to follow as the semi-official representative of the IRB. To this letter were attached a copy of the Supreme Council's general circular on the Treaty issue and a copy of a communication headed 'The Organisation' which had been given to Joe McGarrity of Philadelphia, who had come to Dublin seeking recognition from the 'parent organisation' for the section of the Clan na Gael he represented. Recognition was in fact given, but it was explained that it extended only to the inner organisation and not to the public political movement. The ideal position in America, McGarrity was told, would be to reunite the contending forces.

McCullough's mission was a failure, despite enormous efforts on his part. Among the leaders of the Cohalan–Devoy faction he found an implacable bitterness, and on the other side a firm conviction that the split was irremediable. McCullough told Collins that matters that rankled with the Cohalan–Devoy group and made them bitter and hard to deal with were a resolution of condemnation of them standing in the minutes of the Dáil and lack of connection with the IRB at home.

The opponents of the Treaty in Ireland alleged that the Supreme Council of the IRB, through its pro-Treaty majority, employed all its resources to influence the groups and meetings by which the Treaty was discussed. De Valera, writing to Joe McGarrity on 21 December 1921 while the debate in Dáil Éireann on the Treaty was still in progress, declared that Collins, of whose preliminary work with the IRB he said he had heard

something, had got the IRB machine working. 'The Dáil
members of the IRB were told that the acceptance of the Treaty
would be the quickest way to the Republic; and a lot of other
stuff which time only will explode. . . . Curse secret societies!
. . . I have been tempted several times', he said, 'to take drastic
action, as I was entitled to legally, but then the Army is divided
and the people wouldn't stand for it, and nobody but the enemy
would win if I took it.'[51] And when the debate was over and the
Treaty carried by a small majority no one was more incensed
than Seán T. O'Kelly.

> How could it be accepted [he wrote] that that crowd who
> renounced their allegiance so promptly were honest men? I
> could never understand or explain how those who called them-
> selves the Supreme Council of the Irish Republican Brother-
> hood could order the members of their circles in the Dáil to
> cast a vote in favour of the Treaty. It made me sick to think
> that it was the Brotherhood which was responsible for the
> Dáil's final decision. The majority would have gone against
> the Treaty only for the Brotherhood's votes in the Dáil. What
> sort of people were those who were in control of the Brother-
> hood?[52]

O'Kelly's account then proceeds to examine the motives of
Collins and others to their detriment.

Ó Muirthile, however, denies that undue influence was brought
to bear on Dáil members. No member of the Dáil had been able
to say truthfully that he had been ordered to vote one way or
the other. Whatever was done from an IRB standpoint was done
in an official way, and no instructions, verbal or written, were
issued except by or on behalf of the Supreme Council, which at
that time contained several members who were opposed to the
Treaty, notably Harry Boland, Austin Stack and Liam Lynch.
'Before the Dáil debates on the Treaty', Ó Muirthile says, 'I
issued to the IRB men, who were also TDs [members of Dáil
Éireann], on behalf of the Supreme Council, the following
document:

> The Supreme Council having due regard to the Constitution
> of the Organisation, has decided that the present Peace Treaty
> between Ireland and Great Britain should be ratified. Mem-

bers of the Organisation, however, who are to take public action, as representatives, are given freedom of action in the matter.

By Order,
Supreme Council,
12.12 1921'[53]

The debates in the Dáil began on 14 December 1921 and ended on 7 January 1922. On the 12 January, while the anti-Treaty members were still on it, the Supreme Council issued a statement explaining that the document of 12 December, to which objection had been raised particularly in the South, was for the information of its members in the Dáil. It had always been the policy of the IRB, the statement said, to make use of all instruments, political and otherwise, which were likely to aid in the attainment of a free independent republican government. The Supreme Council had decided that the Treaty should be ratified but that no action for or against it should be taken by the IRB as such. Some such situation as that presented by the Treaty had been obvious from the time of the Truce, and it would be inexpedient for the IRB to interfere in a situation that might have the result of bringing Ireland nearer to its ultimate goal. Until the issues were clearly defined, which could not be until the draft Irish Constitution based on the Treaty had been considered, the sole policy of the IRB, the army and the nation as a whole should be to maintain unity, so that these forces would be available to support the Republic when the proper opportunity arose. When the proposed Irish Constitution was published the policy to be adopted by the organisation would be discussed in accordance with Article 35 of the IRB Constitution as revised for 1920, which prescribed that the amendment of other relevant articles could only take place with the consent and approval of a majority of the County Centres in Ireland. In other words the County Centres would have a voice in deciding the IRB's attitude to the Constitution, when published, of the Irish Free State.

By the end of January 1922, however, the South Munster Division had unanimously decided to ignore this lead[54] and Harry Boland handed over to the members of the Army Council who opposed the Treaty a sum of $60,000 that Luke Dillon had cabled to him. Dillon subsequently asked for the return of this money, but Boland refused, speaking of a convention of the IRB to be held which he hoped would select a new Supreme Council that would throw all its strength behind the defence of the Republic. McGarrity then came over from America to assess the situation and, hopefully, to bring the opposing sides together and prevent a civil war. He found the IRB intact and almost solidly for the Treaty: this, of course, was the organisation with which the Clan was pledged to work in harmony and co-operation. That did not long continue to be the case. McGarrity himself from being a Treatyite moved to the support of the anti-Treaty forces; and in those of his papers that have been published there is no further reference to the possibility of a new Supreme Council of the IRB being elected to undo the decision of its predecessor.[55]

Collins's personal lead was widely followed in the IRB, the IRA, and throughout the country. Men frequently said that what was good enough for Mick was good enough for them. The phrase recurs in a contemporary anti-Treaty verse:

> God save the Southern part of Ireland,
> Three-quarters of a nation once again.
> To the Treaty we will stick,
> Sure it's good enough for Mick
> And the Father and the Mother of Sinn Féin.

P. S. O'Hegarty declared that Collins had come to dominate the whole movement. The IRB and IRA Executives had become mere machines for registering his plans, and through the group more particularly attached to him—the IRB no doubt—he also controlled Dáil Éireann and Sinn Féin.[56] And O'Hegarty does not hesitate to call him a dictator.[57] There is exaggeration in these statements, but it is undeniable that Collins exercised great power to great effect. He was the 'Big Fellow', in more senses than one. During the war with the British his determination to win was such that he never hesitated to overstep the theoretical jurisdiction of his office or to usurp the legitimate functions of others. Cathal Brugha, as Minister for Defence, was nationally responsible for all the armed forces of the Dáil, but Collins's Intelligence work expanded so much that it was him, not Brugha, that the military leaders were anxious to see when they came to Dublin for instructions. Collins had other advantages. As the guiding genius of the IRB he was in a position to pull strings here, there and everywhere, and insert his nominees in positions that fell vacant through death or imprisonment. And the British assessed the relative values of Collins and Brugha by offering £10,000 for one dead or alive and nothing for the other.[58]

It was, of course, a ridiculous situation that Collins *qua* Director of Intelligence should be Brugha's subordinate, and *qua* Minister of Finance his equal; however, it was not this but the legendary position Collins had acquired that affected Brugha most. He became jealous, publicly described Collins as a 'subordinate in a subordinate department of my office', and endeavoured at times to act independently of the army chiefs. One particularly mad idea of Brugha's, which Collins and Mulcahy scotched when they heard about it, was to take some of the best flying column leaders with him to London and, with machine-guns smuggled into the House of Commons, to annihilate the British cabinet as they sat on the front benches.[59] It does not seem to have crossed his mind that British ministers would be easier to replace than the few men who had made a name for themselves in the fighting in the Irish countryside, or that these same men, sticking out like sore fingers in the streets of London, if they ever got so far, would almost invite arrest.

Another enemy Collins made was Austin Stack, a member of the Supreme Council of the IRB and Minister for Home Affairs at the time of the Treaty negotiations. He was undoubtedly an indolent man in comparison with Collins but could be excused for feeling aggrieved when the 'Big Fellow', always critical of any inefficiency he observed, openly described Stack's department as 'a bloody joke'. Clearly there were some people who had reason to dislike the Treaty apart from the terms of the document.

5

Dáil Éireann decided in favour of the Treaty on 7 January 1922 and elected Arthur Griffith as President in place of Éamon de Valera. Collins as Chairman of a Provisional Government took over Dublin Castle from the Lord Lieutenant. The formal ceremony was as brief as could be. There was an exchange of courtesies between the two men and later between companies of outgoing khaki-clad and incoming green-clad soldiers. Collins must have sensed that he was making history. For that day, marred as it was by the division over the Treaty, was a great day for Ireland, for the forces, civil and military, in whose creation or functioning he had played so major a part, and not least for the IRB, whose supreme leader he was and which, through him, was recording its first and only unquestionable achievement: he was accepting the surrender of what for centuries had seemed impregnable, the centre and symbol of British government in Ireland. But Collins, we may imagine, had no time that particular day for deep recollection. He was, as always, a man hurrying on to his next appointment, and there was much to be done. So when an official greeted him with 'We're glad to see you, Mr Collins,' the 'Big Fellow', with a grin all over his face, replied 'Like hell you are!' and strode in to the Castle chamber to confront the uneasy Viceroy.

An effort was made to get more out of the Treaty immediately than was feasible. On this Collins and his supporters depended to win over men like Liam Lynch and, through them, such hesitating IRB and IRA men as from the outset were extremely critical of the Treaty's obviously obnoxious features. A republican constitution which 'knocked the Treaty end-ways' was therefore submitted as soon as possible to the British, but the British would not have it and the draft had to be substantially amended[60] before being presented to the Dáil, by which body it was approved in October 1922. In the meantime the Provisional Government was opposed in arms, protracted negotiations at leadership level to heal the divisions in the IRB and IRA having proved fruitless. This happened despite the production of a revised IRB Constitution[61] which accepted 'the present governmental position of An Saorstát' but declared once more that the Supreme Council of the IRB would remain the sole government of the Irish Republic until Ireland's complete independence was achieved, and that the President of the Supreme Council was the President of the Republic. Florrie O'Donoghue gives particulars of the IRB meetings in this connection, the last held on 19 April 1922, and he lists those he remembers who attended.[62]

A revealing decision was taken by the Supreme Council in the early weeks of 1922, namely to spend a £1,000 on a national political weekly, which was to attempt to maintain IRB principles during the developing crisis. This paper, *The Separatist*, with a sub-title invoking Tone's call 'to break the connection with England', was edited by P. S. O'Hegarty and ran from February to September 1922. It would have lasted longer had not an ominous strike in the Post Office made it impossible for O'Hegarty, who had become secretary of that department of the new state, to devote further time to it. *The Separatist* was in no sense an official IRB organ, and O'Hegarty was given a completely free hand in running it, but a declaration of policy in its first issue said nothing with which the Supreme Council would have disagreed :

> We stand for the complete separation of Ireland from England, without any association external or internal, save such association as independent nations normally conclude with each other for the mutual regulation of trade etc. That is the minimum and maximum of the Separatist demand. And in working for that we will use, as Separatists have always used, every movement which we can use, and take advantage of every situation which can bring us advantage.[63]

It was May 1923 before the anti-Treaty forces, at the end of a bitter and ruinous war, acknowledged defeat and dumped their arms. For some time they observed the fiction that theirs was the *de jure* government of a Republic that still existed, and for that purpose they maintained a council of deputies, a council of ministers or cabinet, and a Sinn Féin party, as well, of course, as an IRA that regarded itself as in direct descent from the original. The political side of this resistance ended with a split and the entry into the Dáil in 1927 of a new, but essentially anti-Treaty party, Fianna Fáil, leaving Sinn Féin thereafter as the party of political extremism. The military element had by this time more or less severed the connection with the politicians, and from that element there began a series of outcroppings culminating in the present-day Provisional and Official IRA, both of which have links with, or are fronted by, contemporary manifestations of political Sinn Féin.

The Treatyites meanwhile had revived for their political party the name of Cumann na nGaedheal which, it will be remembered, the police translated as 'The Confederation of the Gaels' when it made its first appearance in 1900. The new Cumann na nGaedheal was likewise to be a sort of confederation inasmuch as it was intended to bring together men of different classes, origins and creeds who were prepared to contribute to the building of the new state. There was room for other constitutional parties, of course, and these likewise began to emerge at the first general election held under the new dispensation in August 1923.

But by that time Michael Collins, the guiding genius of the IRB through the most vital years of its long history, was dead. The Civil War, which had been simmering from the early months of 1922, came to a head in June of that year, when the government, provoked by the arrest of the Deputy Chief of Staff of a rapidly expanding national army, built upon IRA and IRB men who had taken the Treaty side, attacked the Four Courts in Dublin which the anti-Treaty forces had seized and made their headquarters. Six weeks later Collins, the Commander-in-Chief of the national army, was killed in an ambush at Béal na mBláth in his native county. Griffith had died a few days before of a cerebral haemorrhage brought on by exhaustion. On the other side Harry Boland and Liam Lynch, both members of the Supreme Council of the IRB, met equally tragic deaths.

Much has been written about the manner of Collins's death, but all that really requires to be remembered about it is contained in a dispatch sent by Liam Lynch from his field GHQ to the officer commanding the 1st Southern Division on 28 August 1922. It read :

(i) Yours of the 24th inst. reporting attack on the enemy at Béal na mBláth to hand yesterday. Considering the very small number of men engaged, this was a most successful operation, and they are to be complimented on the fight made under such heavy fire and against such odds; (ii) Considering you were aware of the fact that the convoy contained an armoured car, it is surprising you had not mines laid to get this; (iii) Nothing could bring home more forcefully the awful unfortunate National situation at present than the fact that it has become necessary for Irishmen, and former comrades, to shoot such men as Michael Collins, who rendered such splendid service to the Republic in the late war against England. It is to be hoped that our present enemies will realise the folly of trying to crush the Republic before it is too late.[64]

The End of the Road

I

IT SEEMED already to some people that the IRB had not
survived the amputation of the Treaty issue, though it appeared
at the head of a list of associations proscribed in Northern
Ireland by the Civil Authorities (Special Powers) Act of 1922.
James Hogan thought it was dead and done with: within a
few months of the outbreak of the Civil War he no longer heard
any talk of the IRB and believed it was for practical purposes
extinct.[1] Kevin O'Higgins thought the same. The IRB died of
inanition, he said, in 1922 but was galvanised into life in the
first six months of 1923.[2]

But within days of the Dáil's acceptance of the agreement,
P. S. O'Hegarty, who had begun to act as a kind of spokesman
for 'the Organisation', declared that the Treaty would not settle
the Irish Question. Ireland's destiny was to be an independent
nation, not a member, associated or otherwise, of any empire.
The Irish Republican Brotherhood, which had been the political
sheet anchor of Ireland since Stephens founded it more than
sixty years before, would go on.[3]

Richard Mulcahy also denied that it had died. Its existence
was continuous, he said. This had to be so, because of the
commitment to work for a republic undertaken by those of its
members who had recommended the acceptance of the Treaty.[4]
He had, at the end of 1922 and the beginning of 1923, attended
at least one meeting in connection with the revision of the IRB
Constitution, to bring it into line with the new conditions in
Ireland. Ó Muirthile enlarged on this by saying that the activities of the IRB at this time were concerned with the physical
defence of the state. The IRB stood by the right of the will of
the people.[5] In 1919 the organisation's policy had been changed
to enable members loyally to accept and obey the authority of

Dáil Éireann which the IRB had succeeded in establishing. And again, after the withdrawal of the British forces, the acceptance of the new position and the consequential obedience to the public authority, was declared. By the public authority was meant Dáil Éireann as a whole as distinct from any party or section of it.[6]

By 1923 W. T. Cosgrave's government was facing up to its responsibilities as a member of the British Commonwealth of Nations, with Mulcahy as Minister for Defence, O'Higgins as Minister for Justice, Joseph McGrath as Minister for Industry and Commerce, Ernest Blythe as Minister for Finance and Desmond FitzGerald as Minister for External Affairs. All of these had belonged to the IRB and were now criticised by anti-Treaty acquaintances for having changed their ways and their company. 'The IRB days were brought to my mind yesterday', Diarmuid O'Hegarty, the secretary of the government, himself previously an IRB leader, was told, 'when I read of Desmond FitzGerald and Eóin Mac Néill being present at a Royal Dinner given at Buckingham Palace by the King and Queen. How Desmond made it fit in with his old IRB principles I could not understand.'[7]

The 'galvanising into life' mentioned by O'Higgins occurred in the following fashion. Towards the end of 1922 a number of prominent army officers, led by Major-General Liam Tobin and Colonel Charles F. Dalton, set about reviving the IRB in the army and met in Circles and groups at Portobello Barracks and elsewhere in Dublin. The first meeting may in fact have been held in the Viceregal Lodge, where Tobin was ADC to the Governor-General, T. M. Healy. Later, concluding that they would be unable to obtain a controlling influence over the Supreme Council, they proceeded to form a new body which they called the Irish Republican Army Organisation (IRAO). They received considerable encouragement from serving senior and junior officers in all parts of the country who had formerly belonged to the IRA and to whom, with a few exceptions, membership of the IRAO was confined. The exceptions included Sam Maguire, the Post Office official who brought Collins into the IRB when they worked together in London and who was a considerable force in Collins's Intelligence Department during the Anglo-Irish struggle. The IRAO found support

within the government party in the Dáil; and in Joseph Mc-
Grath, the Minister for Industry and Commerce, they had an
active influential sympathiser who helped to finance their activities.

At their first formal meeting in January–February 1923 Tobin
did some 'plain speaking'. They had followed Collins and
accepted the Treaty in exactly the same spirit as he did. 'We
firmly believed with him that the Treaty was only a stepping-
stone to a Republic. The late C-in-C [Collins] told me that he
had taken the oath of allegiance to the Republic and that oath
he would keep, Treaty or no Treaty—this is our position exactly.
The actions of the present GHQ staff since the C-in-C's death,
their open and secret hostility to us, his officers, has convinced
us that they have not the same outlook as he had.' The army
was not, Tobin insisted, a national army at all. It was composed
roughly of 40 per cent of the old IRA, 50 per cent ex-Britishers
and 10 per cent ex-civilians, the majority of whom were hostile
to the national ideals. A reorganisation was pending threatening
the future of many of their comrades and he demanded on their
behalf a committee of inquiry on which they should have equal
representation. In a *Brief History of Events* prepared by the
IRAO their objects were summarised as, firstly, a strong voice
in army policy with a view to securing complete national independence when a suitable occasion arose, and, secondly, the
control of vital sections of the army and the ousting of un-
desirable elements.

At a general meeting held in April 1923 Major-General
Patrick O'Daly objected to the action proposed, left the meeting
and, it was alleged, went straight to the C-in-C (Mulcahy) and
the Chief of General Staff (Seán MacMahon) and told them
everything that had happened at the meeting and the names of
those present. 'As a result of this unexpected development we
decided', the *Brief History of Events* recorded, 'to drop things
for a while as it meant reorganising again. The GHQ staff had
started to reorganise the IRB to counteract our efforts but had
said "Drop your organisation and we will drop ours." ' They
had secured a place for Major-General O'Daly on the Supreme
Council of the IRB and had also elected to the Council a
number of other senior officers who up till then had been working
for the IRAO as well as the general officers commanding the

military districts. One of these, Major-General Seán Mac Eóin, was a member already, and in his papers is a 'new' IRB Constitution dating from this period which gave the army substantial 'vocational representation' on a greatly enlarged Supreme Council. But a surviving GOC to whom the present writer has spoken has no knowledge of this part of the allegation. It does appear certain, however, that the army sometime in 1923 was given 'vocational representation' on the Supreme Council.[8]

To prevent 'Mick's ideals' being perverted, Tobin, Dalton and their friends succeeded in securing discussions with President Cosgrave and Mulcahy, the C-in-C. At the first of these, on 25 June 1923, feelings ran so high that Mulcahy walked out. He had found Liam Tobin 'very hard and bitter', Frank Thornton 'talkative and negative', Christy O'Malley 'in very bad aggressive humour', and Charlie Dalton with 'nothing to say'. But the atmosphere was better when they met again the following month. Mulcahy on this occasion gave the IRAO representatives an assurance that he was quite prepared to deal directly at any time with them—he conceded their absolute honesty of purpose and ideals—and to consider any representations they might wish to make on matters considered vital to the complete independence of Ireland, it being understood that this was, of necessity, a private and personal arrangement and not indicative of sectionalism of any kind in the army. But the IRAO declared that the representations subsequently made were of no avail, and a promise of one seat on the Supreme Council of the IRB (an allocation which they considered insufficient) was broken.

In a deteriorating situation in which the organisation of disgruntled armed men proceeded, the authorities, it was said, resorted to 'other attentions besides the policy of the cold shoulder'. According to *The Truth about the Army Crisis*, to which Tobin contributed a foreword, the government's 'secret service agents became very active. Spies [were] employed to dog our footsteps. Dictaphones to record our conversations were placed in offices where we were likely to meet. Men of the Intelligence Branch were put on to "make friends" with us. The agent provocateur came up from his underworld to suggest to one of our officers the murder of a member of the Army Council.'[9] The suggestion was presumably objectionable only because of its source. Assassination was for these men a means of dealing with their problem they would not have overlooked and, if what we have been told is true, one of them at one time did consider disposing of the Minister for Justice in this fashion. Attempts were to be made on O'Higgins as he attended a concert in the Metropole Cinema or as he left Kingsbridge railway station for his family place in the country, but these intentions, it is said, were frustrated as a result of information leaked to the government.

A secret approach to the anti-Treaty IRA with a view to bringing off jointly a *coup d'état* likewise came to nothing. This move is revealed in contemporary documents that were available to the authors of a recent Irish-language biography of de Valera. The anti-Treaty IRA understandably rejected the proposition. They would have been delighted, of course, to see the Irish Free State overthrown, but they had no regard whatever for the army officers who were scheming to bring this about and had no intention of becoming embroiled in their plans. Those officers, after all, had arrested and imprisoned the defenders of the Republic, as they conceived themselves to be. Anyhow, the anti-Treaty IRA had shortly before this reached a decision to bring the IRB to an end in so far as they could do so and had issued an order for their members to have nothing further to do with it.[10]

The trouble which had been brewing in the army since the early days of 1923 reached a crisis point in March 1924 on the release of the report of reorganisation. A number of officers with very good pre-Truce records were demobilised and others allegedly with none were retained. Tobin and other leading members of the Irish Republican Army Organisation were reduced in rank. This was seen immediately as a direct assault upon the IRAO and drew from it an ultimatum to the government to which a reply was required within a stated short time. A conference was demanded to discuss the IRAO's interpretation of the Treaty which, they repeated, was the same as Collins's, and conditions were laid down for the removal of the Army Council and the suspension of demobilisation and reorganisation. In the event of the government rejecting these 'proposals', the IRAO declared their intention to take such action as would make clear to the Irish people that they were not renegades to the ideals that induced them to accept the Treaty. They knew what they were doing was serious but they could no longer, they said, be party to the treachery that threatened to destroy the aspirations of the nation. It should, in passing, be said that the members of the Army Council they wished to see removed (Mulcahy, Mac-Mahon, O'Sullivan and Ó Muirthile) had been at least as close to Collins as the leading dissentients were. Of Ó Muirthile, Collins had written that 'at best there is no one else I would have as a friend'.[11]

The government reacted to the ultimatum by ordering the arrest of Tobin and Dalton and bringing in Eóin O'Duffy, the head of the police, another old IRB man, to command the army. Some raids and searches were made; some desertions took place; some officers absconded with military material; but on the whole the army stood loyal to the government. Tobin and Dalton managed to evade capture.

The Dáil, when it next met, heard a denunciation of the ultimatum from President Cosgrave; it was a challenge which no government could ignore without violating the trust it had received from the people. McGrath, the Minister for Industry and Commerce, announced his resignation. He did not agree with the IRAO's ultimatum, he said, but he was thoroughly satisfied that the situation had been brought about by muddling, mishandling and incompetence on the part of the Department of Defence. In a few days, however, he was able to make an announcement to the mutineers which they conceived as a *volte face* on the government's part. A committee of inquiry into the administration of the army was to be set up, and in the event of the committee making a recommendation for the removal of the Army Council, neutral officers were to be appointed in their place. The personnel of the army was to be reviewed with the object of making it effectively a republican army. All men with active service records, even though demobilised, were to be given appointments, subject to a control on the cost of the operation. Members of the IRAO who had taken part in the mutiny would return to their posts with any arms they had removed from them. There was to be no victimisation, no further raids or arrests, and both sides were to co-operate in preserving order.

That was the situation as Tobin, Dalton and company understood it on the 12 March when, in acknowledgment of what McGrath had told them, they sent a further letter to the President assuring him of their full recognition that the army, like the police, was subject to the absolute control of the civil authority. On the same day, however, one of their men was allegedly fired on in the street, and was arrested some days later. A few days later still a raid was made on Devlin's public house in Parnell Street, which had been a meeting place for Michael Collins and his chief Intelligence lieutenants during the War of Independence and where now a number of the mutineers were assembled, possibly with the intention of staging a coup. (Years later one of them disclosed to a journalist that the purpose of the gathering in the pub was to finalise arrangements for the kidnapping of the entire cabinet.)[12] The building was surrounded by troops with machine-guns and armoured cars, and, following a protracted operation, a number of officers were arrested, among them the ADC to President Cosgrave. Cosgrave's greater dilemma, however, arose from the fact that in proceeding against the mutineers in this fashion the army had acted independently of the government : the action had been ordered by the Adjutant-General (O'Sullivan), who had consulted the Minister for Defence (Mulcahy) but not General O'Duffy, the new C-in-C and the government's 'strong man'.

In the absence of Cosgrave through illness, O'Higgins, the Minister for Justice, faced the crisis with customary determination. He called upon the Adjutant-General, the Chief of Staff (MacMahon) and the Quartermaster-General (Ó Muirthile) to resign, and was about to put the same pressure on the Minister for Defence when Mulcahy forestalled him by offering his own resignation. O'Higgins had seen the threat by Tobin and Dalton as 'mutiny plus treason', but he was also critical of Mulcahy's failure to keep the government informed of what was going on in the army, in particular of the emergence—and in opposition to each other—of what somebody called 'the old IRA and the new IRB'. He was determined that the army should be completely under government control, that nobody within its ranks should be able to invoke or exercise influence because of IRB or IRA associations, and in support of his case he told the Dáil that Ó Muirthile, when Assistant Adjutant-General, had summoned officers from the country to sit in uniform under his chairmanship for the purpose of reorganising the IRB within the army. In fact, he alleged that the army staff for all practical purposes were an inner or upper IRB Circle. This was strenuously denied.[13]

By now, as we have seen, two ministers representing opposing points of view had resigned in the crisis. So, too, had a number of deputies from the government party, and those submitting themselves to their constituencies for re-election as a National Group were wiped out. MacMahon, O'Sullivan and Ó Muirthile were relieved of their appointments, and a regulation was made requiring officers of the army to take an oath of allegiance to the democratic government of the state and to have nothing to do with secret societies of any kind whatsoever.

2

The committee of inquiry set up in April 1924 by President Cosgrave was completely satisfied that there would have been no mutiny but for the existence of the 'old IRA' within the army; it was equally satisfied that the activities of that organisation were intensified by the revival or reorganisation of the IRB with the encouragement of certain members of the Army Council. Ó Muirthile had told the committee that the IRB had been re-organised to prevent the anti-Treaty forces, otherwise known as the Irregulars, from getting control of it if it were left derelict and using its name to stir up disaffection against the state; but the committee was satisfied that the 'old IRA' group regarded the reorganisation as directed against them, and were confirmed in that belief by the fact that the group, IRB men themselves one and all, were not allowed to share in the control of the re-organised IRB. The committee also considered that the re-organisation, carried out as it appeared to have been by the actual heads of the army, had been a disastrous error of judg-ment and had accentuated a mutiny which might not have occurred at all, and which could have been more firmly sup-pressed if those in authority had not weakened their position by leaving themselves open to the charge of acting in the interest of a hostile secret society. The committee accepted that Mulcahy had left the government in the dark; and the chairman, James Creed Meredith, in a separate note, accused him of mismanage-ment. Ó Muirthile he saw as the prime mover, with MacMahon and O'Sullivan little more than assenting parties. As the surviving member of Collins's IRB Executive, he had thought it incum-bent on him to make some move and obtain a decision as to policy. His own opinion was in favour of resuscitating the IRB, but it did not appear that he had brought any pressure to bear on Mulcahy, whose precise position in the IRB had not been established. (He had in fact been an ordinary member since 1908 and a member of the Supreme Council since 1921.)[14] Meredith, in this connection, drew attention to a letter which he obviously regarded as extraordinary, which on 31 August 1922 Ó Muirthile, then only a commandant in charge of Kilmainham Detention Prison, addressed to Mulcahy, the Commander-in-Chief, calling him to a meeting in the office of O'Sullivan, the Adjutant-General, to consider certain questions in connection with the IRB following the death of Collins nine days before. No doubt the first business was to elect a President in succession to Collins, but Ó Muirthile explained that other purposes of the meeting, in connection with which he said important papers existed, included the IRB relations with Irishmen abroad, the question of the Wolfe Tone memorial, and the disposal of certain 'national funds' which Collins had collected. We do not know what those 'national funds' were.

In December 1922, as the fighting ceased, Ó Muirthile had begun consultations with prominent members—among them army men, civilians and members of the government parliamentary party—and found them agreed that 'the Organisation' should be saved from the Irregulars, and its tradition preserved and handed on. As most of the principal members were either in the army or the government or had gone 'Irregular', this would have to be done by survivors of the old Supreme Council, even though these might be army officers; but the government, some of whose ministers were IRB men, were not to be prejudiced in any way. This was a reference to the possibility that members of the government might be inhibited in their relations with the British if it could be said that the IRB was functioning with their full knowledge and connivance.

Further discussions were held later as to the means by which this consensus should be implemented, and at these talks army officers were naturally present.

We learned [said Ó Muirthile] that the Minister for Home Affairs [O'Higgins] had expressed himself dissatisfied, but we felt that it was because of his not being in possession of information as to our intentions, and I felt that he should be seen by somebody who would give him an outline of what we proposed, more especially as he was himself a member of the Irish Republican Brotherhood; but, owing to information regarding growing bitterness on his part against myself and my colleagues at Headquarters, it was felt that no useful purpose could be served.

O'Higgins was probably received into the IRB in the 1920–21 period by his friend Gearóid O'Sullivan, who was now involved in the official inquiry as the Adjutant-General of the national army and was committed to the revival of the IRB.[15]

A meeting, however, was held in President Cosgrave's room in Government Buildings in June 1923 at which O'Higgins, in the company of the President and the Minister for Education (Eóin Mac Néill) met the IRB protagonists. The two sides produced utterly different accounts of what took place. O'Higgins told the Review Committee that when Mulcahy invited him to the meeting he replied that he did not wish to leave him under any misapprehension; that although he had been a member of the IRB in pre-Treaty days, he had the strongest possible objection to it or to any other secret society in the altered condition of things; and that he believed that an organisation of that nature would be bad for the army and the country. He said that at the meeting Ó Muirthile introduced the subject of organising the IRB within the army and stated that the Constitution of the IRB had been altered to meet the altered situation. Mulcahy had spoken in a similar strain, stating that the real idea was to keep the IRB from falling into the hands of the Irregulars or other violent or irresponsible people and to enable the organisation the better to control restive elements within its own ranks. But the project of a revival within the army was vigorously and emphatically opposed by Mac Néill and himself and 'finally the President stated that it must not be allowed to develop into a debate or degenerate into a wrangle and dispersed the meeting'.

Ó Muirthile in his account, which O'Higgins said was 'garbled', denied that the President had dispersed the meeting to prevent a wrangle. On the contrary, he and his colleagues left the meeting satisfied that they were 'understood and trusted'. In the course of the discussion Mac Néill had made a passing refer-

H

ence to the events of Easter Week—we can well imagine how he felt on that subject—and had said that he would greatly prefer there to be no IRB at all. He realised, however, that the IRB was a living thing and, that if it had to be controlled, it would be better to have its control in the hands of men who would be likely to keep it in line with government policy. O'Higgins had suggested certain alterations in the Constitution of the IRB in view of the altered state of things, and was told by Ó Muirthile that this had actually been done.[16] It does not appear that he showed O'Higgins the alterations. The 'new' Constitution, as we have seen, provided 'vocational representation' for the army. It also contained a policy clause in the following terms:

> (a) Whereas National Sovereignty is inherent and inalienable and, while acknowledging that political authority is exercised through instruments legitimately established, the Irish Republican Brotherhood pledges itself the custodian of the Republican Ideal, the traditional expression of National Independence.
>
> (b) The policy of the IRB shall be to utilise every power and movement in the Nation: it shall influence them in their activities so as to secure that the maximum organised strength of the Nation—armed, economic, political, social and otherwise—shall be at all times available for the achievement of its objects.

These objects, as in the earlier Constitution, were to 'establish and maintain a free and independent Republican Government in Ireland', but no longer included the obligation to train and equip its members as a military body for the purpose of securing that independence by force of arms and to co-operate with other Irish military bodies for the same end. Candidates for membership were to be required to swear that they would do their utmost to establish the national independence of Ireland; but whereas in the 1917 and 1920 Constitutions the inception oath provided that true allegiance was to be promised to the Supreme Council *and* Government of the Irish Republic—they were then one and the same thing—true allegiance was now promised to the Irish Republic and *obedience* to the Supreme Council. The oath, as before, enjoined the inviolability of the secrets of the IRB; and the risk of punishment with death for any wilful betrayal of matters vital to the organisation's objects was retained, though this could hardly have been maintained in the presence of a national sovereign government.[17]

It is difficult to know what to make of Ó Muirthile's statement that he and his colleagues left President Cosgrave's room satisfied that they were understood and trusted. Their position was no doubt well understood, but could they be trusted to do the right thing? And what was the right thing? In the minds of the ministers there was no doubt that the right thing was to discontinue the IRB, not only within the army, but outside as well. That this was President Cosgrave's conviction was made evident in June 1924 in a debate in Dáil Éireann on a motion of censure tabled by General Mulcahy. In a placatory speech, delivered in what was for him and his government an extremely embarrassing situation, Cosgrave said that he was putting it in the mildest possible fashion when he said that the IRB served no useful purpose in the army, though he would not go so far as the committee of inquiry in saying that in the move to develop it there had been a disastrous error of judgment. He explained that he had never been a member of the IRB himself but, in justice to Mulcahy and his colleagues, he realised and admitted that in the past the IRB *had* served a useful purpose : 'It was a political institution which within the last couple of years served a most important purpose in the national life of the country.' It drew a great deal of support from the most prominent and most useful young nationalists and it was regarded as an instrument of the greatest political consequence. He was sure it would not be easily possible to disintegrate gradually an organisation of that particular character, but, looking back to the interview in his room and the dispute as to what occurred there, it was his recollection that the ministers recommended that the IRB should be disembodied and disestablished.[18]

According to Ó Muirthile, it was not he but General Mulcahy who had opened the proceedings in the President's room—his own role was that of a subordinate—and the object of the meeting was to deal with a letter, which Ó Muirthile had handed round, in which an appeal was made to the IRB on behalf of the leading uncaptured Irregular leader in Cork, Tom Barry, which contained the possibility of a surrender of arms. It was understood that Barry was appealing to the IRB to stop what he

described as a man-hunt for Republicans. He wanted to arrange
to release the Irregulars—those who opposed the Treaty in arms
—from their allegiance to de Valera's executive. He would then
propose the open destruction of arms and the disbandment of
the IRA, and would ask for the formation of a national organisation in which the best elements of both sides could co-operate,
and which would comprise both a political organisation and a
secret organisation. He would ask for an amnesty in respect of
all persons not yet rounded up, and for the release on parole of
some prisoners for the purpose of consultation. Mulcahy, as he
later told the Dáil, was impressed by Barry's appeal which,
first and foremost, revealed the continuity of the IRB and indicated the regard in which it was held by certain elements in the
country. The Irregulars had made an attempt to form an IRB
of their own and had failed. The recognition of the Supreme
Council meant that a body existed to whose wishes the Irregulars
could acquiesce in matters of disbandment and disarmament
without feeling humiliated. Mulcahy did recognise, however, that
his and his colleagues' position as military officers, and the fact
that there was no one else to handle the crisis but they, made the
situation very delicate from the point of view of the government.
Nevertheless, the more he thought about the problem, the more
he saw that the IRB was the only organisation that provided a
pivotal point for arranging the disbandment of the IRA, which
had become a blind-alley organisation. The policy of the IRB
was 'fully controlled by us', Mulcahy said, and he added that the
IRB policy could bear the light of day: in two years' time,
perhaps, it would, as a political organisation with political ideals,
be as open, as it had become previously, as the Irish Volunteers.[19]
But how open really had the IRB ever been?

A correspondence seen by the present writer throws some light
on Mulcahy's reference to the attempt made by the Irregulars to
form an IRB of their own. In this correspondence with some of
his Southern comrades in 1922 Florrie O'Donoghue pointed to
the confusion of mind from which Liam Lynch was suffering.
Lynch, a member of the Supreme Council of the IRB who had
voted against the acceptance of the Treaty, wanted the Council
to summon a meeting and give an account of themselves, but
simultaneously he confessed that such a meeting would be useless.
O'Donoghue agreed: 'The Supreme Council was a Treaty party

pure and simple.' Lynch also had an idea that 'the Organisation' could remain intact. This, said O'Donoghue, was absurd : it was split from top to bottom like everything else in the country, and Lynch should have the sense to see this. O'Donoghue was not sure what sort of organisation Lynch thought the IRB would be in the future. If it was to be one for anti-Treaty men only, he could go ahead at any time, but the result would not help the cause of separatism and republicanism. The present position of 'the Organisation' was hopeless in any event; but 'sooner or later some settlement of the army squabble would be made and then the IRB reorganised honestly and honourably would be a vital necessity'. They could not start, however, with the assumption that every man in the Free State army was ineligible if there was to be a united IRB. Men in the British army had not been ineligible in the past, and they had taken an oath to England!

The correspondence is inconclusive, but the subject was obviously never far from the minds of the anti-Treatyites, and in January 1924 their army executive directed the Adjutant-General to get the names of all IRB County Centres who were still in service with them and order them to disband the IRB. In the following November seven of eleven men summoned to a meeting formally and unanimously agreed to do this and to take the necessary steps to ensure that Circle Centres and, through them, individual members, knew of the decision. Paradoxically, four of the County Centres at the meeting expressed themselves as being opposed to disbandment. In their view it would be better to set about reorganising the IRB, which, if properly controlled, would uphold the national tradition. The IRB represented the physical-force movement since Tone's time and had not outlived its usefulness.

3

Ó Muirthile, before the committee of inquiry, denied absolutely that up to the time they were removed from office the Army Council had speeded up the IRB within the army. He challenged anybody to produce proof that they had done anything to tamper with the allegiance of soldiers to the government, and he invited the most exhaustive inquiry for evidence that the IRB functioned within the army either in organised units or in a general way, though, or course, large numbers of officers and men were members. He said nothing, nor indeed could he have been expected to say anything, as to the circumstances in which the IRB in the army had attained special representation on the Supreme Council in 1923, a representation that was subsequently withdrawn in a 'final Constitution'.[20] The books and moneys of 'the Organisation' were handed over by Diarmuid O'Hegarty to trustees.

It had been intended to insert in the Defence Forces Act, Ó Muirthile said, a clause prohibiting serving soldiers from belonging to any political society, but the men who had proposed to do this had been removed from the army for the offence of having fostered secret societies within it. He had personally always stressed that the IRB was a people's organisation, most of whose work was done by the time the national army came into existence. He was satisfied that continuity and tradition had been preserved and consolidated 'after the crisis that had taken place, and that it could not be said in the future that it [the IRB] expired in the hands of this generation'.[21] Ó Muirthile was being unduly sanguine, for there is no evidence that the IRB, which had been 'a living reality and a present force in shaping the destinies of the nation from 1867 onwards',[22] survived the crisis. It could be said that having reached the apex of its power with Collins, it disappeared in a controversy over his name and intentions.

'The IRB does not exist now,' Mulcahy told his family circle in 1961 : 'the end was when GHQ Parkgate Street was handed over by the British to us.' This statement did not deny the effort to revive the organisation in 1923, because he also told his family that the end of the IRB was when the principal executive persons who had roots in it were dismissed from the army and put through the humiliation of an inquiry in order to show that the army was subordinate to the government. In that situation the IRB and its work and its spirit was 'sublimated to a full stop'.[23]

Mulcahy could have added that 'the Organisation' had died without reaching the end it had set out to attain sixty-six years earlier, though it would claim, and did, that on the way it had brought about the Rising of 1916, the establishment of Dáil Éireann, and the Treaty of 1921. In that time it had gone through nine discernible phases. The first stretched from 1858 when the IRB, then the Irish Revolutionary Brotherhood, was founded, till the abortive rising of 1867; the second, a period of decline, lasted roughly till 1873 : the third, from 1873 to 1877, was a time of reorganisation and of experimental alliance with Home Rule; in the fourth period, from 1877 till 1891, the Brotherhood, playing second fiddle to Land Leaguers and not very constitutional parliamentarians, projected its own ideas through Young Ireland Clubs; in the fifth period (1891–98) it was caught up in the defence of Parnell and in fighting off the attacks of the rival INB; the sixth period, from 1898 till 1904, witnessed another decline after the effervescent '98 centenary reunions; a remarkable revival occurred in the seventh period (1904–16), the Ulstermen McCullough, Hobson and Mac-Dermott, producing with Clarke the conditions in which, with Irish-American stimulation, the Easter Rising became possible; the eighth and ninth periods (1916–22 and 1922–24) were so dominated by the exciting, inspiring and charismatic Collins, living and dead, that it is not unreasonable to conceive everything that went before as a preparation for him and for his remarkable leadership in the Anglo-Irish conflict.

Seán Mac Eóin, a member of the Supreme Council in its final stage, verified that the IRB dissolved itself in 1924,[24] and we have no reason to believe that it was revived in any shape or form. Neither do we know whether any formal decision was ever taken to wind 'the Organisation' up : the Supreme Council may have just stopped meeting. The funds lay until 1964 in a bank in the names of trustees, the first of whom were Seán Ó Muirthile, Martin Conlon, and Eóin O'Duffy. In that year the surviving trustee, Martin Conlon, with Seán Mac Eóin, passed the funds—a mere £2,835—to Kathleen, the widow of T. J. Clarke, a trustee of the Wolfe Tone Memorial Fund Committee which, surviving in one fashion or another since 1898, had been reconstituted through her initiative.[25] A deed was set up to carry on the trusteeship and, with the IRB contribution, the Memorial Committee was able to contribute £11,635 towards the cost—something over £27,000—of erecting a statue of Tone with suitable surrounds at the north-eastern corner of St Stephen's Green, not too far from the place where the original stone had been laid in 1898. The site and the balance of the cost were contributed by the Irish government, and President de Valera unveiled the statue on 18 November 1967.

4

In 1924, as the IRB dissolved, John Devoy visited Ireland for the first time in forty-five years. When he had been there in 1879 he was in the eyes of officialdom a most unwelcome visitor and only managed to do his work of reorganising the underground movement by sedulously avoiding the attentions of the police. He was then a man very much 'on the run'. Now it was different. As he came ashore at Cobh, formerly Queenstown, he was greeted, not by British policemen but by the Minister for External Affairs of a native Irish government, and formally invited to consider himself the guest of the Irish people. He stayed six weeks, receiving many courtesies, including the freedom of several cities as well as a presentation from erstwhile IRB notabilities, among them a former President and Secretary of the Supreme Council, Seán McGarry and Seán Ó Muirthile. He also met Joseph McGrath, the ex-minister, and others who had been connected with the mutiny in the army. He returned to the United States and died in Atlantic City in October 1928 at the age of eighty-six. An obituary in the London *Times* saw him as the oldest of Irish revolutionaries and the most bitter and persistent, as well as the most dangerous, enemy of Britain which Ireland had produced since Wolfe Tone.

The 'new', 'reorganised' or anti-Treaty Clan na Gael which McGarrity controlled expanded greatly through the influx of post-Civil War Republicans, but in the course of time it suffered, like so many Irish and Irish-American organisations before, from a plethora of feuds and factions. One cause of division was the launching of the Irish Hospitals Sweepstakes. McGarrity, who had made and lost several fortunes, was in deep financial trouble in 1929 when Joseph McGrath, the friend of the army mutineers and now one of the originators of the Sweepstakes, induced him to become their principal American agent. The upshot was that the Clan to a large extent became the Sweepstakes organisation in America and used the old IRB contacts and methods to smuggle material in and out of the country. This did not mean any modification, however, in McGarrity's interest in Ireland's revolutionary progress. On the contrary. He broke with de Valera in the mid-1930s, seeing in him 'a past patriot', and conceded the title of 'Chief' to Seán Russell, who readily implemented McGarrity's ideas of bringing English statesmen to their senses by bombing their cities.[26] The factions are all quiet now, for the members are nearly all old men. One relatively active New York camp supports today's Official IRA, while what is left of another group leans towards the Provisionals. But none of them has much power or influence, so that for all practical purposes the Clan is dead.[27] And if the new Clan is dead, so too, as far as we know, is the original Clan so long identified with the name of John Devoy.

The Irish Free State created by the Anglo-Irish Treaty of 1921 lasted little more than a quarter of a century. It was from the outset what has been well described as a restless dominion. The men in the tradition of Griffith and Collins, who accepted the Treaty as a means of achieving something better, worked through Imperial Conferences and a Statute of Westminster to enlarge the status of the members of the British Commonwealth, of which the Irish Free State was one, transforming them and the Irish Free State from dominions to co-equal partners with Great Britain in a free association and enabling the Irish Free State to pursue a policy of neutrality during the Second World War. The men who opposed the Treaty and who had inevitably and democratically come into power continued the process of dismantling the Treaty, removing one by one the remaining features of it that were obnoxious to them. They then replaced the Constitution that was based on the Treaty with one that conformed more to their general ideas but maintained a tenuous link with the Commonwealth. This link was severed in 1949 by the act of an inter-party government in which successors of the pro-Treaty party formed the largest element, and a free and independent republic, effective over twenty-six of Ireland's thirty-two counties, thus came into being. Among the first ministers of the Republic were two old IRB men, Richard Mulcahy and Seán Mac Eóin, while a third portfolio was filled by Seán, the son of Major John MacBride and Maud Gonne.

In this way, therefore, it could be said that the original and fundamental aim of the IRB had been achieved, leaving the political future of the six north-eastern counties in the realm of

H*

unfinished business. A limited Council for the whole of Ireland was recently rejected by the Northern majority, and a promising experiment in the sharing of power with the minority came to an abrupt ending. Meanwhile the resort to physical force continues. A long-drawn-out campaign conducted by the latest, competing, outcroppings of Sinn Féin and IRA, and the Unionist and British reaction to it, has caused great loss of life and destruction of property, north and south of the Border, leaving no apparent hope that a totally united Republican Ireland is any nearer realisation than when the idea of a Brotherhood of Irish Republicans was first conceived.

References

[Numbers quoted without other distinguishing mark refer to the Chief Secretary's Office's Registered Papers, now in the State Paper Office, Dublin. Full references to the printed sources will be found in the bibliography.]

PREFACE (pp. ix–x)
1. O'Hegarty, *The Victory of Sinn Féin*, 12–14.

I. REPUBLICANS AND HOME RULERS (pp. 1–23)
1. Larcom Papers, NLI MS 7517.
2. Ó Broin, *Fenian Fever*, 239–40.
3. Fenian Papers, 4421.
4. Pearse, *Political Writings and Speeches*, 127.
5. Doran Papers and Fenian Papers, 6001R.
6. Fenian Papers, 6450R. 7. NLI MSS 16695–6.
8. Doran Papers. 9. NLI MSS 16695–6.
10. Bulmer Hobson in *Irish Times*, 6 May 1961.
11. Doran Papers. 12. *Freeman's Journal*, 1 Jul. 1879.
13. O'Brien and Ryan, ed., *Devoy's Post Bag*, I, 159.
14. McCullough Papers: P. S. O'Hegarty to Denis McCullough, 10 May 1952. 15. 13229/1876.
16. Fenian Papers, Government Memoranda, 47.
17. Doran Papers: Father Richard Galvin to Father Thomas Hickey, 23 Mar. 1875, quoted *in extenso* in Leon Ó Broin, 'A Charles J. Kickham Correspondence', *Studies* (Autumn 1974).
18. Doran Papers: W. Dillon to W. H. Madden, 27 Mar. 1875, and W. H. Madden to C. G. Doran, 28 Mar. 1875.
19. 463/1877. 20. Doran Papers. 21. A Files, 518.
22. Ibid., 500. 23. Ibid., 534. 24. Doran Papers.
25. O'Brien and Ryan, ed., *Devoy's Post Bag*, I, 209.
26. A Files, 506.
27. 5572/1877: Lake to Burke, 7 Apr. 1877.

28. *Archivium Hibernicum*, Kirby Papers : Cullen to Kirby, Oct.–Dec. 1861.
29. A Files, 591.
30. O'Brien and Ryan, ed., *Devoy's Post Bag*, I, 90, 114, 141, 142, 207, 209, 282, 288 and 292.
31. 283/1879.
32. O'Brien and Ryan, ed., *Devoy's Post Bag*, I, 546–55.
33. Moody, 'The New Departure in Irish Politics, 1878–79'.
34. Bourke, *John O'Leary*, 161.
35. Fenians, Memoranda of Government Files, 75 and 87.
36. 20998/1878 : Mallon to Chief Commissioner DMP, 25 Nov. 1878.
37. Doran Papers.   38. A Files, 612.

2. THE IRISH NATIONAL INVINCIBLES (pp. 24–35)
1. 6330/1878.   2. 7008/1878.
3. O'Connor, *The Parnell Movement*, 244.
4. Richard Hawkins in Williams, ed., *Secret Societies in Ireland*, 101.
5. B Files, 267.
6. Leon Ó Broin in Williams, ed., *Secret Societies in Ireland*, 113–25.
7. B Files 249 : Mallon to E. G. Jenkinson, 23 Aug. 1883; *Irish Times* obituary, 2 Dec. 1886.
8. Bourke, *John O'Leary*, 219.
9. O'Hegarty, *A History of Ireland under the Union*, 522.
10. Ó Broin, *Fenian Fever*, 217–21.
11. Devoy, *Recollections of an Irish Rebel*, 211–12.
12. Cabinet Papers, 37/14.
13. 501/1416S and Colonial Office Papers, 904/183.
14. 501/1415 and 523/2201S.   15. 17037/1875.
16. 8334/1875.

3. THE YOUNG IRELAND SOCIETY (pp. 36–45)
1. Leon Ó Broin in Williams, ed., *Secret Societies in Ireland*, 113–25.
2. Daly, *The Young Douglas Hyde*, 86–8.
3. Copy in possession of author, a gift from the late George A. Lyons.
4. St Aldwyn Papers, D 2455/PCC.46 : E. G. Jenkinson to D. Harrel, 6 Oct. 1886.
5. Cabinet Papers, 37/23.   6. 501/548.
7. Bourke, *John O'Leary*, 204–5

4. THE PARNELL SPLIT (pp. 46–59)
  1. 5006/S.   2. 7928/S.   3. CBS 1895.   4. 6627/1878.
  5. Ó Broin, *The Prime Informer*, 71–4.
  6. Colonial Office Papers, 904/18, 8008 and 11207/S.
  7. Colonial Office, Précis of Police Reports, 1896.
  8. McGarrity Papers, NLI MS 17550.
  9. 15091/S.   10. 10712/S.   11. 9204/S.   12. 10878/S.
 13. 9001/S.   14. 10712/S, Oct. 1895.
 15. Redmond Papers, NLI MS 15164/2.   16. 9117 and 9255/S.
 17. 9246/S.   18. Ibid.

5. INB *versus* IRB (pp. 60–83)
  1. *Gaelic American*, 17 Jan. 1925.   2. 9234/S.
  3. Yeats, *Memoirs*, 83.   4. 24838/76S.
  5. Yeats, *Memoirs*, 109.   6. Ibid.   7. Ibid, 82–3 and 109.
  8. Précis of Police Reports, 1896.   9. 9995/S.
 10. 12631/S.   11. 11518/S.
 12. *Irish Weekly Independent*, 22 Sep. 1894.
 13. *Irish Republic*, 10 Nov. 1895.
 14. 10574/S; *Evening Herald*, 21 Sep. 1895; *Irish Daily Independent*, 26 Sep. 1895.
 15. *Irish Weekly Independent*, Apr.–Jul. 1894.
 16. *Gaelic American*, 21 Mar. 1925.
 17. *Irish Republic*, 13 Oct. 1895.
 18. 10711/S.   19. 10750/S.   20. 11811/S.
 21. 11001/S.   22. 10584/S.   23. 10584/S.
 24. 8 Oct. 1895.   25. 12 Nov. 1895.   26. 10839/S.
 27. Intelligence Notes, XI, Apr. 1896.
 28. 10850/S.   29. 10811/S.
 30. Intelligence Notes, B Series, IX, Mar. 1896.
 31. 10870/S.   32. Ibid.
 33. 10779/S.   34. 11676/S.   35. 13217/S.
 36. Dublin Secret Societies. Précis, 1897.
 37. O'Brien and Ryan, ed., *Devoy's Post Bag*, II, 338.
 38. Young, *Arthur James Balfour*, 469.   39. Ibid.
 40. O'Brien and Ryan, ed., *Devoy's Post Bag*, II, 342–6.
 41. 10819/S.   42. 12836/S.   43. Ibid.
 44. O'Brien and Ryan, ed., *Devoy's Post Bag*, II, 343.
 45. Ó Broin, *The Prime Informer*, 66.
 46. MacBride, *A Servant of the Queen*, 168.
 47. 17115, 17319 and 17156/S.
 48. MacBride, *A Servant of the Queen*, 61.
 49. NLI MS 8576/26.

6. COMMEMORATING 1798 (pp. 84–96)
1. 15170/S.   2. 15219/S.   15200/S.
4. 15327/S.   5. 15438/S.   6. 15240 and 15475/S.
7. 16160/S.   8. Ibid.   9. 159/22409/S and 17894/S.
10. 15275/S.   11. 18291/S.   12. 16285/S.
13. 17005/S.   14. 17560/S.
15. Greaves, *The Life and Times of James Connolly*, 87.
16. Ibid., 87.   17. 17025/S.   18. 17042/S.
19. Ibid.   20. 24838/76S.
21. 17087/S.   22. 17957 and 17977/S.
23. *An tOglach* (Summer 1962).
24. *Capuchin Annual* (1971), 101.
25. 19044/S.   26. 76/2394/S.
27. Devoy Papers, NLI.
28. *Gaelic American*, 30 May 1925.
29. 380S/23574 and 19044/S.
30. *Forum* (Jan. 1950).
31. *Lloyd's Weekly News*, 25 Jul. 1909.
32. NLI MS 94108, f.30.   33. *Forum* (Jan. 1950).

7. FRED ALLAN AND THE IRISH INDEPENDENT (pp. 97–107)
1. Redmond Papers, NLI MS 15164/2.
2. 18500/S.   3. 18778/S.
4. 18788 and 18500/S.   5. 18921/S.
6. Allan Papers : Redmond to Allan, 20 Jun. 1899.
7. MacBride, *A Servant of the Queen*, 281.
8. 18354 and 18700/S.   9. 16515/S.   10. 18945/S.
11. 20996/S.   12. 21107/S.   13. *Forum* (Jan. 1950).
14. MacBride, *A Servant of the Queen*, 281; *Irish Figaro*, 14 Apr.
    1900, 240.
15. *Forum* (Jan. 1950).   16. Ibid.
17. O'Brien and Ryan, ed., *Devoy's Post Bag*, II, 354.
18. 22397/S.
19. *Irish Independent*, 7 Oct. 1920; *Freeman's Journal*, 7 and 9
    Oct. 1920.

8. ARTHUR GRIFFITH, AN IRB MAN? (pp. 108–20)
1. *Irish Daily Independent, Irish Weekly Independent* and *Evening Herald*.
2. 91117/S.   3. *Forum* (Jan. 1950).   4. 23489/S.
5. 29597/S, 5 May 1904.   6. 22086/S.   7. 20886/S.
8. 20957/S.   9. 21056/S.   10. 21055/S.
11. 21107/S.   12. 21353/S.   13. 21317/S.

14. *Irish Figaro*, 7 Apr. 1900.
15. Ibid., 14 and 21 Apr. 1900.
16. 181/27373/S and 22340/S.
17. Lyons, *Ireland since the Famine*, 246–7.
18. Hobson, *Ireland Yesterday and Tomorrow*, 4.
19. 23592/S.
20. Allan Papers, 16 May 1901.
21. McCullough Papers : McCullough's undated answers to a Bureau of Military History questionnaire of 25 Sep. 1952.
22. 27633/S.

9. THE CASTLE IN A LIBERAL MOOD (pp. 121–39)
   1. 28813/S.   2. 29992/S.
   3. Bryce Papers, Bodleian MS 19 : Augustine Birrell to James Bryce, 17 Jun. 1907.
   4. 28377/S.   5. 28288/S and CBS Nov. 1903.
   6. 28297/S.   7. 29274 and 29472/S.
   8. 28327/S.   9. 28726/S.   10. 28827/S.
   11. 29841/S.   12. 29989/S.   13. CBS 1903, No 6.
   14. Colonial Office 904 Précis series.
   15. Ibid.   16. Ibid.   17. Ibid.   18. Ibid.   19. Ibid.
   20. O'Brien Papers, NLI MS 15657 : P. S. O'Hegarty to William O'Brien, 13 May 1952.
   21. Colonial Office Papers, 904/13.
   22. O'Brien and Ryan, ed., *Devoy's Post Bag*, II, 401–2.
   23. *Forum* (Jan. 1950).
   24. O'Hegarty, *The Victory of Sinn Féin*, 133–4.
   25. Colonial Office Papers, 904/12, 16 Nov. 1909.
   26. Ibid. : Dougherty to Birrell, 20 Mar. 1909.
   27. Ibid., Nov. 1910.   28. Ibid., Dec. 1910.
   29. Colonial Office Papers, 904/13.   30. Ibid., Mar. 1911.
   31. Colonial Office Papers, 904/18, Jul. 1911.
   32. Colonial Office Papers, 904/13, Jun. 1911.
   33. Ibid., Jul. 1912.
   34. Ibid. : Dougherty to Birrell, Nov. or Dec. 1912.

10. THE RISING OF 1916 (pp. 140–74)
   1. Devoy, *Recollections of an Irish Rebel*, 392.
   2. McCullough to the author.   3. 7583/14249/1875.
   4. McCullough to the author.   5. Ibid.
   6. Cronin, *The McGarrity Papers*, 32–3.
   7. *Evening Herald*, 23 Jan. 1920.
   8. Trinity College, Dublin, MS 3560.

9. Lynch, *The I.R.B. and the 1916 Rising*, 22–3.
10. Emmet Dalton to the author, 19 Aug. 1974.
11. NLI microfilm P.4548.
12. de Blaghd, *Trasna na Boinne*, 123.
13. Cronin, *The McGarrity Papers*, 175.
14. Mulcahy Papers, P7/D/5.
15. Beckett, *The Making of Modern Ireland*, 426–7.
16. *An tOglach* (Autumn 1966).
17. O'Hegarty, *The Victory of Sinn Féin*, 14–19.
18. Martin and Byrne, ed., *The Scholar Revolutionary*, 135.
19. Bulmer Hobson in *Irish Times*, 6 May 1961.
20. McGarrity Papers, NLI MS 17505.
21. Hobson, *Ireland Yesterday and Tomorrow*, 71–2.
22. *The Letters of Seán O'Casey*, ed. D. Krause, I, 697.
23. NLI MS 13162 : Pearse to McGarrity, 19 Oct. 1914.
24. Cronin, *The McGarrity Papers*, 48–9.
25. Le Roux, *Tom Clarke and the Irish Freedom Movement*, 119–27.
26. Devoy, *Recollections of an Irish Rebel*, 403.
27. Hobson, *Ireland Yesterday and Tomorrow*, 71.
28. Devoy, *Recollections of an Irish Rebel*, 404.
29. Ó Ceallaigh, *Seán T.*, I, 139.
30. Ó Lúing, *Art Ó Griofa*, 262.
31. McCormick Memoir, NLI MS 15337.
32. *An tOglach* (Custom House Memorial Number, 1962).
33. FitzGerald, *Memoirs*, 73–5.   34. Ibid.
35. Hobson, *Ireland Yesterday and Tomorrow*, 14.
36. Longford and O'Neill, *Éamon de Valera*, 17–18.
37. Ibid., 25.   38. Ibid., 36.
39. Daly, *The Young Douglas Hyde*, xi, xvii, xviii.
40. Seán Ó Lúing in *Studies* (Summer 1973).
41. Ó Muirthile Memoir (Mulcahy Papers, P7/52), 31.
42. McCormick Memoir, NLI MS 15337.
43. Mulcahy Papers, P7/D/14 and 15.   44. Ibid.
45. Ó Broin, *Dublin Castle and the 1916 Rising*, revised ed. 112–42.
46. Mulcahy Papers, P7/D/14 and 15.
47. Ó Broin, *Dublin Castle and the 1916 Rising*, revised ed., 35 and 62.
48. Bulmer Hobson in *Irish Times*, 6 May 1961.
49. Ryan, *The Rising*, 116.
50. Martin, ed., 'Eoin MacNeill on the 1916 Rising'.
51. Hobson, *Ireland Yesterday and Tomorrow*, 78.
52. Hyde to L. MacManus, Aug. 1916. (Letter through courtesy of Pádraig Ó Fialáin.)

53. Bulmer Hobson in *Irish Times*, 6 May 1961.
54. W. J. Brennan-Whitmore in *Daily Telegraph*, 4 Feb. 1961.
55. FitzGerald, *Memoirs*, 145.
56. Ernest Blythe in *Irish Times*, 30 Dec. 1974.
57. Martin, 'The Origins of the Irish Rising of 1916', 12.
58. O'Hegarty, *The Victory of Sinn Féin*, 3.
59. NLI MS 15188 (10) : Redmond to General L. B. Friend, 9 Mar. 1916.
60. Bulmer Hobson in *Irish Times*, 6 May 1961.
61. Ó Muirthile Memoir (Mulcahy Papers, P7/52), 40.
62. McCullough Papers, O'Hegarty to McCullough, 10 May 1952.
63. Hobson Papers, NLI MS 13170.

11. MICHAEL COLLINS (pp. 175–205)
1. CBS, Carton 23 : Maxwell to Chief Secretary (H. E. Duke), 5 Sep. 1916.
2. Mulcahy Papers, P7/D/2.
3. Ó Muirthile Memoir (Mulcahy Papers, P7/52), 50–1.
4. See Lyons, *Ireland since the Famine*, 395–6, and Younger, *Ireland's Civil War*, 65–6.
5. Ó Muirthile Memoir, 53.
6. Cronin, *The McGarrity Papers*, 64–5.
7. Ó Muirthile Memoir, 59.
8. Béaslaí, *Michael Collins and the Making of a New Ireland*, I, 166.
9. Ó Muirthile Memoir, 64.
10. Taylor, *Michael Collins*, 57 : Collins to Kevin O'Brien, 6 Oct. 1916.
11. Ibid., 88.
12. Lyons, *Ireland since the Famine*, 390.
13. Macardle, *The Irish Republic*, 231.
14. Longford and O'Neill, *Éamon de Valera*, 66.
15. Mulcahy Papers, P7/D/14.
16. Brennan, *Allegiance*, 154–5.
17. *Hansard*, Vol. 110, Col. 1,984.
18. Mulcahy Papers, P7/D/35.
19. O'Connor, *The Big Fellow*, 67–8.
20. Maurice ('Moss') Twomey in conversation with the author.
21. Macardle, *The Irish Republic*, 406.
22. O'Connor, *The Big Fellow*, 36, 116.
23. *Irish Independent*, Michael Collins Memorial Foundation Supplement, 20 Aug. 1966.
24. Ibid.

25. CBS, Carton 23 : Brigadier-General C. Prescott Deane, Limerick, to Assistant Under-Secretary (A. Cope), 1 Jun. 1920. (This letter is quoted in Béaslaí, *Michael Collins, Soldier and Statesman,* 181–2.)
26. Liam de Roiste (25 Jan. 1921), *Dáil Éireann. Minutes of Proceedings of the First Parliament of the Republic of Ireland, 1919–21: Official Report,* Dublin 1921.
27. Ernest Blythe and Seán MacEntee in conversation with or by letter to the author.
28. O'Daly Memoir, NLI microfilm P.4548.
29. Mulcahy Papers, P/D/15.   30. Ibid., 31.
31. Ó Muirthile Memoir, 76–132.
32. James Hogan, Evidence to 1924 Committee, Mulcahy Papers, P7/C/30.
33. O'Donoghue, *No Other Law,* 188–9.
34. Deasy, *Towards Ireland Free,* 258–9.
35. Liam Deasy in conversation with the author.
36. Ó Muirthile Memoir, 133.
37. Cabinet Papers, Cab. 24/109. C.P. 1693.
38. Ó Muirthile Memoir, 160.
39. Ibid., 161.
40. Béaslaí *Michael Collins and the Making of a New Ireland,* II, 233.
41. Lyons, *Ireland since the Famine,* 427.
42. Mulcahy Papers, P7/C/13.
43. Townshend, *The British Campaign in Ireland,* 202–6.
44. Winter, *Winter's Tale,* 290.
45. See Ó Broin, *Dublin Castle and the 1916 Rising,* revised ed., Chapters 10 and 15.
46. Béaslaí, *Michael Collins and the Making of a New Ireland,* II, 221 and 249–50, and an interview with Emmet Dalton in *Agus* (Jul. 1970).
47. O'Hegarty, *History of Ireland under the Union,* 758–9.
48. Ó Muirthile Memoir, 162–3.
49. Béaslaí, *Michael Collins and the Making of a New Ireland,* II, 22.
50. C. G. Duffy, Department of Foreign Affairs, Dáil Éireann, 23 Mar. 1922.
51. Cronin, *The McGarrity Papers,* 108–9.
52. Ó Ceallaigh, *Sean T.,* 2, 176–7.
53. Ó Muirthile Memoir, 174.
54. O'Donoghue, *No Other Law,* 194–5.
55. Cronin, *The McGarrity Papers,* 113–14.
56. O'Hegarty, *The Victory of Sinn Féin,* 61.

57. Ibid., 44.
58. Pakenham, *Peace by Ordeal*, 85.
59. Seán Mac Eóin and Joseph Sweeney in conversation with the author.
60. Jones, *Whitehall Diary*, III, 202–17.
61. Copy in Mac Eóin Papers.
62. O'Donoghue, *No Other Law*, 231–8.
63. *The Separatist*, 18 Feb. 1922.
64. From an article by Major-General Seán Mac Eóin in the *National Observer* (Dec. 1958).

12. THE END OF THE ROAD (pp. 206–24)
 1. Mulcahy Papers, P7/C/30.   2. Ibid., P7/C/23.
 3. *New Ireland*, 17 Dec. 1921.
 4. Mulcahy Papers, P7/D/14 and 15.
 5. Ibid., P7/C/13.   6. Ibid.
 7. Ibid., P7/C/12 : Mícheál Ó Foghludha to Diarmuid O'Hegarty, 13 Oct. 1923.
 8. Mac Eóin Papers, paper headed '1923'.
 9. *The Truth about the Army Crisis*, 7.
10. Ó Néill and Ó Fiannachta, *De Valera*, 2, 155.
11. Taylor, *Michael Collins*, 50.
12. *Sunday Press*, 28 Nov. 1965.
13. *Dáil Reports*, Vol. 7, Cols 3,156–7.
14. Mulcahy Papers, P7/C/42.
15. Ó Muirthile Memoir, 170.
16. Mulcahy Papers, P7/C/13, 22 and 23.
17. Ibid., P7/C/42; Mac Eóin Papers.
18. *Dáil Reports*, Vol. 7, Col. 3,149.
19. Ibid., Vol. 7, Col. 3,123.
20. Copy in Mac Eóin Papers and paper headed '1923'.
21. Mulcahy Papers, P7/C/42.
22. Ibid., P7/C/13.   23. Ibid., P7/D/15.
24. *With the I.R.A. in the Fight for Freedom*, 15.
25. Entries in Seán Mac Eóin's diary for 14 and 15 Oct. 1964.
26. Cronin, *The McGarrity Papers*, 160–74.
27. Seán Cronin in a letter to the author, 4 Aug. 1974.

Bibliography

PRINCIPAL MANUSCRIPT SOURCES

State Paper Office, Dublin: Chief Secretary's Office Registered Papers; Fenian Papers; Crime Branch Special Papers (CBS), A and B files; Monthly Précis of Police Reports (Précis); Intelligence Notes.

National Library of Ireland (NLI): Larcom Papers; Redmond Papers; Devoy Papers; Harrington Papers; Hobson Papers; McGarrity Papers; William O'Brien (labour leader) Papers; Patrick O'Daly and Patrick McCormick Memoirs; Florence O'Donoghue Papers; J. F. O'Brien's unpublished autobiography.

Public Record Office, London: Cabinet Papers; Colonial Office Papers; Monthly Précis of Police Reports (Précis).

University College, Dublin: Mulcahy Papers (including a memoir by Seán Ó Muirthile [P7/52] and some of Diarmuid O'Hegarty's papers).

Gloucestershire Records Office: Earl St Aldwyn Papers.

Privately owned collections: Papers of C. G. Doran, F. J. Allan, Arthur Griffith, Seán Mac Eóin, Roger Sweetman, Denis McCullough, and Maurice ('Moss') Twomey, in the custody of Mrs Michael Clifton, Seán Allan, Nevin Griffith, Alice Mac Eóin, Brigid Sweetman, the McCullough family, and Maurice Twomey respectively.

NEWSPAPERS AND PERIODICALS

Independent newspapers, *Freeman's Journal, Gaelic American, Irish Republic* (New York), *Shan Van Vocht, Forum, Irish Figaro, The Separatist.*

BOOKS CONSULTED

Béaslaí, Piaras, *Michael Collins and the Making of a New Ireland,* 2 vols, London 1926.

—— *Michael Collins, Soldier and Statesman*, Dublin 1937.
Beckett, J. C., *The Making of Modern Ireland, 1603–1923*, London 1966.
Bell, J. Bowyer, *The Secret Army*, London 1970.
Bourke, Marcus, *John O'Leary*, Tralee 1967.
Brennan, Robert, *Allegiance*, Dublin 1950.
Brown, Thomas N., *Irish-American Nationalism*, Philadelphia and New York 1966.
Colum, Pádraic, *Arthur Griffith*, Dublin 1959.
Coogan, Timothy P., *The IRA*, London 1970.
Corfe, Tom, *The Phoenix Park Murders*, London 1968.
Corish, Patrick J., 'Political Problems, 1860–78' in *A History of Irish Catholicism*, ed. P. J. Corish, Vol. 5, Fasc. 3, Dublin 1967.
Cronin, Seán, *The McGarrity Papers*, Tralee 1972.
Curtis, L. P., *Coercion and Conciliation in Ireland, 1880–92: A Study in Conservative Unionism*, Princeton and London 1963.
Daly, Dominic, *The Young Douglas Hyde*, Dublin 1974.
D'Arcy, William, *The Fenian Movement in the United States*, Washington, D.C., 1947.
Davis, Richard, *Arthur Griffith and Non-Violent Sinn Féin*, Tralee 1974.
Deasy, Liam, *Towards Ireland Free*, Cork 1973.
de Blaghd, Earnán (Ernest Blythe), *Trasna na Boinne*, Dublin 1957.
Devoy, John, *Recollections of an Irish Rebel*, New York 1929.
Edwards, O. Dudley, 'Ireland' in *Celtic Nationalism*, London 1968.
Edwards, R. Dudley, 'Parnell and the American Challenge to Irish Nationalism', *University Review* II, 2 (1958).
FitzGerald, Desmond, *Memoirs*, London 1969.
Gaughan, J. Anthony, *Memoirs of Constable Jeremiah Mee, RIC*, Tralee 1975.
Greaves, C. D., *The Life and Times of James Connolly*, London 1961.
Hobson, Bulmer, *Ireland Yesterday and Tomorrow*, Tralee 1968.
Hone, Joseph, *W. B. Yeats, 1865–1939*, London 1942; 2nd ed., London 1962; repr. London 1965.
Inglis, Brian, *Roger Casement*, London 1973.
Jones, Thomas, *Whitehall Diary*, Vol. III: *Ireland, 1918–25*, ed. K. Middlemass, London 1971.
Kee, Robert, *The Green Flag: A History of Irish Nationalism*, London 1972.

Larkin, Emmet, *James Larkin, 1876–1947, Irish Labour Leader*, London 1965.

Le Roux, L. N., *Tom Clarke and the Irish Freedom Movement*, Dublin 1936.

Levenson, S., *James Connolly*, London 1973.

Longford, Earl of, and T. P. O'Neill, *Éamon de Valera*, London 1970.

Lynch, Diarmuid, *The IRB and the 1916 Rising*, ed. F. O'Donoghue, Cork 1957.

Lyons, F. S. L., *The Fall of Parnell, 1890–91*, London 1960.

—— *Ireland since the Famine*, London 1971; 2nd ed., London 1973.

Macardle, Dorothy, *The Irish Republic*, London 1937; repr. London 1968.

MacBride, Maud Gonne, *A Servant of the Queen*, Dublin 1935.

Martin, F. X., 'Eoin MacNeil on the 1916 Rising', *Irish Historical Studies* XII (Mar. 1961).

—— 'MacNeill and the Foundation of the Irish Volunteers' in Martin and Byrne, ed., *The Scholar Revolutionary*.

—— '1916—Myth, Fact and Mystery', *Studia Hibernica* VII (1967).

—— 'The 1916 Rising—A *Coup d'État* or a "Bloody Protest"?' *Studia Hibernica* VIII (1968).

—— 'The Origins of the Irish Rising of 1916' in Williams, ed., *The Irish Struggle, 1916–26*.

—— and F. J. Byrne, ed., *The Scholar Revolutionary: Eoin Mac-Neill, 1867–1945, and the Making of the New Ireland*, Dublin 1973.

Moody, T. W., ed., *The Fenian Movement*, Cork 1968.

—— 'The New Departure in Irish Politics, 1878–79' in *Essays in Honour of James Eadie Todd*, ed. H. A. Cronne, T. W. Moody and D. B. Quinn, London 1949.

—— *The Ulster Question, 1603–1973*, Dublin 1974.

—— and Leon Ó Broin, 'The IRB Supreme Council, 1868–78' *Irish Historical Studies* XIX (Mar. 1975).

Neeson, Eóin, *The Civil War in Ireland, 1922–23*, Cork 1967; 2nd ed., Cork 1969.

Norman, E. R., *The Catholic Church and Ireland in the Age of Rebellion, 1859–73*, London 1965.

O'Brien, Conor Cruise, 'Passion and Cunning: The Politics of Yeats' in *In Excited Reverie*, ed. A. N. Jeffares and K. G. W. Cross, London and New York 1965.

O'Brien, William, *Forth the Banners Go*, ed. Edward MacLysaght, Dublin 1969.
—— and Desmond Ryan, ed., *Devoy's Post Bag, 1871–1928*, 2 vols, Dublin 1948–53.
Ó Broin, Leon, *The Chief Secretary: Augustine Birrell in Ireland*, London 1969.
—— *Dublin Castle and the 1916 Rising: The Story of Sir Matthew Nathan*, Dublin 1966; revised ed., London 1970.
—— *Fenian Fever: An Anglo-American Dilemma*, London 1971.
—— *The Prime Informer*, London 1971.
O'Casey, Seán, *Drums under the Window*, London 1945.
—— *The Letters of Seán O'Casey*, ed. David Krause, Vol. I, New York 1975.
Ó Ceallaigh (O'Kelly), Seán T., *Seán T.*, ed. Proinsias Ó Conluain and Pádraig Ó Fiannachta, 2 vols, Dublin 1972.
O'Connor, Frank, *The Big Fellow*, Dublin 1965.
O'Connor, T. P., *The Parnell Movement*, London 1889.
O'Donoghue, Florence, *No Other Law*, London 1954
—— *Tomás Mac Curtain*, London 1958.
An tOglach, ed. P. Béaslaí and J. Dufficy (1961–71).
O'Hegarty, P. S., *A History of Ireland under the Union, 1801–1922*, London 1952.
—— *The Victory of Sinn Féin*, Dublin 1924.
O'Leary, John, *Recollections of Fenians and Fenianism*, 2 vols, London 1896.
Ó Lúing, Seán, *Art Ó Griofa*, Dublin 1953.
—— *John Devoy*, Dublin 1961.
—— *Ó Donnabháin Rossa*, Dublin 1969.
O'Malley, Ernie, *Army without Banners*, London 1967 (repr. of *On Another Man's Wound*, London 1936).
Ó Néill, T. P., and Pádraig Ó Fiannachta, *De Valera*, 2 vols, Dublin 1968.
Pakenham, Frank (Earl of Longford), *Peace by Ordeal*, London 1935.
Pearse, Pádraic H., *Political Writings and Speeches*, Dublin 1922.
Pender, Seámus, ed., *Fenian Papers in the Catholic University of America* (Cork Historical and Archaeological Society) (in progress).
Pigott, Richard, *Recollections of an Irish National Journalist*, Dublin 1882.
Pollard, H. B. C., *The Secret Societies of Ireland: Their Rise and Progress*, London 1922.

Ryan, Desmond, *The Fenian Chief: A Biography of James Stephens,* Dublin 1967.
—— *The Phoenix Flame: A Study of Fenianism and John Devoy,* London 1937.
—— *The Rising: The Complete Story of Easter Week,* Dublin 1949; 3rd ed., Dublin 1957.
Sullivan, T. D., *Troubled Times in Irish Politics,* Dublin 1905.
Taylor, Rex, *Michael Collins,* London 1958; repr. London 1961.
Townshend, Charles, *The British Campaign in Ireland, 1919–21,* Oxford 1975.
The Truth about the Army Crisis (issued by the Irish Republican Army Organisation), Dublin, n.d.
White, Terence de Vere, *Kevin O'Higgins,* London 1948; repr. London 1967.
—— *The Road of Excess,* Dublin 1945.
Williams, T. D., ed., *The Irish Struggle, 1916–26,* London 1966.
—— ed., *Secret Societies in Ireland,* Dublin 1973.
Winter, O. de l'E., *Winter's Tale,* London 1955.
With the IRA in the Fight for Freedom, Tralee, n.d.
Yeats, W. B., *Autobiographies,* London 1955.
—— *Essays and Introductions,* London 1961.
—— *Memoirs,* ed. Denis Donoghue, New York 1973.
Young, Kenneth, *Arthur James Balfour,* London 1963.
Younger, Calton, *Ireland's Civil War,* London 1968; repr. London 1970.
—— *A State of Disunion,* Dublin 1972.

Index

Allan, Frederick J., 37, 40, 43, 44, 48, 50, 54–9, 63, 66–9, 73–5, 78–80, 85, 90, 91, 98–101, 103, 104, 106–8, 110, 119, 121, 131–5, 144, 145, 169
Allan, Mrs Frederick J., 110
American Land League, 66
Ancient Order of Hibernians (AOH), 59, 72–3, 129, 132, 145
Anderson, Robert, 16–17, 35, 86, 187
Anderson, Samuel Lee, 16, 29, 187
Armstrong, Gloster, 75
Army of Independence, 59
Ashe, Thomas, 176, 177, 183
Association for the Recognition of the Irish Republic, 191
Asquith, H. H. (Home Secretary and Prime Minister), 58, 141, 152
Atkinson, John (Attorney-General), 70
Avengers, the, 55

Balfour, Arthur James (Chief Secretary), 42
Balfour, Gerald (Chief Secretary), 88, 103
Barry, John, 11–14, 44
Barry, Tom, 185, 217
Beach, Thomas, see Le Caron, Henri
Béaslaí, Piaras, 185–7
Bernstorff, Count von, 158–9
Biggar, Joseph Gillis, 11, 44
Birrell, Augustine (Chief Secretary), 132, 136–9
Blake, Colonel J. Y. F., 109
Blythe, Ernest (Earnán de Blaghd), 146–8, 150, 160, 163, 179, 207
Bodkin, Matthew, 46
Boland, Harry, 178, 179, 181–4, 190, 191, 197–201, 205

Boland, James, 43, 49, 52–3, 58–9, 102
Boland, John P., 59, 102
Boland, Michael, 60–1, 94
Bolger, Joseph G., 43
Boothman, 122
Bracken, Brendan (Viscount), 74
Bracken, Joseph K., 44, 74, 125
Bracken, Thomas, 108
Bradlaugh, Charles B., 7
Brady, Joe, 42
Breen, David, 43
Brennan, Robert, 180
Brennan, Thomas J., 27, 28
Broy, Ned, 187
Brugha, Cathal, 179, 182, 201–2
Bryce, James (Chief Secretary), 132, 133
Burke, Martin, 61
Burke, Thomas Henry (Under-Secretary), 28–9
Butt, Isaac, MP, 5, 11, 14
Byrne, Frank, 28
Byrne, Tom, 109

Cadogan, Earl (Lord Lieutenant), 88, 103
Cameron, Major C. A., 187
Carberry, Paddy, 142–3
Carew, John L., 93
Carey, James, 18, 29
Carroll, Dr William, 9, 19, 21–3, 24, 31, 60
Casement, Sir Roger, 153, 159
Cassini, Count, 123
Catalpa, The, 15
Cavendish, Lord Frederick (Chief Secretary), 26, 28
Ceannt, Éamonn, 156, 167

Celtic Literary Society, 104, 118, 122, 126
Chamberlain, Joseph (Colonial Secretary), 76
Churchill, Winston S. (Prime Minister), 74
Cipriani, 82
Clancy, John, 43, 46, 52, 111
Clarke, Mrs Kathleen, 221
Clarke, Thomas J. (*alias* Henry H. Wilson), 68, 87, 110, 111, 119, 133, 136, 139, 141, 144, 146, 153–4, 156, 157, 159, 161, 165–9, 173, 221
Coffey, Denis J., 37
Cohalan, Judge Daniel F., 131, 183–4, 190, 197–8
Colles, Ramsey, 112–16
Collins, Con, 176
Collins, Jerome J., 5
Collins, General Michael, 145, 175–205, 207, 208, 210–14, 221
Conlan, Martin, 173, 175, 221
Connolly, Dick, 161–2
Connolly, James, 81, 84–5, 89, 90, 104, 119, 123, 135, 156, 161, 166, 169, 178
Cooney ('The Fox'), 76
Corcoran, T. F., 58
Corydon, John Joseph, 34
Coughlan, Dan, 60
Cosgrave, W. T., 106–7, 207, 209, 211, 212, 215–17
Cowley, Michael, 144, 147
Cowper, Earl (Lord Lieutenant), 26
Cremont, Comte de, 83
Cronin, Dr Philip Henry, 60–4, 76
Crossin, William, 106
Crowley, Peter O'Neill, 131
Crummy (organiser), 78
Cuffe, T. S., 136
Cullen, Cardinal Paul (Archbishop of Dublin), 18, 71
Cullen, Tom, 185, 186
Cumann na nGaedheal ('Confederation of the Gaels'), 116–17, 119–20, 123, 128–31, 141, 143
Curley, Daniel, 18
Curtis, W. O'Leary, 118
Cusack, Michael, 122

Daily Nation, 98, 100, 108
Dalton, Major-General Emmet, 149, 195
Dalton, Colonel Charles F., 207, 209, 211
Daly, John, 14, 29, 73, 87, 88, 119, 132, 133
Daly, Ned, 168
Daly, P. T., 107, 119, 120, 125, 128, 130, 132–5, 144
Daughters of Erin, *see* Inghinidhe na hÉireann
Davis, Eugene, 43
Davis, Thomas, 36, 81
Davitt, Michael, 19–21, 24, 43, 59, 109, 121
Deakin, James, 153–4
Deasy, Liam, 192–3
Delaney, Daniel, 18, 59
De Roiste, Liam, 188
De Valera, Éamon, 147, 163–4, 179, 180, 182, 184, 188–91, 196, 198–9, 202, 210, 222, 223
De Valera, Sinéad, 147
Devany, John, 34
Devlin, Joseph, MP, 149
Devlin, Liam, 212
Devoy, John, 5, 9, 19–24, 29–32, 42, 45, 48, 60–3, 67–8, 75, 80, 93, 110, 132, 139–40, 141, 154, 158–9, 183–4, 190–1, 197–8, 222–3
Dilke, Charles, 7
Dillon, John, MP, 33, 38, 40, 43, 45, 64, 96, 136, 141
Dillon, Luke (*alias* Karl Dullman), 60, 106, 191
Dineen, F. B., 77, 118
Dixon, Henry, 44
Dobbyn, Henry, 65, 78–9, 86, 91
Dolan, C. J., 133
Dolan, Father, 130
Doran, Charles Guilfoyle, 10–14, 21, 30, 121
Dorr, Frank, 125
Dougherty, Sir James (Under-Secretary), 125, 127, 130, 131, 133, 134, 136–9
Dungannon Clubs, 130, 143
Dunne, Thomas, 52
Dunraven, Earl of, 124

Edward VII, 15, 37, 126
Egan, Patrick, 9, 11, 17, 27, 28
Egan, James F., 63, 69, 73, 87, 104–5, 117–19

Emmet, Robert, 56, 67, 69
Evening Herald, 49, 56, 64
Evening Telegraph, 55
Everard, Colonel Nugent T., 133

Feeley, Denis, 60–2, 94
Fenian Brotherhood, 2, 3, 4, 9
Fianna Éireann, 141, 160
Field, William, MP, 91
Findlater, Mr, 85
FitzGerald, Desmond, 162–3, 175, 179, 207
Fitzgerald, Lord Edward, 72
Fitzgerald, P. N., 21, 44, 50, 55, 58, 63, 68, 74, 125
Fitzharris, James ('Skin-the-Goat'), 115–16
Fleming, Éamonn, 185
Foley, Father Henry, SJ, 149
Foley, J. C., 43
Ford, Patrick, 38
Forster, W. E. (Chief Secretary), 26, 27
Freeman's Journal, 46, 56, 77, 99–100, 111
Friends of Irish Freedom, 191

Gaelic Athletic Association (GAA), 59, 77, 118, 122, 129, 132, 136, 141, 142, 143
Gaelic League, 59, 118, 122, 128–32, 141–2, 164–5, 171, 174, 189
Gaffney, T. St John, 123
Geoghegan, Thomas F., 43
Gladstone, W. E. (Prime Minister), 4, 25, 27, 31, 32, 41, 45, 48, 140
Gleeson, Joe, 161, 166–7, 176
Glina, Michael, 50
Gonne, Maud, 64, 78–85, 91, 96, 100–1, 104, 110, 112–14, 117–19, 122–3, 126, 137, 141, 169–70, 223
Gore-Booth, Sir Jocelyn, 137
Gosselin, Major Nicholas, 50, 53, 59, 65, 70, 71, 74–6, 79, 82, 84, 86–92, 100, 101, 103, 105–6, 108, 112, 115, 120, 122, 126, 127, 187
Gray, Edmund Dwyer, 55
Gregan, Patsy, 106
Griffith, Arthur, 81, 95, 104–5, 108–18, 126, 128–9, 132, 133, 135–6, 141, 143, 150, 156, 160, 180, 184, 202

Haines, T., 76
Harbinson (retired soldier), 78
Harcourt, W. G. (Home Secretary), 27
Harmsworth Brothers, 99, 101
Harp, The, 135
Harrel, David, 102, 115
Harrel, W. V., 125
Harrington, Timothy, 33, 38, 82, 90, 93
Harris, Matthew, 21
Harte, Christy, 186
Healy, Timothy M., MP, 45, 46, 55, 92, 98, 164, 207
Hoare (vice-consul), 75
Hobson, Bulmer, 119–20, 130, 133–4, 136, 137, 139, 141–4, 145, 146, 152–4, 155, 158, 163, 169, 170, 173–4, 179, 221
Hoctor, Patrick, 84, 95
Hogan, James, 191–2, 206
Holland, Dan, 77, 91
Holland, John P., 19
Holland, Stephen, 77, 91
Humbert, General, 92
Hyde, Douglas, 37, 131, 141, 164–5, 171

Independent National Club, 59
Inghinidhe na hÉireann, 118
Irish Daily Independent, 48–9, 54, 56, 59, 65, 68–9, 77, 98–100, 108, 111, 119
Irish Figaro, 52, 112–14
Irish Freedom, 137, 144–6, 154
Irish National Aid, 145
Irish National Alliance (INA), 59, 65–83
Irish National Brotherhood (INB), 59, 65–83, 125, 134, 135, 221
Irish National Federation, 59, 96
Irish National Foresters, 59
Irish National Invincibles, 28–30, 147
Irish National League, 59, 82, 97
'Irish National Party', 83
Irish Peasant, 144, 146
Irish Republic, 54, 62, 64, 66, 68, 73–5, 80, 94
Irish Socialist Republican Party, 123
Irish Times, 99
Irish Weekly Independent, 56–7, 100
Irish Worker, 157

Irlande Libre, L', 82
Ivory, Edward, 76, 79

Johnston, Anna Isabel ('Ethna Carbery'), 79–81, 141
Johnston, Robert, 30, 43, 44, 49, 50,
78, 80, 119
Jones, J. J. (Commissioner, DMP),
70, 102
Jones, Merrick Shaw Copeland, 76–81

Kearney, J. F., 76
Kearney, Peadar, 147, 174
Kelly, Colonel Thomas J., 3
Kelly, John, 43
Kennedy, Luke, 175
Kenny, Dr J. E., 38, 43, 93
Kenny, John, 95
Kenny, Tom, 136, 137
Kickham, Charles J., 9, 12, 14, 16,
18, 20, 24, 29, 30, 183
Kerwin, Michael, 19
Knights of the Plough, 59
Kruger, President S., 106

Labour Advocate, 52
Larkin, James, 123
Leamy, Edmund, 47
Leavy, John, 13–15, 17–18
Le Caron, Henri, 16, 17, 21, 61, 76
Leitrim, Lord, 24
Logue, Cardinal Michael (Archbishop
of Armagh), 73
Lomasney, William Mackey, 32
Lowrey, Dan, 85
Lowther, James (Chief Secretary), 20
Luccan, John, 53
Lyman, Mrs William, 79
Lyman, William, 54–5, 59, 62–6, 68,
73, 76, 78, 79, 85, 93
Lynch, Colonel Arthur, 109, 122
Lynch, Diarmuid, 159, 161, 166, 176,
178, 180, 190
Lynch, Liam, 199, 203, 205, 218–19
Lynam, Inspector, 101
Lynd, Robert ('Y.Y.'), 143
Lyng, Thomas J., 85, 119
Lyng, Murtagh, 85, 119
Lyons, F. S. L., 194
Lyons, George A., 95, 96, 104–5,
108–9, 135, 136–7

MacBride, Dr Anthony, 63, 65, 95

MacBride, Major John, 37, 40, 63,
65, 66, 78, 81, 109–12, 115, 117–
20, 132, 133, 136, 137, 144, 156,
169–70, 223
MacBride, Seán, 223
McCabe, Alec, 161–2, 176
McCafferty, John, 15, 28
McCaffrey, Edward, 18, 59, 84
McCartan, Dr Patrick, 145, 150, 161,
166–7, 174, 175
McCarthy, Denis Florence, 15
McCarthy, J. F., 115
McCarthy, Justin, 45, 97
McClure, Captain John, 131
McCormick, Pat, 161, 176
McCullough, Daniel, 43, 142
McCullough, Denis, 119–20, 130,
136, 142–3, 144, 153–4, 156, 161,
165–8, 172, 179, 197–8, 221
McDermott, Seán (John), 133, 136,
139, 143–5, 153, 154, 156, 159,
161, 165–9, 175, 221
MacDonagh, Thomas, 156, 163–4,
169
MacDonnell, Sir Antony (Under-
Secretary), 124–8, 132, 133
Mac Eóin, General Seán, 149, 182,
209, 221, 223
McGarrity, Joseph, 150, 191, 198,
201, 222, 223
McGarry, Seán, 156, 176, 180, 182,
184, 222
McGrath, Joseph, 107, 207, 208, 211,
222
McGuinness, W., 49
Macken, Peadar, 103
McKee, Dick, 185
Mackey, Anthony, 86
McLaughlin, Charles O'Connor, 63,
68
MacMahon, Lieutenant-General
Seán, 208, 211–13
MacManus, Terence Bellew, 18, 121
Mac Néill, Eóin (John), 128, 152–7,
160, 164, 166, 170–3, 207, 215–
16
Madden, Dr Richard Robert, 84
Maginn, Michael, 165
Maguire, Sam, 175, 207
Mallon, John (Superintendent, DMP),
26–9, 49, 51–5, 65, 69–71, 74,
76, 84, 86–92, 99–103, 110–11,
115–16, 117, 124, 187

Manchester Martyrs, 3
Manning, Michael J., 56, 99, 100
Markievicz, Countess Constance, 137, 142, 161
Martin, Rev. F. X., 152
Martyn, Edward, 128, 143
Massey, Godfrey, 34
Maxwell, Major-General Sir John, 174–5
Meade, Alderman, 99
Meara, James, 34
Menton, John, 50
Meredith, James Creed, 213–14
Merna, John, 52–5, 58, 76, 77, 99, 100, 101, 105–6, 108
Millen, General F. F., 15–16, 19, 21
Millevoye, Lucien, 82
Milligan, Alice, 63, 78–81
Mitchel, John, 12–14, 66
Morgan (informer), 78
Morley, John (Chief Secretary), 58
Moroney, William, 59
Moylett, Patrick, 184
Mulcahy, Dr Denis Dowling, 14–15
Mulcahy, General Richard, 148, 179, 189–90, 194, 202, 206–18, 220, 223
Mulholland, John, 165
Mullett, James, 51, 57–8, 84, 111, 115, 121
Mullett, Joseph, 114–16
Murphy, John Archdeacon, 175
Murphy, William Martin, 98

Naas, Lord (Chief Secretary), 4
Nagle, Pierce, 9, 34
Nally, P. W., 51, 57
National Council, 126, 130, 132, 141
National Press, 47, 51
National Society, 59
Nesbitt, George, 145
Nolan, Jackie, 50, 52–5, 58, 69–70, 74, 76, 77, 85, 101, 105–7, 108, 122
Nolan, Polly, 106–7
Nowlan, Alderman James, 125

O'Beirne, J. W., 56, 99, 118
O'Boyle, Neil John, 142
Ó Briain, Liam, 160
O'Brien, Daniel, 85, 119
O'Brien, Dr, 63

O'Brien, J. F. X., 6
O'Brien, Pat, MP, 64, 71
O'Brien, P. J., 100
O'Brien, William, 33, 38, 43, 45, 46–7, 64, 97, 136, 156
O'Brien, William (labour leader), 85
O'Carroll, Louis Ely, 77, 91
O'Casey, Seán, 146–9, 156–7
O'Connell, Daniel, 1–2, 13–14, 48
O'Connor, Frank, 181
O'Connor, James, 43, 46–7, 132
O'Connor, John, 30, 43
O'Connor, Rory, 185
O'Connor, Séamus, 173
O'Daly, Major-General Paddy, 149–50, 208
O'Dea, Bishop, 137
Odger, George, 7
O'Doherty, Liam, 189
O'Doherty, Séamus, 179
O'Donnell, Frank Hugh, 38
O'Donoghue, Florrie, 192, 203, 218, 219
O'Donovan Rossa, Jeremiah, 12, 15, 22, 31, 34, 38, 40, 41, 62, 66, 68, 130, 160, 161, 164
O'Donovan, T., 85
O'Duffy, General Eóin, 211, 221
O'Farrell, Charles J., 49, 72
O'Growney, Father Eugene, 122
O'Hagan, Thomas (Lord Chancellor), 13
O'Hanlon, John, 50, 132, 134–5, 136, 144, 145
O'Hanlon, Michael, 43
O'Hegarty, Diarmuid, 175, 176, 181, 182, 185, 193, 207, 220
O'Hegarty, P. S., 136, 137, 144, 152, 173, 201, 204, 206
O'Hegarty, John (Seán), 137
O'Higgins, Kevin, 206, 207, 210, 212, 214–16
O'Keeffe, Patrick (Paidín), 150, 181
O'Kelly, James J., 19, 43, 99
O'Kelly, Seán T., 148, 156, 165, 173, 179, 199
Old Guard Union, 131
O'Leary, John, 9, 24, 29, 30, 37–41, 44–5, 49, 50, 57, 69, 74, 88, 91, 92, 95, 105, 109, 110, 116, 119, 131, 132, 141, 161, 183
O'Loughlin, P. F., 58, 118, 122
O'Mahony, John, 2, 18, 56, 121

O'Mahony, John (*Evening Herald*), 64, 99
O'Malley, Christy, 209
Ó Muirthile, Seán, 164–5, 173, 175, 176, 178, 179, 182, 183, 184, 186, 187, 190, 193, 194, 196–200, 206–7, 211–22
O'Rahilly, The, 153
O'Sullivan, Father Denis, 149
O'Shea, J. J., 43
O'Shea, Katharine, 25, 31, 43, 47
O'Shea, Captain Willie, 25–6, 43–4
O'Sullivan, Gearóid, 185, 211–15
O'Sullivan, J. A., 64
O'Sullivan, J. F., 125

Papen, Count von, 158
Parnell, Charles Stewart, 9, 12–13, 19–21, 24–5, 28, 31, 32, 36, 39, 41–5, 47–52, 92, 93, 97, 121, 140, 164, 221
Patrie, La, 82
Pearse, Patrick Henry, 149, 153, 156, 158, 161, 164, 167, 171, 172, 174, 178
People's Protection Association, 126
People's Rights Association, 97
Phoenix Conspiracy, 3
Pigott, Richard, 13, 22, 43
Pile, Alderman Thomas, 100, 103–4, 135
Pius IX, 71
Plunkett, Count G. N., 99
Plunkett, Sir Horace, 122
Plunkett, Joseph, 156, 167, 172, 175
Pollard, H. B. C., 132, 176
Poole, Joe, 95–6
Power, John O'Connor, 11–14, 38, 44
Power, John Wyse, 44, 49–50
Price, Ivon H. (RIC), 124–5

Redmond, John E., MP, 39, 44–5, 56–7, 66, 75, 87, 88, 91–3, 97, 98–100, 113, 126, 136, 141, 149, 151–5, 159, 172–3
Redmond, Willie, MP, 39
Regan, D. B., 106
Reid, Mrs Pat, 53
Reid, Pat, 52–5, 76, 102, 122
Reilly, George, 34
Republic, The, 143
'Richmond', 101–2
Ridgeway, Sir Joseph West (Under-Secretary), 34, 50
Roantree, W. F., 17
Rolleston, T. W., 37, 63
Rooney, William, 81, 91, 108, 110, 116
Rourke, James, 43
Rowan, John, 105–6
Russell, Seán, 223
Ryan, Daniel (Superintendent, DMP), 26
Ryan, Desmond, 17, 96
Ryan, John, 30
Ryan, Dr Mark, 30, 44–5, 49, 57–9, 63, 64, 69, 73, 77, 81, 84, 86, 91, 96, 109, 110, 120
Ryan, Dr Michael, 74
Ryan, Dr Patrick, 63, 74
Ryan, W. P., 129, 144

Salisbury, Marquess of (Prime Minister), 32
Sanderson, Sir Percy (consul-general), 123
Schlippenbach, Baron, 123
Seery, Denis P., 53, 68, 84
Seery, Michael J., 43, 74, 75
Sellers (Primrose League), 64
Separatist, The, 204
Shan Van Vocht, 80–1, 94, 141
Sheridan, P. J., 21, 28
Sheridan, Walter, 52–3
Shortt, Edward (Chief Secretary), 180
Sinn Féin, 130–1, 136, 141, 143, 150, 178–81
Sinn Féin, 130–1, 150
Sinnott, Constable, 51
Smiddy, Professor T. A., 197
Spencer, Earl (Lord Lieutenant), 26, 29, 32
Stack, Austin, 199, 202
Stephens, James, 2–3, 9, 18, 22, 33, 45, 121
Stewart, E. T., 85
Stewart, J., 119
Sullivan, Alexander, 31, 42, 60–2, 64, 67–8, 94, 106
Sullivan, John, 43
Sweetman, John, 128, 143
Sweetman, Roger, 188–9
Synge, John M., 148

Talbot, George (Chief Commissioner, DMP), 27–8

Teeling, Charles McCarthy, 40, 43, 83
Times, The, 51
Thornton, Frank, 186, 209
Tobin, Liam, 185, 186, 207–11
Tobin, Patrick, 68, 77, 78, 79, 84, 91, 101
Tobin, Seán, 161
Tone, Theobald Wolfe, 1, 36, 90, 91, 158, 222
Torley, John, 30
Transvaal Committee, 112–15, 117
Tudor, Major-General H. H., 181, 193
Twomey, Maurice ('Moss'), 189
Tynan, P. J. P., 28, 76, 77

United Ireland, 46–7
United Irish League (UIL), 97, 125, 129, 136, 141
United Irishman, 95, 110, 117, 128, 129, 130

United National Societies, 138
Volunteer Dependants' Fund, 145

Walsh, John, 15, 28, 50, 105–7
Walsh, William J. (Archbishop of Dublin), 46, 92
Wilkins, C. A., 127
Wilson, Henry H., *see* Clarke, Thomas J.
Worker's Republic, 89
Wolfe Tone Memorial Fund Committee, 91–3, 131, 146, 214, 221
Wyndham, George (Chief Secretary), 124

Yeats, J. B., 131
Yeats, W. B., 36, 48, 63–4, 74, 81, 84, 86, 91, 94, 95, 96, 113, 131, 169, 170
Young Irelanders, 2
Young Ireland Society, 36–41, 49, 50, 59, 72